BENJAMIN
FRANKLIN
~ *and* ~
# WOMEN

"*The Tea-Tax Tempest, or the Anglo-American Revolution*" (1778).
*Women, blacks, and Native Americans look on as men squabble
about liberty—wondering what the tempest will mean for them.
(Engraving by Carl Guttenburg of Nuremberg, 1778.
Library of Congress, LC USZ62-1523)*

BENJAMIN FRANKLIN

~ *and* ~

WOMEN

Edited by

Larry E. Tise

The Pennsylvania State University Press
University Park, Pennsylvania

The right to use previously presented or published material cited in the text is grate-
fully acknowledged:

Reprinted by permission of the Board of Directors of The Friends of Franklin, Inc.,
essays and other materials that in whole or in part were originally prepared for a
symposium entitled "Benjamin Franklin and Women," co-sponsored by The Friends
and held on April 9, 1994.

Reprinted by permission of Stackpole Books from *The American Counterrevolution: A
Retreat from Liberty, 1783–1800*, by Larry E. Tise, Mechanicsburg, Pa.: Stackpole
Books, 1998. Copyright © 1998 Stackpole Books.

Reprinted by permission of Yale University Press from *My Life with Benjamin Franklin*,
by Claude-Anne Lopez, New Haven: Yale University Press, 2000. Copyright © 2000
Yale University Press.

Library of Congress Cataloging-in-Publication Data

Benjamin Frankin and women / edited by Larry E. Tise
       p.   cm
   Includes bibliographical references and index.
   ISBN 0-271-02034-2 (cloth : acid-free paper)
   ISBN 0-271-02035-0 (pbk. : acid-free paper)
    1. Franklin, Benjamin, 1706–1790—Relations with women. 2. Franklin,
Benjamin, 1706–1790—Influence. 3. Women—United States—Social conditions—
18th century.   I. Tise, Larry E.

   E302.6.F8 B454 2000
   973.3'092—dc21
   [B]   99-055271

It is the policy of The Pennsylvania State University Press to use acid-free paper for
the first printing of all clothbound books. Publications on uncoated stock satisfy the
minimum requirements of American National Standard for Information Sciences—
Permanence of Paper for Printed Library Materials, ANSI Z39.48—1992.

CONTENTS

LIST OF ILLUSTRATIONS

PREFACE

It began from the first moment I told friends and colleagues in 1989 that I was going to be the first executive director of the Benjamin Franklin National Memorial in Philadelphia. "You will have to figure out how many ladies old Ben seduced," said one male colleague, chortling as he said it. "How many illegitimate children did he have anyway?" asked another—chortling, of course. This seemingly universal reaction of men to the mention of Franklin's name struck me from the outset as an unfair caricature of this world-renowned American scientist, diplomat, author, and founding father of the United States.

Just before starting in that new position I took a long overdue, but welcome, extended vacation in France. Through my friends David and Margaret McGovern, Americans who have lived in Paris for more than thirty years, I was able to meet a number of impressive French citizens as well as other Americans living in France. When I was introduced to French folk as having a connection, as a historian, with Benjamin Franklin, I was immediately greeted with giggles and raised eyebrows. Men asked, "You do know about Franklin and the ladies of Paris, don't you?" Women responded, "Oo, la la, Benjamin Franklin had so many women—too many to count." Even at dinner at the at the official U.S. ambassadorial residence with American Ambassador Walter Curley—successor to the position held by Franklin as America's first official minister abroad—when it came time for toasts, the first one was to honor Franklin and his many conquests of the women of Paris.

A major theme seemed to be developing: the most common reaction to the mention of Franklin's name was to connect him with women. And this became even more obvious after I started my work at the National Memorial. The most commonly asked question by letter or phone and in conversations with thousands of people over a period of seven years had something to do with Franklin and women. Have you ever figured out who was the mother of Franklin's illegitimate son, William? How many illegitimate children did he have? How could he have sex with all of those women in France when he was already seventy years old at the time he arrived there?

How many women *did* he seduce? And so went the litany of endless questions.

That Americans delight in hearing and talking about the subject of Franklin and women was confirmed for me in 1990. As will be detailed in the following pages, while scholars from all over the world gathered on the bicentennial of Franklin's death in Philadelphia to discuss virtually every facet of his life and career, the only articles that appeared in public print during the occasion were gibes about Franklin as "our founding flirt" and his contributions to pornography.

Nor has the persistence of these questions subsided in the twelve years in which I have studied, researched, and tried to explain the life of Benjamin Franklin. But the more I examined the life of this man—both in my work and in researching and writing my book *The American Counterrevolution: A Retreat from Liberty, 1783–1800* (wherein Franklin plays a leading role)—I came to several conclusions. First, I found that the chortles about Franklin and women obscured the very complex relationship that Franklin had with those most basic women in his life—his mother, his wife, and his daughter. And, despite the many flirtatious notes and letters that exist between Franklin and a host of other women—mainly much younger women—his relationship with them was also a complicated affair that always had much less to do with sex than with the fine interplay of minds, with Franklin usually in the role of mentor.

Second, I learned that Franklin had much to say in the age of liberating revolutions about the rights and responsibilities of both men and women. A mere glimpse at Franklin's carefully culled and chiseled Poor Richard sayings on the relations between men and women, the nature of marriage, the dangers as well as the delights of sex, and the importance of education for men and women demonstrates that Franklin gave much thought to these subjects and maintained a keen understanding of them. And as one of the most important arbiters of the American Revolution, the creation of a new American nation, and the establishment of constitutions, laws, and civil institutions to guide the nation, he played a major role in defining a new and important role for women in this society.

Third, as I mined the Franklin historiography ever more deeply, I found that the theme of Franklin's relationship with women had followed a most curious and interesting course beginning with Franklin's first printed words in the Silence Dogood essays in 1722 and his first affairs with "lewd" women in London two years later, continuing with the birth of William and the spread of rumors about his treatment of William's mother, and ending with the many years he was away from his wife, Deborah, and America—almost always living with or next door to women.

And that was just in his lifetime.

The course got richer with the publication of his *Autobiography* in various forms after his death. There he added much to the story with jesting references to his various "errata" in dealing with women. And, as will be seen in the following pages, the story that is the subject of this book took a whole new turn during the Victorian era with the discovery of Franklin's unpublished essay on choosing a mistress. This piece, when it was added to the already riveting saga of Franklin and women, assured that the mere mention of Franklin's name would perpetually conjure the subject of women and concomitant smiles.

As it became increasingly clear to me that this most discussed facet of Franklin's life was little understood, I suggested that the subject "Franklin and Women" be the topic for our annual Franklin symposium in 1994, co-sponsored by the National Memorial and the Friends of Franklin, Inc., an international Philadelphia-based organization devoted to the study of Franklin. Everyone agreed that it was about time an effort was made to bring some clarity and sense to this hoary and constantly dismissed topic.

For me as a historian, one of the greatest pleasures of my professional career was the recruitment of speakers for the symposium and thus also the authors of the essays included in the following volume. Never have I found it so easy to recruit some of the most outstanding historians in our profession today to participate in the discussion of a historical topic. With the advice and assistance of several key individuals, I drew up a list of the most knowledgeable historians who could add luster and light to the subject. Chief counsels were Roy Goodman, reference librarian and Franklin authority at the American Philosophical Society; Barbara Oberg, then editor-in-chief of the *Papers of Benjamin Franklin* at Yale University; Mary Kelley, distinguished Dartmouth historian who both spoke and then wrote for this book; and J. A. Leo Lemay, Franklin biographer at the University of Delaware.

With my list of authorities in hand, I called my top seven choices to participate in the symposium and this book. All accepted. And, fittingly, though not by design, all of the participants (except this symposium organizer and book editor) turned out to be women. Who better to adjudge the record and intentions of Franklin in this most vulnerable facet of his character, life, and place in history?

The acceptors were a cast of stars: Claude-Anne Lopez, author of more about Franklin and women than anyone else in history; Sheila Skemp, author of more about Franklin's illegitimate son than anyone else ever; Jan Lewis, authority on images of sexuality and roles; Mary Kelley, expert on the education of women; Carla Mulford, master on Franklin in literary history; and Susan Stabile, new specialist on salons in Europe and America. What a lineup! What a vast array of learning and erudition! [1]

The symposium held at the Franklin Institute in Philadelphia in early May 1994, was a stunning success in every respect. Speakers and audience were in rapt attention as the age-old subject of Franklin and women was carefully unfolded and elucidated by the authors represented in this volume. And due to the good work by my colleague Kathleen DeLuca in making arrangements for the symposium, it became more than just talk. It was a memorable happening.

There was never any question that their papers should be revised for publication in the first real collection on Franklin and women. The only questions were about when they could be revised and who would contribute the energies to edit the work and find a publisher. Due to changes in careers and other intervening books and responsibilities, *Benjamin Franklin and Women* was postponed and set adrift for a couple of years.

This book might have remained unpublished except for the determination and interest of the contributing authors and the persisting invitation of Pennsylvania State historian William Pencak for me to submit the papers for publication in the journal he edits, *Pennsylvania History*. He had done this to papers deriving from other of our Franklin symposia. But also at the urging of Pencak, I decided to submit the papers for consideration by The Pennsylvania State University Press. There we have had the decidedly positive and professional encouragement of editor Peter J. Potter.

I hereby express my appreciation for the assistance and patience of all those individuals mentioned above. A special word of appreciation to my colleagues in the Friends of Franklin, Inc., who encouraged the symposium that ignited the essays eventually prepared for this book—Ralph Archbold, Ralph Elliot, Elly Fitzig, Roy Goodman, Deane Sherman, Coxey Toogood, George Waters, Doug Whitley, and others. And to my colleagues at the Franklin Institute when the symposium occurred—Irene Coffey and Virginia Ward, librarians; Kathleen DeLuca and Wendy Ellis, fellow producers of great events. And I also bow and kiss the hand (as would have Franklin himself) of each of the six elegant, charming, and inspiring women who joined with me in this little publishing enterprise, which I believe will forever place the subject of Franklin and women in proper perspective.

Larry E. Tise
Philadelphia, 2000

PRINCIPAL WOMEN IN THE LIFE
OF BENJAMIN FRANKLIN
A Biographical Glossary

◡

Are women books? says Hodge; then would mine were
An almanac to change her every year.
—*Poor Richard, 1737*

Addertongue, Alice (1732). One of Franklin's early female pseudo-nyms. A single woman of thirty-five living with her mother, Alice posits a defense of "scandal" as a beneficial habit of women. *Pennsylvania Gazette*, 12 September 1732.

Aftercast, Margaret (1722). Fictional correspondent with Mrs. Silence Dogood. A single woman who turned down many suitors in her youth until she reached an age at which they no longer called, Margaret appeals to Mrs. Dogood "to form a Project for the Relief of all those penitent Mortals of the fair Sex, that are like to be punish'd with their Virginity until old Age, for the Pride and Insolence of their Youth." *The New-England Courant*, 20 August 1722.

Baker, Miss Polly (1747). Franklin's fictional unwed mother who lectured her judges during a trial said to have occurred "at Connecticut near Boston in New-England" during 1747. Having been brought before the court for bearing her fifth bastard child, she protested the fines and public whippings given her following her previous births. Indeed, since she was pursuing "the first great Command of Nature, and of Nature's God, *Encrease and Multiply*," she argued, the court should "have a Statue erected to my Memory." Because of the impression made by her and her arguments, not only was her case dismissed; one of the justices hearing her case asked to marry her the following day. Submitted anonymously by Franklin to the London *General Advertiser*, and published on 15 April 1747, Franklin's clever article on this character was reprinted in fifteen British newspapers and magazines by the end of April and in four American newspapers by the end of August. Written at a moment when the form of fiction was initially emerging in the English language, this brief story has been reprinted hundreds of times, making Polly Baker one of the most renowned women in Franklin's life.

Barbara (d. 1764). Purported mother of Franklin's illegitimate son, William, who was described in a private letter of 9 October 1763 as follows: "tis generally Known here his [William's] birth is illegitimate and his Mother not in good Circumstances, but the report of her begging Bread in the Streets of this City [Philadelphia] is without foundation in Truth. I understand some small provision is made by him [Franklin] for her, but her being none of the most agreeable of Women prevents particular Notice being shown, or the Father and Son acknowledging any Connection with her." Less than a year later, during an election campaign where Franklin's character was smeared in every possible way, one political publication of 27 September 1764, described Barbara somewhat differently: "His [Franklin's] principal Estate, *seeming* to consist, / Till very lately, / In his Hand Maid BARBARA / A most valuable *Slave*, The *Foster-Mother* [Deborah] / Of his last Offspring [Sally], / Who did his dirty Work, ———/ And in two *Angelic* Females [Deborah and Sally] / Whom Barbara also served, / As Kitchen Wench and Gold Finder [i.e., prostitute]. / But alas the Loss! / Providence for wise, tho' se-cret Ends, / Lately depriv'd him of the Mother / Of EXCELLENCY [William, Governor of New Jersey]. / His Fortune was not however impair'd, / For he piously withheld from her / Manes, / The *pitiful* Stipend of *Ten Pounds per Annum*, / On which he had cruelly suffered her / To Starve; / Then stole her to the Grave, in Silence, / Without a Pall, the Covering due to her *Dignity*, / Without a *Groan*, a *Sigh* or a *Tear*. / Without a *Tomb*, or even / A *Monumental Inscription*. / Reader behold this striking Instance of / Human Depravity and In-gratitude; / An irrefragable Proof, / That neither the Capital Ser-vices / Of *Friends*, / Nor the attracting Favours of the Fair, / Can fix the Sincerity of a Man, / *Devoid of Principles* and / *Ineffably mean*; / Whose Ambition is / Power; and whos Intention is / Tyrany." Leonard Labaree et al., eds., *The Papers of Benjamin Franklin*, 40 vols. (New Haven: Yale University Press, 1959—), 11:270–71, 283–84. (Hereafter *PBF*.)

Barwell, Mary (b. 1733). Wealthy, intelligent, and financially influential friend of Polly Hewson and Dolly Blunt, who beginning in 1770 joined the small group of young women with whom Franklin maintained a friendly and affectionate friendship and correspondence. Her father and brother were deeply involved in the East India Company, with which she arranged purchases for Franklin and other members of his family.

Blunt, Dorthea (Dolly) (1733–1809). Friend of Polly Hewson with whom Franklin formed a playful, affectionate relationship as early as 1761 and with whom he corresponded in endearing terms. When Polly married in 1770 Franklin wrote Dolly that they had "agreed to love each other better than we ever did, to make up as much as we can our suppos'd Loss." *PBF,* 9:327.

Brillon, Anne-Louise Boivin d'Hardancourt (1744–1824). Neighbor and mother of Cunegonde Brillon while Franklin lived in Passy, near Paris. She became the most immediate object of Franklin's fantasies when he arrived in France in early 1777. Shy and beautiful, she was a celebrated performer on the clavichord. Despite his amorous and playful overtures over many months, she did not respond, except in the exchange of tantalizing letters.

Caillot, Blanchette (?–?). Mother of William Temple Franklin's short-lived illegitimate son. Wife of a famous French actor, Joseph Caillot, and another neighbor of the Franklins while they lived in Passy, she became the mistress of Temple. In 1785 she bore him a son, whom they named Theodore and who died in infancy.

Chaumont, Therese Le Ray de (?–?). Wife of Jacques Donatien Chaumont, Franklin's landlord, frequent host, and business associate at Passy during his years in France. Mrs. Chaumont was among those French women believed by John Adams to exert too much influence over Franklin.

Davies, Marianne (1744–1816?); and Cecilia (c. 1750–1836). British sisters claimed by early twentieth century historians as potential unacknowledged Franklin offspring. Franklin chose the elder sister,

Marianne, in 1761 to be the first and principal public performer of his glass armonica—the musical instrument he devised about that time while living in London. Marianne traveled about the United Kingdom performing to the adulation of audiences. By 1767 the younger Cecilia joined the performances as a vocalist. The high point of their career was a tour of Europe, culminating in performances in Vienna, in 1769, of music written by various German composers. Marianne later fell ill and had to be confined for more than a year, her malady attributed to the "mesmerizing" effects of the armonica's shrill sounds.

Dogood, Mrs. Silence (1722). Franklin's earliest pseudonym for fourteen essays written while he was sixteen. Mrs. Dogood, being a busybody, do-gooding Boston widow, pokes fun at the morals, manners, and habits of everyone in New England, while also recounting her tragic early life and marriage to a country minister to whom she had been apprenticed. Marriage, the ways of women, of ministers, of Christians, dress, sex, poetry—nothing escapes Mrs. Dogood's sharp eye and witty pen.

Downes, Elizabeth (Franklin) (d. 1777). William Franklin's wife, whom he married in September 1762, shortly after his appointment as royal governor of New Jersey. Born in the West Indies, educated, and literate, she ventured with William to America as he launched his governorship. By 1776 she had become asthmatic and suffered other afflictions. As William's Loyalism emerged and he was forced from his governorship and placed under arrest in June 1776, Elizabeth's growing frailty became a distressing issue to him. When Congress transferred him to Connecticut, she remained at the governor's house in Perth Amboy, friendless and alone. Sally Bache invited her to relocate to Philadelphia, but she declined for fear that American rebels would loot their belongings. William Temple Franklin brought her temporary relief and a loan of sixty dollars from Benjamin Franklin. But when she wrote a pathetic letter to Franklin in August, 1776, pleading for him to arrange William's parole so that he could care for her, Franklin did not respond. Despite her illness and isolation, she remained in the house for another ten months. Eventually forced to take refuge somewhere in New York, she died on 28 July 1777, still separated from William.

Evans, Amelia (Barry) (b. 1744). Deborah's goddaughter and daughter of American cartographer Lewis Evans. She became a world traveler and frequently applied to Franklin for guidance, advice, and occasionally, financial assistance. She visited Franklin in London in 1759 and appealed to him for assistance in 1766. Upon a trip to Tunis with the family of British consul James Traill she met David Barry, a sea captain, and married him. Franklin was always cordial and responsive to her appeals.

Foxcroft, Judith Osgood (m. 1770). Married John Foxcroft, Franklin's associate in the North American colonial postal service, in London in 1770, with Franklin giving away the bride. Franklin addressed her in his letters as "my daughter." Her husband described her in letters to Franklin as "your Daughter." Franklin described Judith Foxcroft's daughter as "little Sally my grandaughter," provoking biographer Sidney George Fisher in 1899 to conclude that she was indeed one of Franklin's unacknowledged offspring.

Franklin, Abiah Folger (1667—1752). Franklin's infrequently mentioned mother. Born on Nantucket Island, in 1689 she became the second wife of Josiah Franklin, who already had seven children with his first wife, Anne Child. Benjamin was Abiah's sixth and last son and the eighth of her ten children.

Franklin, Deborah Read (Rogers) (1708—74). Franklin's wife of some forty-four years. Born probably in Birmingham, England, of John Read, a carpenter, and Sarah White. The family migrated to Philadelphia in 1711. She and Franklin met on a Sunday morning in October 1723, under odd circumstances immortalized by Franklin in his *Autobiography*. When Franklin soon became a boarder with the Reads, a courtship ensued. It ended when he left for a two-year sojourn in London, 1724—26, in the printing trade. Deborah married John Rogers, a potter, who turned out to be already married. The Franklin-Read relationship resumed in 1730 and may have resulted in the illegitimate birth of William Franklin. A common-law bond was established between them on 1 September 1730. Deborah managed the book and stationery shop they developed in connection with their printing business. She also managed their business and family finances from the outset and continued doing so alone while Franklin was away in London for fifteen years. Although she was a capable and faithful business partner and wife, the 175 letters exchanged between them while he was away reflect something other than a close and intimate relationship. Nor did Franklin discuss with her any matters of political, social, or political import. She did not accompany Franklin to England, nor did she see him during the last ten years of her life.

Franklin, Sarah (Bache) (1743–1808). Franklin's only daughter, known as Sally, appeared as Franklin was entering into the most productive period of his career. Although he and Deborah arranged for her to get the rudiments of a female education (reading, writing, arithmetic, and household skills), Franklin denied her the academic studies and travel abroad she aspired to undertake. He did give her musical lessons and one of the armonicas he invented. In 1767 she married Richard Bache (1737–1811), a failed merchant, against Franklin's wishes, during her father's most lengthy stay in England (1764–75). On the death of Deborah Franklin in 1774, Sally became the head of the Franklin household in America, which she ran just as faithfully as had her mother until Franklin's death in 1790. He was sufficiently kind to her in his will that she and Bache could take a grand tour of Britain and in 1794 retire to a farm near Bristol that they named Settle. She bore eight children, including Franklin's favorite—Benjamin Franklin (Benny) Bache. All present descendants of Franklin—of which there are thousands—are the issue of Sally's offspring.

Franklin, Sarah (c. 1753–81). Daughter of Franklin's English cousin Thomas, "a Dyer at Lutterworth, in Leicester Shire"—the only other Franklin in England in 1766 descended from the same grandfather. Sarah (nicknamed Sally), evidently a sickly child, came to live with Franklin and Margaret Stevenson at Craven Street in London in 1766. Mrs. Stevenson provided "a little Schooling and Improvement" for the girl and nursed her to good health. Franklin treated her, as well, as his own daughter. Recovered, she returned to her father's home at Lutterworth in late 1766. She married in 1773 and bore four children before her young death.

Graeme, Elizabeth (Fergusson) (1739–1801). Son William Franklin's lover, disapproved of by Franklin and forsaken by William. Daughter of Ann Diggs (who was the stepdaughter of Governor William Keith) and of Dr. Thomas Graeme, Philadelphia physician and Pennsylvania provincial councilor—and thus friends of the Pennsylvania proprietors—she had little chance of winning Benjamin's approval to marry William. They lived at fashionable Graeme Park, an elegant estate with a house built by Keith. Well-educated, intelligent, literate, and attractive, Elizabeth acquired William's devotion shortly before he departed for England with Franklin in 1757 to pursue his legal training at Lincoln's Inn. Although in passionate love letters William promised to write and to return to her, he ended the affair in 1759. Broken-hearted, she spent the rest of her life in search of knowledge, in intimate correspondence with other women, and in pursuit of an appropriate male relationship. She traveled to England in 1764 and met some of the leading writers of the day while she lived near Franklin. She created something of a salon at Graeme Park, including in it such luminaries as Benjamin Rush and William Smith, provost of the University of Pennsylvania. Her marriage to Henry Hugh Fergusson, a Scotsman, in 1772, ended in disaster. Declaring his Loyalism during the Revolution, he fled to Britain, resulting in her temporary loss of Graeme Park. Though not charged with treason, she lived under a cloud of suspicion and eventual near poverty for the rest of her life.

Helvétius, Anne-Catherine (d. 1800). Franklin's neighbor, a widow, and favorite object of playful attention, flirtation, and potential courtship while he lived at Passy, especially after he was rebuffed by Madame Brillon in 1778. Some of his most charming and wistful letters were addressed to her during his years in Paris and following his return to Philadelphia in 1785.

Hewson, Elizabeth (1774–?). Daughter of Mary (Polly) Stevenson Hewson and Franklin's favorite choice as a good match for grandson Benjamin Franklin Bache.

Hewson, Mary (Polly) Stevenson (1739–95). Daughter of Margaret Stevenson and Franklin's virtual adopted daughter in London; later a frequent guest and companion in Paris and Philadelphia. Well educated before Franklin met her in London in 1757, she instantly won his attention and joined Catherine Ray as a special object of his affections and intellectual interest. He immediately chose her as a proper marital companion for son William. That was not to be. In 1770 she married William Hewson, a physician and avid anatomist. He died four years later from an infection that he probably acquired while dissecting one of the cadavers whose bones were found in 1997 during archaeological excavations at 32 Craven Street. Polly spent the rest of her life rearing and educating two sons and a daughter from her four-year marriage and living with Franklin at Passy during 1784–85 and in Philadelphia during the last four years of his life (1786–90). She died at her son's home in Bristol, Pennsylvania.

Left Hand, The (1785). One of Franklin's late female pseudonyms. "The left hand" resents the superior treatment and responsibility given her sister (the right hand) and parodies inequalities imposed upon women.

Le Roy, Petronille (?–?). Wife of Jean-Baptiste Le Roy, French business associate of Franklin, and another of the French women believed by John Adams to have too much influence over him.

Mecom, Jane Franklin (1712–94). The last child of Josiah and Abiah Franklin, and Franklin's youngest and favorite sister. Although Franklin ran away from Boston when Jane was only eleven, they maintained a lifelong correspondence—among his largest. Married to a Boston saddler, she bore twelve children, all except one of whom died of mental or physical defects as children. Of the three who lived beyond the age of thirty-three, two died insane. Her greatest happiness in life was her association with Franklin. She became the most intimate and trusted woman in his life, the only person with whom he could talk and write in total candor. The only time they lived under the same roof in later life was during 1775 and 1776 when she fled the British occupation of Boston, and lived with the Franklins in Philadelphia. Franklin bought a house for her in Boston where she returned in 1784, and left it to her along with a life income in his will.

Osgood, Judith (?–?). Franklin presented this young English woman in August 1770, in London, for marriage to his Philadelphia colleague, John Foxcroft. The marriage was performed by Thomas Coombe, also from Philadelphia, but lodging with Franklin on Craven Street in London. Franklin thereafter always referred to Osgood as "my daughter," provoking some historians to suspect that she was another of his illegitimate children.

Ray, Catharine (Greene) (1731–94). A favorite gleam in Franklin's eye from the moment they met in Boston in 1754—he was forty-eight and she twenty-three years of age. They were captivated with each other instantly. Born in Rhode Island and given a typical female education, she was lively, opinionated, and vivacious. After he finished his postal business in Boston that year, they departed on a long-cherished trip together that included a visit to Catherine's sister in Westerly, Rhode Island. The mutual joy arising from the trip led to a lifetime of correspondence and four additional meetings. The last of these was in 1776 in Philadelphia and it included her husband, William Greene, whom she married in 1758 and who was rising to a distinguished career in Rhode Island as associate and then chief justice of its Supreme Court and as the state's wartime governor (1778–86).

Shipley, Georgiana (1756–1806). The most colorful of the children of Bishop Jonathan and Anna Mordaunt Shipley, Franklin's close English friends and hosts at Twyford, where he began writing his *Autobiography*. Beautiful and one of Franklin's favorite conversationalists on matters including languages, the classics, and the arts, she studied painting with Sir Joshua Reynolds. Her marriage in 1784 to Francis Hare-Naylor, an impecunious author, was against the wishes of her parents.

Single, Celia (1732). One of Franklin's early pseudonyms, a young woman who writes to complain that Franklin in the *Pennsylvania Gazette* "has broken the Peace of several Families, by causing Difference between Men and their Wives." Celia relates the story of an incident growing from an article ridiculing the laziness of a woman. She has "several times in your Paper seen severe Reflections upon us

Women, for Idleness and Extravagance, but I do not remember to have once seen any such Animadversions upon the Men." She then describes the behavior of several men: Mr. Billiard, Mr. Husselcap, Mr. Finikin, Mr. Crownhim, Mr. Bookish, Mr. Tweedledum, and Mr. Toot-a-toot and other idle scoundrels.

Stevenson (Mrs. Addinell), Margaret (1706–83). Franklin's almost perpetual landlady on his two lengthy sojourns in London, 1757–62 and 1764–75. A widow, she received Franklin and son William along with their two black servants, Peter and King, almost immediately upon their arrival in November 1757, at No. 7 Craven Street (now 32 Craven Street). She and her daughter Mary (Polly) provided Franklin and his frequent guests with a warm and ample London base and home. Soon quite intimate with Franklin, both of them became virtual members of the extended Franklin family on both sides of the Atlantic.

T., Mrs. Unmarried woman with child and lover of Franklin's early London roommate, James Ralph, between 1724–26. In the *Autobiography* Franklin acknowledges that while Ralph was away, "being at this time under no Religious Restraints, and presuming on my Importance to her, I attempted Familiarities, (another Erratum) which she repuls'd with a proper Resentment." The event resulted in the loss of Ralph's friendship and his refusal to repay his debts to Franklin.

Thompson, Emma (?–?). British admirer of Franklin, whose exchange of letters with her in February 1777 from Saint Omer in France reflects a previous intimate relationship.

Wheatley, Phillis (1753–84). American slave poet. Taken in the African slave trade to America as a young teen and sold to the Massachusetts family of John and Susannah Wheatley, Phillis quickly learned English and began writing poetic elegies to liberty and the liberators of the age: Lord Dartmouth, George Whitefield, Lady Hastings (the Countess of Huntingdon), George Washington, and many others. With the publication of her *Poems on Various Subjects* in 1773, she became the most famous black woman, slave or free, of the eighteenth century. Her owners arranged a book tour of England for her with the assistance of the Countess of Huntingdon. The twenty-year-old Phillis arrived in London on June 27, 1773, with her young master, Nathaniel Wheatley. Greeted there by Benjamin Franklin at the request of his Massachusetts cousins, master Wheatley became inexplicably annoyed with Franklin's visit. Three weeks after her arrival, Phillis Wheatley reported to the Countess of Huntingdon—whom she still had not seen—that she was being returned to America. Master Wheatley evidently believed that Franklin had come to inform the poet that, as a result of the Somerset Case decided by High Justice Lord Mansfield in 1772, she was automatically freed when she touched English soil. So as not to risk the loss of the valuable poet, her owner abruptly returned her to America. Although freed by her Loyalist owner in 1778, she died in abject poverty in 1784. As a free black she could not peddle the poems that made her famous as a slave poet.

CHRONOLOGY OF BENJAMIN FRANKLIN'S ENCOUNTERS WITH WOMEN

BOSTON, 1706–1723

1706   Born to Abiah Folger Franklin, second wife of father, Josiah Franklin in Boston

1708   Deborah Read born to John Read and Sarah White in Birmingham, England

1711   The Reads migrate to Philadelphia

1712   Jane Franklin Mecom, his favorite sister, born in Boston

1722   Creates his first female pseudonyms—Mrs. Silence Dogood and Margaret Aftercast

PHILADELPHIA, 1723–1724

1723 Oct. Meets Deborah Read (age 15) as he first arrives in Philadelphia and soon becomes a boarder in the Read home; a romance shortly ensues

LONDON, 1724–1726

1724 Nov. Travels to London where he becomes involved with "lewd women" and attempts to seduce Mrs. T, the lover of his roommate and friend James Ralph

1725 Aug. Deborah Read marries John Rogers in Philadelphia

      Dec. Rogers disappears forever

PHILADELPHIA, 1726–1757

1726 Oct. Arrives in Philadelphia and learns that Deborah is married but does not know the whereabouts of Rogers

1729 [?] Illegitimate son William born to BF (age 23) by an unknown woman

1730 Sept. Common-law union formed with presumably still married Deborah (age 22)

1732   Creates new female pseudonyms, Alice Addertongue and
            Celia Single and publishes first *Poor Richard's Almanack*
            always filled with pithy sayings about women

1743 *Aug.* Daughter Sarah (Sally) born to BF and Deborah

1745   Begins electrical experiments and writes "Old Mistresses
            Apologue," his most risqué statement about women

1747   Creates Miss Polly Baker, his most famous fictional
            female

1752 *May* Abiah Franklin dies in Boston

      June Conducts the kite experiment in Philadelphia

1754   Meets and is charmed by Catherine Ray (age 23) while
            visiting Boston

1755   William Franklin and Elizabeth Graeme (age 18) fall in
            love

LONDON, 1757–1762

1757 *June* Sails from NYC, taking William with him

      July Moves into No. 7 (now 36) Craven Street with landlady
            Margaret Stevenson (his own age) and her daughter
            Mary (Polly) (age 18)

1759   Amelia Evans (age 15)—Deborah's godchild—visits
            Craven St. and becomes dependent on BF for
            assistance from time to time

1761   Forms a playful relationship with Dorthea Blunt (age 28)
            and chooses Marianne Davies (age 17) to perform his
            glass armonica publicly

1762 *Feb.* Illegitimate son William Temple born to William (age 32)
            and an unknown woman

      Aug. Departs for Philadelphia disapproving of William's
            plans for marriage

      Sept. William marries Elizabeth Downs (age ?) in London and
            is commissioned as royal governor of New Jersey

PHILADELPHIA, 1762–1764

1762 *Nov.* Arrives in Philadelphia

1764 Death of Barbara, a Franklin family servant

Aug. In electoral campaign his enemies charge that Barbara was William's mother and that BF buried her in an unmarked grave to maintain the secret

Nov. Departs Philadelphia for London

LONDON, 1764–1775

1764 *Dec.* Returns to his residence with Margaret Stevenson on Craven Street

1766 Sarah Franklin (age 13), an ill English cousin, begins living with BF and Margaret Stevenson on Craven Street

1767 Cecilia Davies (age 17) becomes vocalist traveling with her sister performing BF's glass armonica

Oct. Sally Franklin (age 24), with the support of Deborah, marries Richard Bache (age 30), against BF's wishes in Philadelphia

1770 Mary Barwell (age 37) enters BF's circle of favorite women

BF presents Polly Stevenson in wedding ceremonies to marry William Hewson and later does the same for Judith Osgood ("my daughter") to marry John Foxcroft

1771 *June* Becomes charmed with Georgiana Shipley (age 25) while visiting the Shipley home at Twyford where he also begins writing his *Autobiography*

1774 William Hewson dies from infection deriving from an autopsy he performed

Dec. Deborah Franklin dies in Philadelphia

1775 *Feb.* BF leaves London for Philadelphia

PHILADELPHIA, 1775–1776

1775 *May* Arrives in Philadelphia

Nov. Visits Washington's Massachusetts encampment; brings sister Jane, a refugee from occupied Boston, back to Philadelphia

1776 *June* William arrested as a Loyalist in New Jersey, leaving the severely ill and asthmatic Elizabeth isolated in governor's residence in Perth Amboy

 July Declaration of Independence issued

 Aug. Elizabeth sends letter to BF pleading for assistance, which he ignores

 Oct. Departs Philadelphia for Paris, taking William Temple (age 14) and Benjamin Franklin Bache (age 7) with him

PARIS, 1776–1785

1776 *Dec.* Arrives in Paris

1777 *Feb.* Moves to Paris suburb Passy and lives with Jacques Donatien Chaumont and his wife Therese Le Ray de Chaumont, who becomes a strong influence over his social life

 Begins a flirtation with Anne-Louise Brillon (age 33) and participates in the salon of Anne-Catherine Helvétius (age 65?)

 July Elizabeth Franklin dies helpless and alone in a New York refuge

1778 Madame Brillon rejects BF's courtship; he then diverts his attention more fully to Madame Helvétius and other ladies of Paris

1784 Polly Hewson and her children move in with BF at Passy

 BF buys a home for sister Jane Mecom in Boston and gives her a life estate

PHILADELPHIA, 1785–1790

1785 *July* After sad departure meetings with Madame Helvétius and other of his Paris friends, departs with William Temple and Benny for Philadelphia via Le Havre and Southampton, England

 Last meeting with William and the Shipleys at Southampton

Illegitimate son Theodore born to William Temple (age 23) and the married Blanchette Caillot in Paris (he died in infancy)

Sept.   Arrives in Philadelphia

Creates his last female pseudonym, "The Left Hand"

1786   Polly Hewson and children move to Philadelphia and reside with BF and the Baches until his death

1790   *Apr.*   BF dies with Sally and Polly by his side

INTRODUCTION
Benjamin Franklin and the World of Women

⌒

Strange! that a man who has wit enough to write a satire
should have folly enough to publish it.
—*Poor Richard, 1742*

Benjamin Franklin had a life-long, admitted, extended, and well-documented interest in women—particular women: his mother; a sister; some acknowledged "errata"; a wife; his daughter; a landlady; the landlady's daughter and her friends; and the cosmeticized, bejeweled, and exotic ladies of Paris on the eve of the French Revolution; plus various other women he encountered in his far-flung and lengthy eighteenth century journeys among the American colonies, in London and across the United Kingdom, through the Low Countries and at posh spas in Germany, and in the drawing rooms and salons of France. There were many female associates—old, young, and always interesting—in the world of Benjamin Franklin and women.

But he was also fascinated with ideas about the role of women in society and the ways in which they were often stereotyped. In his earliest writings in Boston, he paraded as Mrs. Silence Dogood (1722), lampooning images of busybody women. During his years of greatest business and public success in Philadelphia (1747), he introduced Polly Baker—one of his most memorable female voices—to mock America's legal system and its treatment of unwed mothers. And even in his twilight years, as he was returning to Philadelphia after almost a decade of fame in France, he persisted in using the female voice in 1785 in "A Petition of the Left Hand" to decry the unequal treatment of human beings—including women.[1]

Never was he short on observations about women—in his newspapers, his almanacks, and his bagatelles and in letters of advice and counsel to the hundreds of women who crossed the broad pathway of his life over eight decades, including twenty-six years abroad. In his *Poor Richard's Almanacks*, which appeared yearly from 1732 to

1758, he frequently included spicy sayings about women: eleven specifically on women, twenty-four others about wives, four on mothers, three on maids, four on daughters, and the like.[2] Indeed, an examination of his ideas about women over time reveals that there is as much to be said about the changing world of women and Benjamin Franklin's role in it as about his fascination with particular women.

And he was without question one of the world's first and best mentors. Everywhere he went he encountered young women whom he loved to guide through life (while he also clearly adored their sprightly personalities and undying faithfulness to him): Catherine Ray (1754); Polly Hewson (1757); Marianne Davies (1761); Dorthea Blunt (1762); Mary Barwell (1770); perhaps, also, Madame Brillon (1777).[3] These were all women twenty-plus years his junior with whom he developed deep and abiding relations that continued across decades of contact and correspondence. But in all cases, his role was that of mentor and guide, not meddler or pedophile.

In the process of mentoring, counseling, or socializing with women, there was some magic in the encounter that brought forth the most playful facets of his personality, his most compelling humor. Whether describing his first clownish meeting in 1723 with his future wife, Deborah—as he juggled "three great Puffy rolls" of bread on Market Street in Philadelphia; or advising a "dear Friend" in 1745 in his roguish "Old Mistresses Apologue" that "in all your Amours you should *prefer old Women to young ones* . . . [because] they are *so grateful!!*"; or in testing the waters to see if Madam Brillon might be wooable in 1784 ("That when he shall be with her, he shall be obliged to take tea, play at chess, listen to music, and do all that she may demand of him [Of course, only that which he is able to do!]"), the mere opportunity of dealing with a female being brought forth the most charming and witty elements of his character.[4]

And, as a result of his well-documented interests in women and the ways in which he sought to charm those selected for special attention, Franklin paid a price during his lifetime and has continued to do so historically over the centuries since his death. During his life he was often accused of being a lecher when it came to his dealings with women. Rumors followed him throughout his political career concerning the Franklin penchant for entering affairs with women and for producing illegitimate children: his fathering of son William out of wedlock; William's fathering of William Temple; and Temple's fathering of a son, Theodore, under the same circumstances. Each time Franklin came under the close scrutiny of doubting eyes—when he ran for reelection to the Pennsylvania assembly in 1764 (and was defeated); when he whiled away his time under the ever-vigilant eyes of Abigail and John Adams during 1779 in Paris; and, in the period surrounding his death, when his political motives came into question—the subject of his relationship to women became controverted.[5]

But after his death and the upheavals of the 1790s when grandson Benjamin Franklin Bache became the Franklin focus—"lighting rod, junior" in the words of Peter Porcupine—the subject of Franklin's connections with women got less attention. For most of the nineteenth century it was a topic universally known, but little mentioned. Although in various versions of his *Autobiography* he acknowledged that his life had not been flawless, the public discussion of his views on women and involvements with them was pretty much put aside (except in one extraordinary sense) until 1939 when the Peter Pauper Press of Mount Vernon, New York, brought forth a little book titled *Dr. Benj. Franklin and the Ladies: Being Various Letters, Essays, Bagatelles, & Satires to & About the Fair Sex.*[6]

Published in a private, high-quality, boxed, and limited collector's edition of 1,450 copies, *Franklin and the Ladies* appeared at the culmination of a period of fifty years during which historians almost uniformly considered it improper and ungentlemanly to talk about Franklin's dealings with women. And there was even less of an inclination to explore his views on the subject of women in society. The little book, however, combined usefully, in one place, a rich selection of Franklin's letters to his mother, his sister Jane Mecom, and his wife, Deborah; his correspondence with various of his young admirers; his letters to those French women he attempted to charm; and his various "bagatelles and satires on the sex [women]." This combination of letters, essays, and private advice made it possible to look at the broad spectrum of Franklin's views and flirtations.[7]

The most extraordinary inclusion in the seventy-page booklet was the last item: Franklin's short letter titled "On the Choice of a Mistress," or as he dubbed it, "Old Mistresses Apologue." Indeed, the inclusion of this last piece on pages 67–69 of the book culminated fifty years of some of the strangest efforts by historians, collectors, and public officials to protect Franklin's historical reputation with regard to women and other matters of decency. For this piece, incontrovertibly written and titled by Franklin himself, was long viewed as too indelicate and outlandish to be associated with one of America's idolized founding fathers.[8]

Wholly unknown publicly until its existence leaked out in a most unusual manner in 1881, it is in this brief essay—written as a letter to an unknown friend—that Franklin set forth some of his wittiest and most memorable statements about women. And it is through the discovery of this essay that a perpetual cloud came over and universal snickers came to characterize any reference to Franklin and the subject of women.

He began the letter with a defense of matrimony "as the most natural state of Man." "It is the Man and Woman united that make the compleat human Being," he wrote; "together they are more likely to succeed in the World." A single man is "an incompleat Animal" and "resembles the odd Half of a Pair of Scissars." "If you get a prudent, healthy Wife," Franklin could attest from his own experience, "your Industry in your Profession, with her good Economy will be a Fortune sufficient."[9]

These wise counsels he shared with a young man who, Franklin says, persisted "in thinking a Commerce with the Sex inevitable." In view of his reluctance to marry, Franklin suddenly turns the tables to record one of his now most famous set of sayings about women. If the young man simply would not marry, then Franklin advised that "in all your Amours you should prefer old Women to young ones." Admitting that this advice might seem like a "Paradox," Franklin listed his "Reasons" for giving it.

And, in that these various statements became the basis of historic rumor-mongering about Franklin in the twentieth century, it is worthy to list them here briefly:

1. Because they have more Knowledge of the World . . .
2. Because when Women cease to be handsome they study to be good . . . there is hardly such a Thing to be found as an Old Woman who is not a good Woman.

3. Because there is no Hazard of Children, which irregularly produc'd may be attended with much Inconvenience.
4. Because through more Experience they are more prudent and discreet in conducting an Intrigue to prevent Suspicion.
5. Because in every Animal that walks upright the Deficiency of the Fluids that fill the Muscles appearrs first in the highest Part. The Face first grows lank and wrinkled; then the Neck; then the Breast and Arms; the lower Parts continuing to the Last as plump as ever; so that covering all above with a Basket, and regarding only what is below the Girdle, it is impossible of two Women to tell an old one from a young one. And as in the Dark all Cats are grey, the Pleasure of Corporal Enjoyment with an old Woman is at least equal, and frequently superior; every Knack being by Practice, capable of Improvement.
6. Because the Sin is less. The debauching a Virgin may be her Ruin . . .
7. Because the Compunction is less. The having made a young Girl miserable may give you frequent bitter Reflection; none of which can attend the making an old Woman happy.
8thly and Lastly. They are *so grateful!!* [10]

Although paradoxical in the hearing and contemplations of a young man, this statement—on the surface written in jest—profoundly reflects the bitter experiences, disappointments, and emotional suffering already felt by the thirty-nine-year-old Franklin at the time he wrote it. In a cunning and transparent sleight of his literary hand, Franklin here summarized how he could have sidestepped the admitted sexual errata of his youth. [11]

The existence of this important document and window on Franklin's soul was wholly unknown—except to William Temple Franklin, Franklin's grandson and secretary—until the short letter was discovered by a London bookseller, Henry Stevens, some time after he acquired Temple's still-intact collection of more than three thousand manuscript letters and documents in 1850. Nevertheless, during the thirty-one years in which he held the collection, he did not reveal the document or its existence (even though he had it twice set in type, but did not publish it). [12]

But when Stevens decided to sell the Franklin collection in 1881, he alluded to the document and a few others in such a way that it was certain to capture the attention and imagination of the Victorian world. In a sales catalog listing the items in the collection he wished to sell, he described one small cluster of letters in this manner: "Essays in form of Letters, on 'Perfumes' and 'Choice of a Mistress,' witty and explosive, but perhaps too Dean Swiftian for the press." [13]

Wittingly or not, Stevens not only cranked up the long-silent rumor mill about Franklin and women again, he also revved it to the highest pitch ever. And when he sold the collection to the United States government in 1882 to be housed initially at the Department of State, he made the situation even worse. He did not mention in the catalog that there were three separate copies of this curious document about women. He was thus able to withdraw the best of the copies—the one bearing Franklin's title and his signature—and keep this unique version in private hands. This most prized copy passed among several parties until it was purchased in 1926 by the renowned Philadelphia collector and book dealer Dr. A. S. W. Rosenbach. Rosenbach then kept it under cover until he placed it on exhibit at the Free Library of Philadelphia in 1938 with the claim that it was "the most famous and the wittiest essay" ever written by Franklin. [14]

Meanwhile, the two copies of the essay left in the collection bought by the U.S. government—and the letter on perfumes—caused something of a sensation when they were located and read by Department of State librarians. They were quickly placed under close restriction, only to be viewed—certainly not copied or printed—by qualified gentlemen. There was thus established another source of rumor, the kind that both official and unofficial Washington, D.C., are well able to create and perpetuate. [15]

When these two copies were eventually closely examined in relation to the third Rosenbach version, there was yet another revelation that would help stoke the rumor mill. It became clear that the Rosenbach copy was the most authentic and complete and the only one that bore Franklin's autograph. The first State Department copy was a transcript copy of the original with a few modifications, also in Franklin's hand, but without title or autograph. The second copy at the State Department, however, was the most curious in the puzzle. It was a transcript of "Old Mistresses Apologue," made in the early nineteenth century by or for William Temple Franklin as he was gathering materials for his long-delayed publication of Franklin's letters and papers.

Franklin specifically left his library and papers to Temple so that the grandson/former secretary—who had transcribed many of the papers—would arrange, edit, and publish them. Temple dallied and postponed the project for twenty-eight years following his grandfather's death. Himself something of a playboy who made all of the same mistakes as his grandfather—and many more—he could well understand the double entendre of Franklin's message. He thereby transcribed the "Old Mistresses Apologue" for publication. But when his three-volume work finally appeared in 1817–18 under the title *Memoirs of the Life and Writings of Benjamin Franklin*, the mysterious essay on choosing a mistress had been silently deleted from publication! Evidently, even Temple had ultimately decided that the piece was too risqué to print.

Meanwhile, as rumors began to radiate around and out of Washington in 1882 about the existence of the essay, various energetic individuals vied for the right to publish what was becoming, after the *Autobiography*, Franklin's most famous writing. Secretary of State Thomas F. Bayard (1828–98) between 1885 and 1889 turned down every request to publish the piece because of what he considered its indecency. He would not allow Franklin biographer and editor John Bigelow to add it to new printings of his three-volume *The Life of Benjamin Franklin Written by Himself* (1875). However, as a gentleman and a politician he lent a manuscript copy of the essay to be read aloud at a great New York society dinner party—after the ladies in attendance had left the dining room!¹⁶

One by-product of this special social airing of Franklin's essay was a demand on the part of the "gentlemen" present to have a copy for their own use. Realizing that he had got himself into an embarrassing predicament—Bayard did not want to be responsible for publishing something indecent, but he also could not disappoint his political contributors—he turned to a trusted friend for help, the twenty-two-year-old historian and bibliographer Paul Leicester Ford (1865–1902).

Ford was perfect for the task. Although young at the time, he had already become a prolific editor and bibliographer. At eleven he had published the genealogy of his great-grandfather Noah Webster. At age sixteen he had published letters exchanged between Webster and George Washington and completed a bibliography of Webster's works. Already he was at work on his massive *Franklin Bibliography* that would appear in 1889. And he was gearing up to do editions of the papers of Christopher Columbus and Thomas Jefferson.[17]

Knowing that Ford had his own printing press and that he could be trusted, Bayard asked him to print twenty-five copies of the essay for private distribution. Bayard, described as "cautious and conservative, . . . known for his tall, stately stature, good looks, courtly manners, and personal integrity," agreed that Ford could retain two copies—one for his bibliography project and the other for his printing files. Ford was happy to oblige. Adding more burlesque to the piece, he gave it a title page, calling the essay "A Philosopher in Undress." And he later told the story of this private printing on the condition that his name not be revealed. He wrote, "You are at liberty to use as much or as little of this story as you please, only kindly omit my name, as I do not care to harness it, even with that of B.F. to such a cart." He, too, thought the essay was offensive. Thus in his popular biography of Franklin, *The Many-Sided Franklin,* published in 1899, he gave the opinion that it would "shock modern taste" should it ever be published.[18]

Ford's squeamish view of Franklin's essay on mistresses despite the fact that he was a professional historian—was not at all unique. John Bach McMaster (1852–1932), another productive giant of the historical profession—though prone to moral judgments, reported that the essay was "unhappily too indecent to print" when he published his *Benjamin Franklin as a Man of Letters* in 1887. A few years later McMaster would be even more specific about his objections: "Morality he [Franklin] never taught, and he was not fit to teach it. Nothing in his whole career is more to be lamented than that a man of parts so great should, long after he had passed middle life, continue to write pieces so filthy that no editor has ever had the hardihood to print them." Sidney George Fisher (1856–1927), another eminent Franklin biographer and esteemed gentleman historian from Philadelphia, who published *The True Benjamin Franklin* in 1899, also would not print the essay—although he did quote parts of it.[19]

8

If historians would not touch Franklin's affront to Victorian manners, one can imagine the views of other proper preachers, pedagogues, and politicians. Clergyman/educator and founder of Macalester College at Saint Paul, Minnesota, Edward D. Neill (1823—93) told his students and faculty in 1892 about the "real" Benjamin Franklin by referring to the offensive and oft rejected essay as the one in which Franklin advised a young man how "to sustain a relation of neither maid nor wife."[20]

Perhaps the most telling judgment on Franklin's morality was rendered a few years later when honored senator George F. Hoar (1826—1904) of Massachusetts, Franklin's birthplace, got a list of nominees to be included in America's newly established National Hall of Fame. Grandson of founding father Roger Sherman, chief of decorum in the U.S. Senate, regent of the Smithsonian Institution, president of the American Historical Association, and translator of Thucydides' histories, Hoar looked over a list containing the names of Washington, Franklin, Jefferson, Webster, and Lincoln. And then he marked through Franklin's name, explaining: "Dr. Franklin's conduct of life was that of a man on a low plane. He was without idealism, without lofty principle, and on one side of his character gross and immoral. . . . [His letter] on the question of keeping a mistress, which, making all allowance for the manners of the time, and all allowance for the fact that he might have been partly in jest, is an abominable and wicked letter; and all his relation to women, and to the family life were of that character."[21] Such was the universal opinion and judgment of nineteenth-century Americans. Franklin, for his deeds in life and for the despicable words found a century later to have emanated from his pen, was a morally condemned man.

The embargo against revealing Franklin's essay continued until 1926—a time when attitudes about human habits and desires were undergoing rapid change. In that year the version of the essay that was by then housed at the Library of Congress—away from the political controls of the State Department—was finally published in full by a new Franklin biographer. Phillips Russell, a popular writer, issued a new biography titled *Benjamin Franklin: The First Civilized American* in which he chose to present Franklin in his entirety, warts and all. His intent to be candid about Franklin appeared on the first page, where he presented a "prefatory catechism." Russell asked,

"Were there any inconsistencies in his career?" The answer, "Many." "Can you specify?" he continued. "He [Franklin] disregarded his own maxims as uttered by 'Poor Richard' and lamentably failed to observe the principles set up in his own 'Art of Virtue.' " [22]

Russell titled the chapter containing the mistress essay "Franklin's Humorous Year" (chap. 19), discounting this and other pieces written at about the same time and attributing them to Franklin's business success and newly won confidence at the age of thirty-nine. Yet he also alluded to the controversy surrounding the document: "Certain writers and biographers have listed it or hinted at its existence in such a way as to excite a curiosity which they might as well have allayed. Since the letter is in a sense a public document which helps reveal Franklin just as he was, there is no longer any reason for not publishing it in full." But having thus dared to cut through the tedium of Victorian attitudes and mannerisms, Russell proceeded to prove that not everything Franklin wrote could yet be revealed. "Not even this writer, however, has the hardihood to include another of Franklin's suppressed documents," he wrote, referring to Franklin's essay on "perfuming farts," which had been placed by bibliophile Stevens in the same batch of papers as being too indecent to be printed. While pretending to remove the mystery surrounding Franklin's manners and morals, he managed to perpetuate the image of this founding father as morally defective. [23]

While historians and the pundits of public opinion treated Franklin as morally flawed, they nevertheless in their biographies had to deal in some manner with the subject of the many women in Franklin's life. Paul Leicester Ford, although he would not print the essay on mistresses for public consumption, meticulously analyzed and categorized Franklin's numerous female relationships. But he dismissed moral judgment on these connections because, as he averred, Franklin lived in another era with different standards of behavior. Bernard Faÿ, a French historian, and author in English of a spate of books about Franklin, dealt only with Franklin's involvements with women in France. From his point of view, Franklin's vast popularity opened many elegant parlors to the wily American, and he rarely declined the welcome invitations to join the company of charming females. [24]

By 1938—the year in which the Benjamin Franklin National Memorial at Philadelphia was completed and dedicated—it seemed that historians were no longer pinching their noses when they spoke of various parts of Franklin's career. Carl Van Doren published that year the most definitive biography yet produced on Franklin, simply titled *Benjamin Franklin.* Van Doren in an expanse of 845 pages did not hold back on any aspect of Franklin's life or any of his writings, nor did he editorialize about their moral character. He described the essay on mistresses as "the best known of his surreptitious writings" and the letter on perfuming farts as "a burlesque of such preposterous scientific schemes as Rabelais and Swift had ridiculed." [25]

Van Doren set the tone for future serious Franklin historians and biographers. Indeed, the first biographers to confront Franklin warts and all and who sought to understand Franklin's much rumored private life were Claude-Anne Lopez and Eugenia W. Herbert, who on the eve of the American Revolution Bicentennial commemoration produced probably the most accurate description of this man and his relations with other human beings—including women. In this work, titled *The Private Franklin: The Man and His Family,* Lopez and Herbert delve into Franklin's "Errata Committed, Errata Corrected" (chap. 2) intimately and constructively, acknowledging that his relations with women—family and otherwise—encountered rocky periods. [26]

In the most recent serious treatments of Franklin's life and legacy, the subject of Franklin and women is barely mentioned. Sir Esmond Wright in his *Franklin of Philadelphia,* published on the eve of the bicentennial of the U.S. Constitution, merely describes Franklin's many women friends without comment. And, even more remarkably, in a fat volume of twenty-four essays arising from a major symposium held in April 1990 on the bicentennial of Franklin's death, *Reappraising Benjamin Franklin,* no paper was devoted to the subject of Franklin and women. Nor was there any reference to the subject—except in passing—in any of the essays. [27]

But while scholars sidestepped discussions of Franklin's morality in relation to women, the popular image of him did not change. It was probably inevitable in the 1960s, during the heyday of Hugh Hefner and *Playboy* magazine, that some wag would compare Franklin and the creator of the Playboy empire. [28] Such a charge was seriously made in 1967. It was likewise destined that Franklin would be portrayed during the 1970s and the bicentennial of the American Revolution as an unprincipled philanderer. And such was the case in the Broadway musical and subsequent Hollywood movie 1776—where he also was made to look as something of a buffoon.[29]

Nor could the bicentennial of Franklin's death in 1990 pass without some pokes at his personality and his proclivity for women. Two days before a major commemoration of Franklin's death in lavish proceedings in Philadelphia, a Washington publicist put forth the only article on the occasion that circulated nationally. Aaron Goldman's spoofy "Our Founding Flirt: Cuddlesome Ben Franklin, the Randy Rebel with a Cause," appeared on 15 April in the *Washington Post* and was then reprinted in newspapers throughout the nation. The only other article about Franklin that got national circulation during the 1990 bicentennial year appeared in a July issue of *Newsweek*, titled "A Quick Look at the History of Smut"! So much for the rehabilitation of Franklin by historians.[30]

It was athwart this long and overwhelming tradition of ridiculing Franklin's relationship with women that a group of very capable historians—themselves mainly women—came together on 9 April 1994, to explore quite seriously for the first time the subject "Benjamin Franklin and Women—Women and Benjamin Franklin." None scoffed at the topic or the task. All produced rich new perspectives on the often complex relationship between Franklin and particular women in his life and on the subject of the changing role of women in eighteenth-century society. Although convened on a topic that continued to elicit snickers even as the conference began, all of the speakers peeled away the mold of history to bring new light and understanding to this often trivialized subject.

The speeches—subsequently written for inclusion as chapters in this volume—fell into two categories. The authors of the first group of chapters examine the relationship between Franklin and particular women—his wife, Deborah; his daughter, Sally; and some of the women he courted while he was married and after Deborah's death in 1774. In the second set of chapters, their authors look more fundamentally at the evolving role of women in the eighteenth century as juxtaposed to Franklin and his involvement with various women.

Included here, then, is much more than a look at Franklin's flirtations. These chapters shed much-needed light on women in the era of liberating revolutions—their hopes, aspirations, views on education, citizenship, motherhood, and spousal responsibilities.

Sheila Skemp, author of the definitive biography of William Franklin (*William Franklin: Son of a Patriot, Servant of a King* [1990]), sets the standard for this work in her depiction of the life of Deborah Read Franklin, whom she describes as being denigrated by Franklin from the time he arrived in Philadelphia until her death in 1774. Nevertheless, from their first unification in a common-law marriage in 1730 until her death, she was a faithful, obedient, and trustworthy business partner. Indeed, when Franklin chose to make Europe more his residence than America in 1757, Deborah became Franklin's "deputy husband" and business manager. Despite the fact that Franklin's letters to and descriptions of Deborah reflect a minimum of romantic interstices between the two of them, Skemp sees theirs as generally a successful marriage.

The second most important female connection in Franklin's life after Deborah (he had almost nothing to say about his mother), was his daughter, Sarah or "Sally." His relationship with her, described in the second chapter of this volume, was a most regrettable one. She was born when he was thirty-seven years old, working as hard as he could to amass wealth and fortune. By the time she was four years old, he was totally enthralled with electrical experiments. And when she reached her early adolescence, he was removed to Europe. Sadly, Franklin did not take the time to get to know her, to understand her aspirations, or to give her the education and privileges he eventually thought women should have.

Claude-Anne Lopez, the acknowledged authority on the subject of Benjamin Franklin and women (to wit: *Mon Cher Papa: Franklin and the Ladies of Paris* [1966] and *The Private Franklin: The Man and His Family* [with Eugenia Herbert, 1975], employs her inspired French-language charm to reflect on the nature of Franklin's relationship with the many women he courted. But she chooses to make this analysis based on three specific relationships with very young women. She concludes that the much rumored tales of Franklin's flirtations is an American, not European, myth. And she firmly believes that, despite Franklin's many letters intimating a deep coziness with a number of women, his principal aim was to charm, not to seduce them.

These introductions to the women in Franklin's life are followed by four aggressive chapters that look at four facets of the role of women in Franklin's world. Jan Lewis, an authority on women and views of their sexuality in the eighteenth century, looks at the roles women played in Franklin's world. She finds that there was an almost total bifurcation between Franklin's world as "patriarch," procreating husband and father, and sexual being and his world as a "republican" and lover. In his family he did business, had sex, and produced offspring; in his other relations he practiced republicanism, promoted the rights of women, and—most notably—found love. His deep need for romantic stimulation and the warmth of love was found in his social dealings with women in the republic, not in his family.

Mary Kelley, a renowned authority on women, their education, and their reading habits (*Private Woman, Public Stage: Literary Domesticity in Nineteenth-Century America* [1984]), applies her skills to examining ideas about the education of women in Franklin's world. Although Franklin in his mature years became a proponent for the education of women, he did not practice that in the case of his daughter Sally. She got a traditional schooling in domestic skills. But as the American Revolution eventuated into an American republic, opportunities and regard for the value of female education abounded.

Carla Mulford, an accomplished literary historian, provides a completely new and refreshing understanding of the history of Franklin and women—through literature. Historians and politicians have not been the only culprits in perpetuating a negative image of Franklin's involvements with women. His exploits and adjudged misdeeds have been the subject of poets, novelists, essayists, and proponents of the rights of women. Some found that he had many more illegitimate children than the acknowledged William. Others portrayed him as being sought by women to fulfill their passions rather than as in pursuit of them to satisfy his own needs.

Susan Stabile, a rising star in interpreting the education of women in the eighteenth century, looks at Franklin's mentoring role with quite a few women in London and Paris, and a few in America.

She also focuses on the evolution of salons—especially in France and America—as institutions where the differences between men and women melted away. Through salons, in conversation, and with Franklin's elaborate letters (epistles) to young women, Franklin proved to be a formidable educator who touched the lives of many young women. But since he lived so much of his life abroad, he had much more influence on the education of women in England and France than he did on women in the United States.

The end result of these new searches into the world of women and Benjamin Franklin is the revelation that there is much more texture to this realm than could ever have been imagined. It is more complex, less lurid, and more multidimensional than tradition would have it. In a sense, Franklin ultimately seems to hide behind a cloak of light humor rather than to reveal his deep needs for the respect, affection, and love of women. But it is clear that throughout his life, his connection with women, particular women, was his greatest need, his most prized possession.

His reliance on women was nowhere more clearly revealed than in his 1733 *Poor Richard's Almanack*:

> *The proof of gold is fire;*
> *The proof of a woman, gold;*
> *The proof of a man, a woman.*

PART ONE

Franklin's Women

FAMILY PARTNERSHIPS:
The Working Wife, Honoring Deborah Franklin
Sheila Skemp

The good or ill hap of a good or ill life
Is the good or ill choice of a good or ill wife.
—Poor Richard, 1745

In Benjamin Franklin's words, Deborah Franklin was a good "help-meet."[1] She assumed considerable responsibility for raising the Franklin children, managed her domestic duties with apparent ease, worked beside her husband in his printing establishment and post office, and virtually ran his stationery shop. She also served as her husband's surrogate during his long absences from home. For the most part, Benjamin admired her business acumen, relying upon her to handle his business affairs whenever he was away.

Deborah's contributions to the family business, even her often "aggressive" behavior, were not unique. Eighteenth-century women did not pretend to be protected flowers; they did not sit demurely upon a pedestal that both elevated and confined them. The middle-class woman who claimed to be a good "businessman" was not a rarity in Deborah Franklin's world.[2] But in the eighteenth century, a woman's contributions to the economic and domestic welfare of the family did not necessarily give her power or authority in the household, much less in the wider world.

Despite Deborah Franklin's many attributes—her ability, her industry, her devotion to friends and family—historians almost invariably patronize her. They willingly enumerate her accomplishments and skills; but in the end, they offer her their pity rather than their praise. Part of the problem, of course, is that Deborah invariably suffers in comparison to her famous husband. But then so does virtually everyone with whom Franklin came into contact. Benjamin's work was significant. Deborah's was not. His letters home were witty and urbane, brimming with optimism, reflecting the intelligence and wide-ranging interests of their author. His wife's missives, on the other hand, were often melancholy, filled with complaints, poorly written, at times almost incomprehensible, and filled with "unimportant" details about the family, the children, the neighbors. The contrast is painfully obvious. No matter that Deborah wrote as well as almost any American woman did in the mid-eighteenth century—and probably better than most. No matter that her inability to spell and to punctuate properly does not reflect poorly on her intelligence or charm. We might admire Deborah's devotion to her husband and her skills as a helpmate, but Benjamin, we cannot help but feel, could have done better. Deborah may have been a fine companion for an ordinary Philadelphia artisan, but not for the man who stole the lightning from the skies.

What historians know about Deborah Franklin before 1757 comes almost exclusively from her husband's perspective. Franklin's account of his own entry into Philadelphia is a familiar story. Poor, dirty and suffering from fatigue, he wandered the streets in search of food and shelter. Walking up Market Street, his pockets "stuff'd with Shirts and Stockings," carrying "three puffy roles" that he had bought at a local bakery, he encountered Miss Deborah Read, who was standing with her father in the doorway of their house. She giggled at Franklin's "awkward, ridiculous appearance." At least once in her life, Deborah clearly had the upper hand.[3]

Or did she? Franklin's self-serving account of the incident was written many years later and inserted into his *Autobiography* after Deborah's death.[4] He was "Doctor" Franklin by this time, revered throughout the Western world for his scientific experiments, a man of considerable political importance on both sides of the water. Even the most casual reader of the *Autobiography* knew that Benjamin Franklin had risen to great heights despite his ignominious beginnings. Indeed, Franklin lavished such detail on his arrival in Phil-

I. ⌒

Deborah Read (Rogers) Franklin—Franklin's devoted wife and faithful
business partner. (Oil on canvas by Benjamin Wilson, c. 1759, American
Philosophical Society)

adelphia precisely *because* he wanted to highlight the contrast between his present and his past. Seen in this light, Deborah's laughter does not represent her superiority to the homeless ex-apprentice
from Boston. Rather, it makes Benjamin's success all the more admirable—even as it denigrates Deborah Franklin. Her laughter—
seen from a distance—takes on an ironic quality. It is amusing that
this middle-class daughter of a Philadelphia carpenter would ever
have been able to mock the great Benjamin Franklin.

The would-be printer was desperate for a place to stay, and he ended up as a lodger in the Read household. There, he began to view Miss Read with "Respect and Affection," and he had, he said, "some Reason to believe she had the same for me."[5] A marriage to the daughter of a respected artisan who owned two half lots on Market Street would not be a bad bargain. Franklin might well have considered such a match as a way to advance his status.[6] But fate intervened. John Read died, leaving Sarah, his wife, in charge of their daughter's fortunes. Benjamin, lured by the feckless promises of Governor William Keith, left for England in hopes of purchasing the printing equipment he needed to start his own business. He and Deborah "interchang'd some promises," but at Sarah Read's insistence, the couple did not marry.[7] Once in London, Benjamin forgot his promises and Deborah—again at her mother's urging—married another man, John Rogers—a "worthless fellow," according to Franklin, who treated his wife shabbily and ended up deserting her altogether.[8]

Franklin returned to Philadelphia in 1726, no better off financially than when he had left the city two years earlier. But after a couple of other false starts, he was, by 1730, on the road to financial security. He was also ready to think seriously of marriage. He had reestablished contact with Deborah and her mother after his return to Philadelphia and had been struck by the change in his future wife's personality. She was, he said, "generally dejected, and seldom cheerful, and avoided Company." Still, while he claimed to have felt guilty about his own "Giddiness and Inconstancy" he cast about for a better match before turning to his former fiancée.[9]

He had hoped for someone who could bring a respectable dowry to the marriage, but his efforts along those lines were fruitless. Under the circumstances, marriage to Deborah was the best alternative. She could free him from that "hard-to-be-govern'd Passion of Youth" that often led him into "Intrigues with low women."[10] She would be a good woman, a hard worker, and a suitable mother for his illegitimate son, William, who was born shortly after the couple's common-law marriage in the fall of 1730. And the marriage assuaged his guilt, helping him erase one of his many "errata."[11]

Franklin's decision to marry—at least as he presented it in his *Autobiography*—was cool, deliberate, practical, the product of the ledger book mentality for which he was so famous. And once again, Deborah was denigrated. She became a victim. Franklin appears magnanimous—he rescued her from the unhappy position in which his own actions had placed her. He erased his "great erratum." The reader must assume that Deborah was abjectly grateful to Franklin for marrying her.

To some extent, this characterization is correct. But it is hardly the whole story. The marriage was a good one for Benjamin, as well—and not only because he found a wife who was willing to serve as a mother to another woman's child. Deborah may not have brought a dowry to her marriage, but by 1729 his mother-in-law had obtained clear ownership of John Read's former property on Market Street, and in 1734 she divided the eastern half of that lot, plus a dwelling house, between her two sons-in-laws—Francis Croker and Benjamin Franklin.[12]

Moreover, as a native Philadelphian and a member of Christ's Church, Deborah's roots in the city were deep and her contacts were significant. One of her closest childhood friends, for instance, was Deborah Norris, sister of Pennsylvania assembly Speaker Isaac Norris.[13] Both Deborah and her mother—who sold her "well-known Ointment for the ITCH" in Franklin's store—brought their share of customers to the establishment.[14] Benjamin had been rejected by more than one candidate for marriage before he turned his attentions to Deborah. He had no family connections in Philadelphia; he was still in debt; his prospects remained very much in doubt. Benjamin, as much as Deborah, should have been grateful to have secured such an attractive partner.[15]

Indeed, for the first twenty years or so, the marriage served both Benjamin and Deborah well. Historians know very little about Deborah's life in these years. The *Autobiography* does not devote much space to the Franklins' private life. And because Benjamin remained at home throughout most of the period, there are no letters from Deborah to tell us about her experiences. Still, the evidence indicates that they enjoyed a traditional marriage based on affection if not passion. Franklin admired his "plain Country Joan," a faithful nurse, who kept his household in "Peace and good Order," who was industrious and parsimonious, a good "Friend" and a useful partner.[16]

He shared his letters to acquaintances with his wife. She played the flirtatious coquette, laughed at his jokes, and occasionally tried to dissuade him from indulging a sense of humor that was a bit too earthy for her tastes.[17] Her material contributions to the Franklin household were considerable. She took care of a house that was also a place of business. The tiny residence was, at one time or another, home to Deborah's mother, brother and sister, Benjamin's journeyman and apprentice, and his nephew James, as well as to her stepson William and her own daughter Sarah, and for four short years, to her son Francis Folger Franklin, as well. And there were always countless friends and relatives to feed and entertain.[18]

It was no doubt impossible for Deborah to draw a clear line between her duties as "housewife" and "businessman." Indeed, the thought of doing so probably never entered her mind. Even in the eighteenth century, the division between home and work, male and female responsibilities remained fluid. Men were the unquestioned authorities in political affairs. They were also the heads of their households; they were patriarchs who raised children, dispensed discipline, taught morals, manners and academic skills, and enjoyed ultimate authority over all domestic affairs. Women had the responsibility for certain gender-defined tasks—cooking, cleaning and the care of small children. But they also were expected to "pitch in" when their services were needed in the shop or on the farm. So long as a woman acted with her husband's permission, and in the interest of the family, she could perform many duties that would later be reserved for men. And performing those duties threatened neither her husband's dominance nor her own "femininity."[19]

Thus, after her marriage, Deborah was mother and wife, cook and seamstress. She ran the stationery shop, keeping track of the purchases and sales that she made, and she assisted her husband in his printing establishment, as well.[20] While she did not keep her accounts as carefully as she might have, she was generally able to carry out often complex transactions. She spoke with ease of the difference between "Barbadoes Currency" and "sterling value."[21] And she did not shrink from passing judgment on the way other people conducted their business. When an acquaintance bought some houses in Philadelphia, Deborah was frankly contemptuous. "I," she sniffed, "wold not a given a bove halef he has for them."[22] After

1737, when Franklin became the postmaster of Philadelphia, running yet another business from the family's already crowded quarters, Deborah assumed partial responsibility for postal affairs as well. She had, said Benjamin, "a great deal of Experience in the Management of the Post Office," and he had no qualms about leaving her in charge of the operation when he was out of town.[23] If the Franklins "throve" in these years, it was in no small measure due to Deborah's "Industry and Frugality."[24]

Deborah's involvement in the family business gave her neither power nor independence. While she no doubt took pride in her accomplishments, and may even have enjoyed her work in the shop and post office, she performed her services in the name of the family, not as a means of advancing her own individual prospects. Her identity, her sense of purpose and importance, as well as her security were based on her role as wife and mother. While she was a good business-woman, and worked in the public sphere on a regular basis, she was, above all, in Laurel Thatcher Ulrich's terminology, a "good wife." Indeed, her duties as good wife demanded that she be a good businesswoman as well.

In 1748, Benjamin Franklin retired from the printing business. As a result, his life and the lives of everyone else in the family changed dramatically. The Franklins moved away from their crowded house and shop; Benjamin became absorbed in the electrical experiments that would one day earn him international fame; and he also began what would be a lifelong obsession with "publick affairs," a passion that would cause him virtually to abandon his wife and daughter.[25] Many historians see Benjamin's retirement as a major turning point in Deborah's life. No longer was she the valued "helpmeet" whose services were needed in shop and post office. As he moved out of the house—psychologically and eventually physically as well—she was less involved in his activities, more removed from his interests.[26]

It is doubtful that Deborah saw the changes in her life in such a dramatic—or so negative—a fashion. She may well have welcomed a life of leisure and enjoyed the luxuries that her new life afforded. She surely must have felt that she had earned them. During the Stamp Act crisis, Benjamin recalled with nostalgia that there had been a time when he had "been cloth'd from Head to Foot in Woollen and Linnen of my Wife's Manufacture." But Deborah no doubt relished the opportunity to buy satin, silk, and the "Richest Damask" for "New England made" dresses for herself and for Sally.[27] She could enjoy the purchase of a "China Bowl with a Spoon of Silver" for her husband, a little "luxury" that even frugal Benjamin obviously relished.[28] She could afford to hire someone else to do the family wash.[29]

Moreover, in the beginning, her husband's interests did not take him too far afield. He performed his electrical experiments at home, using the everyday items Deborah provided in order to entertain friends with his little exhibitions and to carry out his famous kite experiment. As co-deputy postmaster, he traveled throughout the colonies in his effort to improve and rationalize the American postal system. But he was never gone for long. Even in 1755, when he, along with his son William, traveled to rural Pennsylvania to organize the defense of the colony's war-torn hinterland, Deborah could not have felt unduly threatened by her husband's political interests. She served her colony indirectly, by attending to the needs of her husband—keeping him up to date on Philadelphia news, tending to his business affairs, and sending apples and pies, roast beef and roast veal—"the best that ever were of the kind"—to the men at Gnadenhutten.[30]

Beginning in the spring of 1757, however, when Benjamin left for London to represent the Pennsylvania Assembly's interests in the capital city, Deborah's life changed dramatically. Benjamin was gone for five years, returning only briefly to Philadelphia before heading back to London, where he remained until the eve of independence. Deborah Franklin would, for all practical purposes, live the last eighteen years of her life without a husband.

Two paradigms exist to describe the experiences of eighteenth-century women who became husbandless without being widows. Mary Beth Norton has drawn an appealing picture of women who became "perfect statesmen" during the American Revolution, as they tended to their husbands' businesses and took charge of their own lives, becoming stronger, more confident, and more independent the longer they were left alone by their soldier-husbands.[31]

Both Laurel Thatcher Ulrich and Edith Gelles offer a different perspective. Gelles tells us that Abigail Adams may have been equal to the responsibilities she shouldered when her husband left Braintree to direct America's fortunes during the Revolutionary War, but she certainly did not relish them. Indeed, she resented John's prolonged absences from home and longed for the day when he would return to take over tasks that she clearly saw as belonging rightfully to him. She was, in Ulrich's terms, a "deputy husband," a woman who stood in her husband's place in his absence, but who considered her task a duty—even a burden—not an opportunity.

No one in the eighteenth century, argues Ulrich, denied that women had the *ability* to serve as their husbands' surrogates. Indeed, to refuse this role would invite censure from friends and family alike. But serving as a deputy husband did not lead to equality and independence. A woman could assume responsibility for her husband's duties without challenging the patriarchal family structure that to a great extent still characterized America in the revolutionary era. She continued to fuse her identity with his, working for him, making it possible for him to leave home and tend to public affairs. A wife's willingness to assume her husband's duties contributed to his independence. But it did not lead to her own autonomy. If anything, it underscored her traditional role.[32]

Deborah Franklin was an excellent deputy husband. But her years alone did not imbue her with self-confidence and a sense of independence. On the contrary, her spirits as well as her health steadily deteriorated in the years Benjamin was in London. Moreover, even from a distance, Benjamin clearly remained the head of the Franklin household. His absence did nothing to diminish his role as patriarch. Franklin may have been, as historians have argued, a modern man in numerous ways. But in family affairs, in his relationship with his wife and daughter in particular, he was profoundly traditional.

In some ways, of course, Deborah's life did not change at all during her husband's long sojourn in England. She continued to serve as neighbor and nurse to friends and family—working, sometimes, until she was "no longer abel to baer [her] waite on [her] feet."[33] She entertained visitors, boasting of her ability to outdo even herself when she made buckwheat cakes for unexpected guests.[34] And she remained Benjamin's good wife, sending him apples, cranberries, and peaches, flour, meat, and meal to supplement his London diet and to remind him of home.

Still, no one can deny that Benjamin's absence profoundly altered Deborah's life. Especially in the beginning, she served effectively as her husband's surrogate. She took care of his correspondence, managed his post office accounts, and made decisions about those matters that could not await his return.[35] When Josiah Davenport needed to settle an outstanding loan with his uncle Benjamin, he wrote to Deborah. Benjamin, Josiah said, had told him that he could deal with Deborah "as Well as if [he] was present."[36] She supervised the construction of the Franklins' new house, and, without consulting her husband, purchased an adjoining lot at what Benjamin thought was a "great Price."[37] With the help of her husband's friends, she obtained tenants for the Franklins' rental property, and she put money down on land "in Novascosha or sum such plase." She was, she said somewhat proudly, becoming a "raile Land Jober."[38]

Deborah served as more than a "businessman" in her husband's absence. She was also his source of personal news and the conduit through which Benjamin and his many friends kept in touch with one another so long as he remained in London. She kept her husband apprised of all the comings and goings of his friends and neighbors. Thanks to her letters, he knew about every death and birth, every illness and recovery in Philadelphia.[39] It was also Deborah's duty to thank all of her husband's friends for their various kindnesses. "I have not time to name Names," he would say. "You know whom I love and honour. Say all the proper Things for me to every body."[40] Especially during the 1760s, friends gathered frequently at the Franklin home, begging to be remembered to Benjamin, awaiting news from London, and sharing Deborah's joy when a long-awaited letter arrived in Philadelphia.[41]

Deborah assumed responsibility for family affairs as well as for Benjamin's business concerns. She looked after Benny Mecom, Benjamin's hapless nephew, the son of his favorite sister, Jane.[42] When her own niece, Debby Dunlap, fell ill, and in a fit of delirium began calling for Benjamin, Deborah literally took her husband's place, holding the woman in her arms for two hours, promising to take as good a care of her as Benjamin would have done had he been home. It was bad enough, she thought, to be "father and mother" to her own children. But now, "by inkley nashon and for Credit Sake," she had to serve in Benjamin's stead for "poor Debbey," as well.[43]

One of Deborah Franklin's most onerous burdens involved her duties as surrogate parent to her daughter, Sally. When he first left for England, Benjamin had left her in charge of the "Education of my dear Child," a task that he clearly thought would have been his had he remained at home.[44] Most of the time she handled her role with confidence. But when Sally fell in love with Richard Bache, a newcomer to the colony and, in the eyes of her stepson and many of her husband's friends, a "mere fortune hunter," she was overwhelmed.[45] She no doubt remembered how her mother's interference had almost destroyed her own chances for a good marriage and may well have wondered if a mother was capable of making such a momentous decision without the help of a husband. It was not a responsibility she relished. While she sympathized with her daughter, she was afraid to defy her husband, and she enlisted the support of everyone she could think of to defend her handling of the crisis. She told Benjamin that Joseph Galloway, his ally in the Pennsylvania assembly, thought she acted "correctly."[46] And she made sure that her husband knew that Jane Mecom supported the match.[47] Benjamin pretended to leave the matter in Deborah's hands, but when he learned that the marriage had taken place, he did not accept the fait accompli with good grace. Nothing would mollify him. The Baches named their first son after him. Deborah constantly remarked on little Benny's resemblance to his grandfather and noted that Richard Bache, too, bore an uncanny physical similarity to Benjamin.[48] Only in December of 1771 did Deborah rest easy, when her son-in-law visited Benjamin in England and the elder Franklin received him "with open arms."[49] Deborah may have been compelled, in her husband's absence, to be both father and mother to her daughter, but ultimately it was Benjamin's opinion that counted.

Deborah exhibited little interest in public affairs. But she served her husband in a political capacity when the occasion demanded it. He sometimes used her to leak "secret" news about the Pennsylvania proprietors to his Philadelphia cohorts.[50] But usually she served her husband's political purposes more passively, heeding his advice to avoid any involvement in "Party Disputes." Women, Benjamin told her, should never "meddle" in political matters, "except in endeavors to reconcile thier Husbands, Brothers and Friends who happen to be of contrary Sides." "If," he went on, "your Sex can keep cool, you may be a means of cooling ours the sooner, and restoring more speedily that social Harmony among Fellow Citizens that is so desirable after long and bitter Dissensions."[51]

In only one instance did Deborah take an active political role. During the Stamp Act crisis, Philadelphia was in turmoil. Benjamin was in London trying to obtain a royal charter to replace Pennsylvania's proprietary government. Consequently, while they opposed the Stamp Act, neither he nor his friends wanted to do anything that would bring royal disfavor to the colony. David Hall refused to print antistamp propaganda in the *Pennsylvania Gazette,* and one of Benjamin's closest friends, John Hughes, accepted the unpopular position of stamp distributor. Thus, when opponents of the unpopular legislation decided to imitate rioters in other towns, threatening to destroy the houses of Benjamin Franklin and John Hughes, Deborah's friends were understandably frightened.

Governor William Franklin left his home in New Jersey to urge his stepmother and sister to flee there for safety. While Deborah urged her daughter to take advantage of William's offer, she herself refused to budge. "I was," she told her husband, "verey shuer you had not given aney ofense to aney person att all nor wold I be maid unesey by aney bodey nor wold I stir or show the leste uneseynis but if aney one Came to disturbe me I would show a proper resentement."[52] Benjamin's nephew Josiah Davenport and Deborah's brother helped her defend the Franklin home. They "maid one room into a Magazin," she said, and I "ordered sum sorte of defens up Stairs such as I could manaig my self."[53] Like the pioneer woman of old, Deborah stood ready to defend her husband's house from enemy attack. Benjamin's friends came to the rescue, patrolling the streets and keeping the would-be rioters at bay. Still, it had been a close call, and Deborah had reason to be proud of the way she handled herself during the crisis.

Her subsequent actions indicate, however, that Deborah gained neither confidence nor a sense of independence as a result of her experience. She continued to be uncomfortable even discussing public affairs with her husband. When she sat down to write "sumthing . . . a bought publick afairs," she was virtually tongue-tied. "I would distroy it," she said, "and then begin a gen and burn it a gen and so on." In the end, she simply gave up, hoping that other, more competent observers would keep him up to date on the political climate in his native land.[54]

In fact, the Stamp Act crisis did not pique her interest in public affairs at all. Conversely, it made her turn in on herself, to be more reclusive, to avoid political matters. Benjamin had often told her to do nothing in his absence that would "draw Reflections" on him, and she was determined not to disappoint him. As her husband's surrogate, her actions were not her own. They were always viewed in terms of their effect on Benjamin Franklin. Thus, it was better simply to avoid the public eye.[55] "I don't go much to town," she said after her ordeal. "I donte go ought aney whair if I Can helpe it [.]" Rather, I "keep my self to my self." Above all, she added, " I donte due aney thing to give aney bodey room to say any thing a bought me att all." It was the best way to serve her husband's interests.[56]

Whether he intended to do so or not, Benjamin Franklin dominated his family from his vantage point in London as much as he would have done had he remained in Philadelphia. Deborah always hoped that she had "dun as you wold have me or as you wold if you had bin at home your self," but at times she found it virtually impossible to act in his place.[57] Before Benjamin left for England in 1764, he and Deborah had begun to build a house together. It would be the first residence that the couple had owned outright. Public affairs soon called him away, however, and Deborah was left to supervise the building of the home on her own—"your house," she always called it, although she and Benjamin never lived in it together.[58]

Deborah kept her husband informed about the progress—such as it was—on the house, and Benjamin in turn was interested in every detail. He inundated his wife with marble fireplaces, a new stove for the kitchen, blankets, cloth for the curtains, and reams of advice. This would be, he thought, a house of which an Englishman would be proud, and he wanted it painted, furnished, and decorated in the latest fashion.[59] At times Deborah was simply overwhelmed by the entire business. She wanted her husband's approval, and she feared that her own taste was "all wrong." "O my Child," she complained, "there is graite odes between a mans being at home and a broad as every bodey is a fraid they shall doe wrong so everey thing is left undun[.]"[60] The Philadelphia house was—literally—her sphere. Yet even from a distance, her husband's wishes were paramount.

If Deborah's letters are any indication, Benjamin always remained at the center of her life. She continued to celebrate her husband's birthday in his absence.[61] When friends came, she told him, they always "talked much of you."[62] She eagerly anticipated his letters and was both disappointed and worried when he did not write. And as year after year rolled by, and Benjamin seemed in no hurry to return home, she grew increasingly depressed. The death of old friends such as Deborah Norris, one of her "first playmaites," exacerbated her sense of isolation, reminding her that she was growing old and that she had no one with whom to share her old age.[63] Each year friends asked her when Benjamin was coming home. Each year, she had to reply that her "life of old age [was] one Continewd State of suspens."[64]

Sometime in the winter of 1769, Deborah suffered a stroke. Her letters, difficult to read under the best of circumstances, became almost incomprehensible. She suffered lapses of memory and loss of appetite. She had difficulty speaking, and her ability to write lucidly on one subject for any length of time degenerated. Benjamin dutifully sent her medical advice, but he ignored her when she claimed that her symptoms were psychological—the result of "too much disquiet of mind"—and not physical. She was more and more often "verey lonley," and she only hoped that she would survive to see her husband before she died.[65]

Deborah's condition improved somewhat over the next year or so, although she never recovered completely. By 1770, she could report that she had "recovered flesh." And while her memory was still poor, she looked more like herself than she had for nearly a year.[66] She was a devoted grandmother to Benjamin Franklin Bache, or the "Kingbird," as she affectionately called him. The Baches lived with her in the Franklin home, and her son-in-law, Richard, quietly assumed responsibility for many of his father-in-law's business affairs.[67] But when Sally tried to take over her mother's housekeeping chores, she was unsuccessful. Her efforts caused Deborah "so much uneasiness" that Sally finally had to admit defeat.[68]

After 1772, Deborah's condition deteriorated. She was, she said, "growing verey febel verey faste."[69] She found it increasingly difficult to compose a simple letter. "I cante write to you," she told her husband, "as I am so verey unfitt to expres my self and not a bell to due as I yousd."[70] She was, not surprisingly, "verey Low sperreted."[71] And while she always insisted—with good intentions if not with total honesty—that she tried never to complain about his continued absence, nearly every letter to London asked about his plans for returning home.

And what of Benjamin? What were his thoughts as he remained in London, caught up in the political and social whirl of England's capital city? When he had left Pennsylvania for London in 1757, his heart had clearly remained in America. Despite his occasional comments that he longed to live out his days in England, he expressed genuine "uneasiness" at his absence from his family, as he believed that "domestic comforts afford[ed] the most solid satisfaction."[72] He sent chatty letters home, discussing business, family, and friends; describing his accommodations; and complaining about his expenses. He even tried, on occasion, to persuade Deborah to join him in London, but her nearly phobic fear of travel by water rendered that option virtually impossible.[73] So, Benjamin continued to innundate Deborah and Sally with gifts from London, most of which he picked out himself, many of which reflected his affection for Deborah, in particular. He fell in love with a "large fine Jugg for Beer" because he "thought it look'd like a fat jolly Dame." It put him "in mind," he said, "of——Somebody."[74] When he returned to London in 1764, he intended to remain there only briefly. And at first, his letters were nostalgic. One letter especially pleased Deborah. I read it "over and over a gen," she said. "I Cole it a *husbands Love Letter.*"[75]

In time, however, Benjamin's thoughts of home faded. His efforts to persuade his wife to cross the ocean and join him in London diminished and then stopped altogether. Deborah continued to use her letters to discuss their mutual friends, or simply to "Chat a littel."[76] His letters grew shorter and more perfunctory. This was partly because he always thought he was about to return home. But it was, no doubt, just as much a product of the growing physical and psychological distance that divided husband and wife. She could continue to fill her letters with news about people and places they had once shared. His world, however, was for Deborah literally and figuratively a foreign country. He lived among strangers, hobnobbed with the rich and famous, and was totally involved in a political life that, almost by definition, excluded her. Consequently, he either used his letters to answer her questions in a brief, almost mechanical manner, or, more often, he simply promised to "write more fully per next Opportunity."[77]

Only once did Benjamin abandon his tone of affectionate detachment. He had often exhibited a little irritation when Deborah failed to keep her accounts straight. And from time to time he had also cautioned her to live more frugally, so that they would not be forced to spend their old age in poverty.[78] But in the spring of 1771, he exploded. He had put her on a monthly allowance of thirty pounds, and when she exceeded the allotment and borrowed money from printer David Hall to make up the difference, Benjamin was furious. You were never, he said, "attentive to Money matters in your best Days." Now, however, your "Memory is too much impair'd for the Management of unlimited Sums without Danger of injuring the future Fortune of your Daughter and Grandson." He forbade her to borrow money from "his" friends, and he insisted that the money he provided her was sufficient if only she would manage her affairs more carefully.[79]

It was an uncharacteristically cruel letter, and Benjamin's reference to Deborah's inability to attend to business matters in her "best Days" was unfair. She had served him well as a deputy husband for some forty years. Her careful supervision of his affairs had made it possible for him to remain in England. Her determination to do her duty had given him the independence he needed to play out his role on the imperial stage.

Deborah was devastated by her husband's criticism and eagerly sought to justify her conduct. She offered to send him all the receipts of her expenses, but Benjamin told her this would not be necessary. He would be content with an account of the "considerable Sums" she spent.[80] But more than two years later, the effects of her husband's criticism lingered. She worried about the price of silk and lace that he sent her. She wrote and re-wrote her letters, fearing that they would not pass muster. She even doubted her ability to take care of her precious "Kingbird." I want, she said, to "plese you," and not to be "two trubel sum."[81] For his part, Benjamin's letters home became more personal, more affectionate. Perhaps he genuinely regretted his outburst. Perhaps he was simply correcting another erratum.[82] In any event, he continued to assume that she would take care of his property and the various business transactions that needed attention, despite Deborah's admission that she was "verey uncapall [incapable] of dueing aney bisnes."[83]

Every year Benjamin said that he planned to come home soon. "Positively nothing shall prevent, God willing, my Returning in the Spring," he wrote in the fall of 1773.[84] But in February 1774 he was still in London, assuring her that he would be in Philadelphia in May. And that spring, he was delayed once more. He received no correspondance from Deborah after October 1773. He worried about her silence and missed her letters, but was determined to believe that she failed to write because she thought he was headed for home.[85] To be fair, no one had told him that his wife's condition was worsening. Everyone always assured him that "all the Family are in good Health."[86]

Deborah was not, of course, in good health, as her letters to London surely should have indicated. On 14 December 1774 she suffered another stroke, and a few days later, on 19 December, "without a Groan or even a Sigh, she was released from a troublesome World."[87] In February 1775, Benjamin began, at last, to make serious plans for returning to Philadelphia. He was no longer needed in England. Indeed, it was becoming dangerous for him to remain in the capital city. Moreover, as he told Lord Hyde, his wife, "in whose Hands [he] had left the Care of [his] Affairs," had died.[88] He no longer had a deputy husband. It was time to return home.

Deborah Franklin's contributions to her family's well-being were enormous. As wife and mother, nurse and companion, woman of affairs and deputy husband, she easily crossed and recrossed the boundaries between "women's" duties and "men's" responsibilities. In the 1730s and 1740s she and her husband had developed a thriving business from their little house on Market Street. Beginning in the late 1750s, her attention to the financial and emotional concerns of the family made it possible for Benjamin to live an independent life. Her dependence resulted in his independence.

Neither her contributions to the family business, nor her long career as deputy husband, gave Deborah Franklin power or independence. Nor did she expect that they would. She saw her role as complementary. Her duty was to her husband and family, not to herself. If she had any complaints—and she surely did—they did not arise from her frustrated ambition. She exhibited no desire to have her "own" career or to attain the political rights for which her husband was fighting. Rather, she hoped that her contributions would be appreciated. She longed above all to be relieved of some of her husband's responsibilities. She simply wanted him to return home.

LIBERTY AND THE RIGHTS OF WOMEN:
Sarah Franklin's Declaration of Independence
Larry E. Tise

An undutiful daughter will prove an unmanageable wife.
—Poor Richard, 1752

When he died in April 1790, Benjamin Franklin left behind a will that was just as creative and inspiring as virtually every other act of his uniquely prolific life. He used his last will and testament to produce something of a sideshow that would go on for at least two hundred years. A thousand pounds each from his uncollected salary as president of the Commonwealth of Pennsylvania (he did not believe elected officials should be paid!) he left to the cities of Boston and Philadelphia to be invested for two full centuries at 5 percent interest. The cities were then told to use the resulting funds to make small loans to young male "artificers" (artisans) who were setting themselves up in business—also at 5 percent interest. Such loans were to be made for two hundred years.

At the end of the first century, however, two-thirds of the principal in each city was to be used for such public projects (bridges, dams, buildings, street lighting) as may be chosen by the officials of Boston and Philadelphia. At the end of two hundred years, Franklin ordered, the entire program would be concluded and the funds divided between the respective cities and their states for additional public projects.[1]

But this creative scheme for financing young tradesmen (actually, it failed) across two centuries—assuring national headlines at the bicentennial commemoration of his death—was not the only special feature of Franklin's will. He also employed the document to settle accounts with particular members of his family. For his illegitimate and estranged son, William, Franklin left virtually nothing: a set of worthless claims for land he once wanted in Nova Scotia; whatever papers William had retained that were once his father's; and the cancellation of any debts due Franklin's estate (there were none). Digging in the knife once again for William's disloyalty during the American Revolution, Franklin wrote: "The part he acted against me in the late war, which is of public notoriety, will account for my leaving him no more of an estate he endeavored to deprive me of."

Franklin was much kinder to the two grandsons he had virtually raised himself—William Temple Franklin and Benjamin Franklin Bache. To Temple went Franklin's coveted library, his personal and literary papers (including title to the *Autobiography,* itself worth more than its weight in gold), and, upon marriage, title to Franklin's farm properties in New Jersey. Bache got a thousand pounds in printing and typemaking equipment, a selected set of books, and a quarter of Franklin's remaining cash.[2]

The largest portion of Franklin's estate with direct cash value was left for his daughter Sarah Franklin (1743–1808), and her husband, Richard Bache (1737–1811). Together they inherited Franklin's very fine home at Franklin Court in Philadelphia and various new houses and undeveloped lots owned by Franklin in and around Philadelphia, and all the contents of those properties (china, silver, portraits, pictures, furniture, musical instruments, and so on) excluding the library and his papers. Specifically for Richard Bache, he gave all the lands he owned in Ohio and a number of newly acquired lots in Philadelphia, along with the cancellation of debts of more than two thousand pounds—with the single proviso that Bache "manumit and set free his negro man Bob." To Bache he also bequeathed his musical instruments and his gold watch with a fabulous gold chain "of the Thirteen United States." To assure that daughter Sarah should not be wholly dependent upon her never-successful husband, Franklin left "as her private money" one-half of the funds in his estate and income on his shares in the Bank of North America.[3]

Franklin also singled out his daughter, known to everyone as Sally, to receive the most precious treasure in his entire estate: a miniature porcelain portrait of King Louis XVI presented to Franklin by Louis himself. Studded with 408 diamonds and conferred as a testament of international recognition, the miniature was of enormous monetary value either in cash or as a commemorative asset.

The 408 diamonds surrounding the tiny portrait, Franklin further stipulated, were not to be removed for any cause. Especially prohibited was the use of any of these diamonds for any purpose of making ornaments for Sarah or her daughters that would introduce the "expensive, vain, and useless fashion of wearing jewels in this country." [4]

Each Franklin child and grandchild—no matter their designated inheritance—had a unique reaction to the motives of their renowned patron. William (1730–1814) was driven to total distraction. He used the occasion to declare his final and total independence of America: "The Revolution in America and the Shameful Injustice of my Father's Will have in a manner dissolved all my Connexions in that Part of the World of a private as well as publick Nature." Bitter, impoverished, and spiritually broken, William spent his last years in London in virtual obscurity. [5]

William Temple Franklin (1762–1823), given his behavior as adolescent and young man, responded in what Franklin should have figured a predictable manner: he squandered land, money, reputation, and literary possession until there was virtually nothing left to support his international-playboy style of life. After he sold Franklin's prized library and having laid waste most of Franklin's papers, nothing remained to exploit but the literary rights to the *Autobiography* and a few prized papers.

Not until 1817—twenty-seven years after he was given the solemn responsibility of publishing Franklin's *Autobiography* and his papers—did Temple come forth with his three-volume *Memoirs of the Life and Writings of Benjamin Franklin*. This was a small sampling, indeed, of the total works. Whatever financial rewards came from the venture evidently sustained him for another six years in Paris. There he died, like his father, in abject anonymity. [6]

Like the reactions of William and William Temple, those of Benjamin Franklin Bache were also probably predictable. While he got much less than either his mother or Temple, his portion of the legacy (the Franklin printshop and business) was about what he expected. Within months he launched his *General Advertiser* and raced into a brilliant, albeit short-lived, career of representing his grandfather's spirit and interpreting his principles in a world of revolution. Although when he died in Philadelphia's yellow fever epidemic of 1798 he was in financial peril, he had valiantly carried on the rich Franklin tradition.[7]

If Franklin's male heirs played out their parts with calculable precision, Sarah Franklin, dutiful daughter of one of history's firmest friends of liberty, surprised Philadelphia and the world with her reaction to the terms of the will. Within months after getting her inheritance, Sally and her impecunious husband Richard began to systematically dismantle and spend the core of Franklin's substantial estate. The Philadelphia properties were sold to extract their cash value. Household goods, irrespective of their historic or symbolic value, were sold for cash.

Even Franklin Court, Franklin's personally designed landmark—lovingly built to his specifications by Deborah and Sally while he was away in England—was abandoned for an estate they called "Settle" on the upper Delaware River. It would eventually be demolished for a more lucrative use of the land it occupied. Every trace of Franklin's presence in Philadelphia, save the printshop where Benjamin Franklin Bache labored on, was over the next twenty years obliterated to enable Sally and her family to pursue their life of leisure at Settle. Even Bache's "negro man Bob," although he was legally manumitted in accord with Franklin's wishes, was unable to support himself outside slavery and was restored—not legally, but factually—to his position of servitude for the duration of his life.[8]

If this were not enough, Sally also soon defiled that other sacredly held portion of the Franklin trust, the Louis XVI miniature. She removed a circle of the diamonds and sold them to finance a yearlong trip to Europe. At age forty-nine, Sally Franklin fulfilled a lifelong dream to travel to Europe. She, husband Richard, and daughter Elizabeth sailed for England in the spring of 1792. By June they were settled in comfortable quarters near her renegade brother William.

2. ◡

Sarah Franklin Bache—Franklin's daughter and the only progenitor of his descendants, but who rebelled against his patriarchal control. (Wood engraving, artist unknown [n.d.], after a painting by John Hoppner, 1791, Free Library of Philadelphia, Lewis Collection)

Although Franklin permanently broke his ties with William during the Revolution, Sally and her brother continued a cordial, even warm bond for the rest of their lives. Despite his relative poverty, William served the touring Baches as guide, host, and advisor for their lengthy sojourn.[9]

And a fancy visitation it was. They were wined and dined across England. Temple Franklin joined them in the festivities. This odd claque of descendants basked in the reflective glory of the great Dr. Franklin wherever they went, while on a junket fully financed by his fortune.

Sally sat for a portrait executed by John Hoppner, one of the best portraitists around. Bache, not to be outdone, had his painted as well. Hoppner put Sally in a *fichu Marie-Antoinette* and the type of Phrygian cap fashionable during the French Revolution. Despite the stylish dress, she looked plump and plain and fully fitted with the elder Franklin's large, rosy nose and wide jaw. Bache, who everyone thought looked remarkably like his father-in-law, by contrast, appeared in his portrait as stern and affluent. This was certainly a proper look for a gentleman who was about to head off, with William Franklin, for an extended hunting trip in the North of England.[10]

Sally's goal was to proceed from England to France to meet other of her father's followers and friends on this grandest of tours. In France, where the Franklin name was magical, she anticipated a reception appropriate for a queen. In August 1792, she wrote ahead to Franklin's old neighbor and friend, and mayor of Passy, Louis-Guillaume Le Veillard (1733–93), indicating that she would soon be on her way to France where she hoped to spend the winter. Confiding as had Franklin in Le Veillard (Franklin had entrusted him with one of three somewhat varied drafts of the *Autobiography*), she asked him to share the truth about what was happening in France.

She could not know that France was just at that moment entering into an upheaval that would in little more than a year's time see the arrest, trial, and execution of that very King Louis XVI whose gift was financing her extravaganza; the guillotining of the queen who had made fashionable the dress she had just worn in her portrait; and the arrest and beheading of virtually every member of Benjamin Franklin's circle of friends in Paris—including Le Veillard himself. Antoine Lavoisier, Jean Sylvain Bailly, Condorcet, Jacques Paulze, and Duc de la Rouchefoucauld—other Franklin associates—also fell victims to the upheaval and slaughter.[11]

In the face of growing carnage in France, concluding with the guillotining of trusted Le Veillard in June 1793, Sally sadly but wisely canceled her imagined triumphal visit to Paris. She, Bache, and Eliz-abeth remained instead in England for a full year, until in July 1793, when—as the Terror seized all of France—she came face to face with her own terror. She and Bache had been living in such a high style that she had exhausted every penny derived from the initial sale of diamonds. There was no money to stay longer and none to pay the passage back to Philadelphia.

In a state of panic, she quickly turned to Temple, begging for money and imploring him not to leak a word of her predicament to either husband Bache or brother William. Much to her surprise, Temple used the moment to inform her that he had already lent money to her husband and that Bache was seriously in arrears on re-payment. Temple, in fact, turned the table on her and demanded that *she* repay her husband's delinquent accounts.[12]

Fearful of Bache's reaction if she confronted him both with the fact that they were penniless and that she knew of his previously undisclosed loans from Temple, Sally did the only thing she could under the circumstances. With husband and brother away on their hunting trip, she faced the predicament squarely. Forth came the Louis XVI miniature to be further shorn of its monetary and historic value. With the assistance of a secreted female comrade, she re-moved another circle of diamonds that would produce the needed cash. Fearful that the less than trustworthy Temple might betray her to Bache, she also demanded his total silence on all of her actions as a condition of repaying his loans.[13]

At the very moment that Louis XVI's troubled career on earth came to an end and life was drained from him, his priceless gift to Franklin became the symbolic focus of everything having to do with the liberty of its inheritor, one Sarah Franklin Bache, who was living out a moment when liberating revolutions seemed to promise rights for all beings—both men and women.

It all began for Sally when she was born into a family that, for all of its worldly successes, was almost dysfunctional. The highly moti-vated Benjamin Franklin was already a successful businessman and distinguished citizen of Philadelphia when she arrived on the scene in 1743. By the time she was three, he had launched into those elec-trical experiments that would make him only the second or third person in Western history to gain world renown as a scientist. Mother Deborah Franklin was doing everything on earth to support and please her innovative husband. Deborah helped with the printing business, serving as bookkeeper and accountant for an ever broadening business enterprise. She was always firmly grounded on earth as Franklin floated in the clouds trying to understand lightning, electricity, and human behavior. Somehow the two of them had a son, William, whose mother was never identified; whom Franklin acknowledged as his son; and whose presence was considered a gift.

Franklin did everything possible to educate his son. William had a tutor at age four, had a full-time teacher at age eight, and was enrolled in Philadelphia's best classical academy until he was thirteen. After his son spent the next several years either in Franklin's printshop or off on some mission as a member of the king's army, Franklin then provided him an education in law. He first read under the tutelage of James Galloway, but then enrolled in Middle Temple, Inns of Court, and matriculated there when the Franklins, father and son, went to England in 1757.[14]

But Franklin treated his first and only daughter very differently. Even though Franklin as a young man had argued, not from conviction, but "for Dispute sake," the affirmative on the "Propriety of educating the Female Sex in Learning, and their Abilities for Study," Franklin demonstrated little commitment to the proposition when it came to Sally. Nor did he do anything elsewise in his long career of abundant innovations to encourage, foster, or promote the education of women generally—even though he mentored quite a few particular young women directly.

But Sally was not one of them. In her case, she seems to have quietly begged for what she thought was a fair education. But she was denied access by Franklin to anything much beyond the traditional home trades of spinning, knitting, and embroidering and that "dreary succession of hair-work, feather-work, wax flowers, shell-work, the crystallization with various domestic minerals and gums of dried leaves and grasses, . . .yarn and worsted monstrosities."[15]

She once had a tutor, but it was so she could learn the business of making elegant buttonholes. When Franklin left for England, she begged for and got a French-language tutor. But she soon lost interest. The only frill in her development that she wanted and that he was willing to support was her interest in music. Franklin sent her a harpsichord from England and supplied her regularly with the most current musical scores. But while she wrote him in England during her crucial adolescent years, seeking his encouragement and love, he mainly lectured her on her spiritual development, devotion to work at home, and duty to her mother.

And when she was but a child of seven, Franklin arranged for her someday to marry William Strahan Jr., the ten-year-old son of his closest friend and business partner in London, the publisher William Strahan. He pursued the match relentlessly when he arrived in England, begging Deborah and Sally when she was sixteen to come to London to consummate the match. Deborah would not cross the Atlantic, and Franklin, at least at the moment, thought it unwise for the enthusiastic Sally, eager at least to make the trip, to sail alone (72–76, 82–83).

Although Franklin took Sally along in 1763 on an extended working tour of New England—he was laying out postal routes through the colonies—and there she met many of their relatives, he turned back her pleas to accompany him when he returned to England in 1765. Although on the New England trip the two of them played duets, she on the harpsichord and he on his self-designed glass armonica, in no other realm of life did they operate as collaborators, partners, or equals. He continued to lecture her about attending church, about spending too much time at social events, and about not attending sufficiently to her work. Back in England in 1767, he showered her with gifts that would enhance her as a social creature—gowns, negligees, gloves, and lavender water—but he also again proposed that either Deborah and she or she alone cross the Atlantic and in England marry Billy Strahan, who was by then wealthy and successful (100–102, 112–13, 119–20, 131–32, 138).

That was not to be, not due to Deborah's reluctance to travel, but because Sally Franklin decided at age twenty-three that she wanted some of the liberty that was beginning to be discussed in America and around the world. She had tired of a life ruled in every particular by a father who did not acknowledge her wishes and did not respect her opinions. If her father would not treat her with consideration, would not let her make her own decisions about religion and life, and would not in reality let her travel to England, then she would marry someone who would give her all of those things and more.

Her opportunity came in the summer of 1766 when her closest friend, Peggy Ross, suddenly died, leaving behind a handsome, thirty-year-old fiancé who just happened to be a most impressive, if not entirely successful, English businessman. With his proper English background and education, all of the doors of Philadelphia society had opened to Richard Bache when he arrived in 1760. From all outward appearances—he seemed to work hard and with proper financial backing and time would doubtlessly succeed—Bache seemed to be a dream come true for Sally (133–35).

But how could she proceed with her rebellion, when both Bache and she would need, at least for a time, Franklin's financial support? When Sally, Bache on his own, and also Deborah wrote Franklin that a match was in the making, Franklin wrote back to Deborah (not to Sally or Bache) expressing little interest in the matter and leaving the decision up to Deborah. His only firm word was an order for Deborah not to "make an expensive feasting Wedding, but conduct every thing with Frugality and Oeconomy." By his own calculation, not more than five hundred pounds total should be spent for the wedding and to "fit her out handsomely in Cloaths and Furniture." "For the rest," he told Deborah, "they must depend as you and I did, on their own Industry and Care" (135–36).

That was not what Sally or Bache wanted to hear. The fact was that Bache's financial affairs, due in part to the effects of the Stamp Act and the foundering of a ship he had bought at risk, were a wreck themselves. From his losses he owed debts of more than thirty-six hundred pounds. William Franklin, by then ensconced as the royal governor of New Jersey, assessed Bache's prospects and wrote the elder Franklin the alarming news, "If Sally marries him, they must both be entirely on you for their Subsistence." In William's estimation Bache had been reduced by circumstances and his innate character to the status of "a mere fortune hunter" (136–37).

Franklin, alarmed that things might be getting out of hand, finally decided to have a word directly with Bache. Responding to several letters in which Bache evidently outlined his financial difficulties and asked for assistance as well as the hand of Sally, Franklin sternly wrote:

I love my daughter perhaps as well as ever parent did a child, but I have told you before that my estate is small, scarce a sufficiency for the support of me and my wife, who are growing old and cannot now bustle for a living as we have done; that little can therefore be spared out of it while we live . . . I am obliged to you for the regard and preference you express for my child and wish you all prosperity; but unless you can convince her friends of the probability of your being able to maintain her properly, I hope you will not persist in a proceeding that may be attended with ruinous consequences to you both.

And in a separate letter to Deborah, he virtually insisted that she place Sally on the first ship to London that could be found on which the captain's wife sailed with her husband. Billy Strahan was still awaiting Sally's arrival (137–38).

But it was too late. Sally's quest for liberty from her overly zealous patriarch was on its own track. Without further notice to the father, the wedding occurred on 29 October 1767: "Last Thursday Evening Mr. Richard Bache, of this City, Merchant, was married to Miss Sally Franklin, the only Daughter of the celebrated Doctor Franklin, a young Lady of distinguished Merit. The next Day all the Shipping in the Harbour displayed their Colours on the happy Occasion." That Franklin was left totally in the dark was evident, when, two weeks after the event, he wrote Deborah to learn the response to his September missives. When he finally got the news from his trusted sister Jane Mecom in December, he angrily responded, "She has pleas'd herself and her Mother, and I hope she will do well: but I think they should have seen some better Prospect" (140).

For the next year Franklin refused to acknowledge either wedding or the acquisition of a son-in-law. He refused to answer three letters from Bache. Bache was never mentioned in letters to Deborah or Sally. But after hearing from Bache that his business prospects were improving, Franklin finally broke the silence with a letter accusing the young man of irresponsibility: "In this Situation of my Mind, you should not wonder that I did not answer your Letters. I could say nothing agreeable: I did not chuse to write what I thought, being unwilling to give Pain where I could not give Pleasure." But then he concluded his letter on a slightly warmer and hopeful note: "If you prove a good Husband and Son, you will find in me an Affectionate Father" (140–42).

Deborah Franklin lost Franklin forever for her role in this betrayal. She never saw him again. Sally Franklin never really recovered him either. She did provide him with a rich progeny of eight grandchildren, the first of which was named Benjamin Franklin Bache. But so delighted was Franklin with little Benny when he finally came home from England in 1775—a year after Deborah's death—that he virtually kidnapped the seven-year-old boy the following year. Heading to France in 1776, he took Benny with him, over the protests of a sobbing Sally Bache. She was no match for a father who thought he knew more about bringing up boys than anyone else on earth. She could only acquiesce in Franklin's promise of providing the boy with an outstanding European education. But he likewise took Temple Franklin with him, in that case without bothering to notify the boy's father, his estranged son, William (215–16).

Nor did Sally reclaim the affections of Franklin when he returned from France in 1785 to spend his final days at Franklin Court in Philadelphia. Although she thought he came home to be with her and her family in his last days, once again her role as loving daughter was supplanted with the arrival of Polly Hewson—the former Mary Stevenson and the young woman on whom Franklin showered his greatest and most loving mentoring energies. All those years he lived in London, Margaret Stevenson, his landlady and Polly's mother, had substituted as a wife and Polly as a daughter. Franklin lavished on Polly the type of attention and affection due his own daughter.

While he could not attend and did not approve of Sally's wedding, he condoned and attended Polly's, and, as substitute father, gave away the bride when she married in 1770. With Franklin still spurning Sally in his last days, it was Polly who sat by his bedside and comforted him in his last illness and who whispered to him that he should accept religion. Sally was there, also, but was to receive even in Franklin's last words yet another reproach. When in his dying moments she gently suggested that he would surely recover and live many more years, he looked her squarely in the eye and said, "I hope not." Even with his dying breath, he would not give her the credence of a dutiful daughter (143, 287–88, 304–5).

Sally's marriage to Bache and her determined sale of the diamonds surrounding the Louis XVI brooch were clear and unmistakable declarations of independence from a man who, while he might stand for liberty, freedom, and equality in the eyes of all others, was for her a tyrant. It was not simply that she was his child. He doted over William endlessly until political differences separated them. He showered affection and endless forgiveness on William Temple, even when the young man demonstrated waywardness. And Benjamin Franklin Bache, clearly a rigid and unforgiving being, could in his eyes do no wrong. But they were all boys becoming men and acting out roles acceptable for men. Sally, on the other hand, was a girl becoming a woman; and dutiful abiding service to father and husband was her role in life. However much Franklin might expound upon the rights of man—and even the rights of black men—like most other white men of his generation, he never thought that those rights extended to women, whatever their race.

Sally, on the other hand, was among those women in America and Europe who became fueled by all of the current discussions about the rights of humans. Many there were who were thereby driven to declare their independence, to seek freedom, careers, education, and refinement. And for a time some of them, like Sally, made great progress in the cities of America and among the courts of Europe. But another age would have to come and new discussions about the rights of humans before men of the likes of Benjamin Franklin would come to believe that women and men alike, mother, wife, and daughter, should share those rights equally.

3

THREE WOMEN, THREE STYLES:
Catharine Ray, Polly Hewson, and Georgiana Shipley
Claude-Anne Lopez

Girls, mark my words and know, for men of sense
Your strongest charms are native innocence.
—Poor Richard, 1747

In Europe, Franklin has always been considered an extraordinary figure—in science, diplomacy, writing talent, humor, and philanthropy. The bicentennial of his death was celebrated in France in 1990 in a variety of ways, including sumptuous brochures underwritten by corporations—one of which was, appropriately, France-Electricité.

The popular image of Franklin in the United States is—regrettably—quite different. While a great symposium ("Reappraising Franklin") was orchestrated in Philadelphia on the occasion of the bicentennial by Professor Leo Lemay, the local papers filled their pages with salacious tales about the supposedly inexhaustible sexual drive of the man being remembered, as if there was nothing else to write about.

While lecturing about Franklin around the country, I have been asked repeatedly how many affairs Franklin had, how many illegitimate children, and so forth. My answer is always the same: I don't know and I don't care. Our function as documentary editors is not to idly speculate over what might have happened but to rely on letters, diaries, and memoirs; and there are no letters, diaries, or memoirs that ever mention a specific liaison after Franklin's marriage to Deborah Read. Even if there were affairs, as there may well have been during those fifteen years that he lived an ocean away from his wife, of what interest are they if they left no trace?

What is true, and captivating, is that Franklin had vibrant relationships with a number of women—American, English, and French; young and old—and that world literature has been enriched by the range of emotions and the language these feelings evoked from both himself and his correspondents.

The secret of his powerful bonds with so many different women resides, I believe, in the fact that he considered each one not merely as an object of conquest but as a unique personality well worth listening to. His writing style varies considerably from woman to woman.

Here follow three samples of Franklin's style, in letters to one American young woman and two English ones. He goes from sensuous to sensible when addressing Catharine Ray, from intellectual to quasi-reverential with Polly (Stevenson) Hewson, from grandfatherly to tender when dealing with Georgiana Shipley. Three love stories? Yes, three facets of love—all of them, I am convinced, platonic.[1]

The episode involving Catharine Ray took place during an interlude as potentially erotic as one can image. It started in Boston, during the Christmas week of 1754, while Franklin was paying a visit to his brother John, whose stepson was married to Catharine's sister. Franklin, a man approaching fifty who, having given up his profitable profession in publishing and printing, was now basking in his scientific triumphs—the stove that bore his name, his discovery of the nature of lightning—and a young woman in her early twenties, euphoric on one of her rare trips away from her aging parents, vivacious, romantic, glorying in her obvious effect on that celebrated man. Catharine chatted away and Franklin listened. He really listened. She made sugar plums and he claimed that they were the best he had ever tasted. He "guessed her thoughts" and she called him a "conjurer."[2]

On 30 December 1754, they set out together for Newport, Rhode Island. When they reached an icy hill, their horses, improperly shod by a dishonest smith, kept falling on their noses and knees, "no more able to stand than if they had been shod on skates." Yet they would both remember with delight, for years to come, how they had talked away the hours "on a winter journey, a wrong road, and a soaking shower," and in middle age she would assert that a great part of her life's happiness was due to the pleasing lessons he had given her on that journey. What those lessons were will remain forever their secret.[3]

A few more days in Newport, a few in nearby Westerly to visit another sister of hers, and then she had to rush home to windswept Block Island, to the bedside of a sick parent. Franklin watched her sail away. "I thought too much was hazarded when I saw you put off to sea in that very little skiff, tossed by every wave. . . . I stood on the shore and looked after you till I could no longer distinguish you even with my Glass." He could not bring himself to leave. After an absence of almost six months he lingered some more in New England. "I almost forgot I had a home," he wrote, "till I was more than half-way towards it."

He had barely reached Philadelphia when her first letter arrived. The northeast wind, he declared, was the gayest wind since it brought him her kisses, as promised, her kisses all mixed with snowflakes, "pure as your Virgin Innocence, white as your lovely bosom, and—as cold."

A romance? Yes, but a romance in the Franklin manner, hovering between the risqué and the avuncular, taking a bold step forward and an ironic step backward, implying that he is tempted as a man but respectful as a friend. Such a relationship was flattering for a woman who could not but feel the depth of his emotion, yet knew that it would not lead to what was, in those days, a catastrophe. And with Franklin's many reminders that he could easily be her father, Catharine must have felt young, always.

His first letter to her was typical. One moment of folly: "I almost forgot I had a home." But it did not last:

> Then, like an old man who, having buried all
> he loved in this world, begins to think of
> heaven, I began to think of and wish for
> home. . . . My diligence and speed increased
> with my impatience. I drove on violently and

made such long stretches that a very few days
brought me to my own house and to the arms of
my good old wife and children where I remain,
thanks to God, at present well and happy.

Saved! Reason prevailed.

When the situation was threatening to become too passionate,
Franklin managed to put it back in perspective in such a way that his
correspondent could have no doubt about his desire for her, spiritual *and* carnal, yet no delusion about his being totally carried away.
And what can be more unimpeachable in appearance yet more
sobering in effect than a pleasant, casual mention of one's dear
mate? There never was to be a letter to "Katy," even a flirtatious one,
without some reference to Deborah:

The Cheeses, particularly one of them, were
excellent. All our Friends have tasted it,
and all agree that it exceeds any English
Cheese they ever tasted. Mrs. Franklin was
very proud that a young Lady should have so
much Regard for her old Husband as to send him
such a Present. We talk of you every Time it
comes to Table. She is sure you are a sensible
Girl, and a notable Housewife, and talks of
bequeathing me to you as a Legacy, but I ought
to wish you a better, and hope she will live
these hundred years; for we are grown old
together, and if she has any faults I am so
used to 'em that I don't perceive 'em. . . .
Indeed, I begin to think she has none, as I
think of you. And since she is willing I
should love you as much as you are willing to
be loved by me, let us join in wishing the old
Lady a long Life and a happy.[4]

Catharine felt no such compunction and remembered Deborah
only in polite postscripts. She wrote breathlessly, effusively: "Absence rather increases than lessens my affections. . . . Love me one

thousandth part so well as I do you."[5] She poured out her soul, then feared she had been indiscreet, and shed many tears when he did not answer her promptly. He reassured her but hinted that since even the most innocent expressions of friendship between persons of different sexes are liable to be misinterpreted, he would be cautious "and therefore though you say more, I say less than I think."[6]

Soon she was consulting him about affairs of the heart and sending—supposedly for translation—the love message that a young Spaniard had written her, with the incongruous result that among Franklin's political tracts and philosophical pamphlets there appears an English rendering, in his hand, of the ardent lines once penned by a Don Laureano Donado de el Castillo to his "dear Heart." Franklin took it all in good spirit, encouraging her to tell him more about her pretty mischief, but refused to help her choose from among her suitors, though he made it clear that he favored any worthy Englishman over the Spaniard.

Finally, he advised her to lead a good Christian life, get married, and surround herself with "clusters of plump, juicy, blushing, pretty little rogues like their Mama."[7] Which is just what Catharine eventually did. The next time Franklin met her, she was Mrs. William Greene, wife of the future governor of Rhode Island, to whom she had already borne the first two of their six children.

Franklin and Catharine remained friends for life. Even though they did not recapture the magic of that first encounter, the spark never went out of their letters, and neither did their gratitude toward fate, which had given them that much and no more—the warmth of the embers without the devastation of the flame. To Catharine Ray Greene the world is indebted for some of Franklin's most poetic letters.

Three years later, he was off on his first political mission to England, a mission that was supposed to last six months but took five years. Accompanied by his son, William, who was to study law in London, he settled near the Strand in the Craven Street house of Margaret Stevenson, an obliging and warmhearted widow.[8] After an interlude of eighteen months back in Philadelphia, during which he started building a home for Deborah and himself, he returned to London and spent almost ten more years under Mrs. Stevenson's roof. They were considered a couple by their mutual friends, who

3. ⌢

The House at 36 Craven Street near Trafalgar Square, where Franklin lived with his landlady, Margaret Stevenson, and her daughter, Mary (Polly), for fifteen years. (Courtesy, The Friends of Benjamin Franklin House)

generally invited them together. In the eyes of those friends, there is no doubt that Mrs. Stevenson was in love with her lodger and that after Deborah's death in 1774, she hoped he would marry her. Joseph Priestley reported to Franklin, by then back in Philadelphia, "Mrs Stephenson is much as usual. She can talk about nothing but you." And shortly after Franklin reached Paris, a certain Emma Thompson, whom he must have known well in London, referred to "your good friend Stevenson who I think would have risqued all tarring and feathering to have paid you a visit in Philadelphia." [9]

But years later, when Franklin invited Mrs. Stevenson to join him in Paris, it was to be again as manager of his household. By then the lady was too ill to travel, and she died the following year.

The person who really captured Franklin's attention in England was young Mary ("Polly"), the Stevenson daughter, who was eighteen when he arrived. Highly intelligent, eager to learn, serious, even a bit straitlaced, Polly was the ideal student, the perfect answer to Franklin's urge to teach. Since she was dispatched to live outside London with an elderly aunt from whom she was expected to inherit a tidy fortune (or was it because of the growing closeness between landlady and tenant on Craven Street?), a large number of letters between Franklin and Polly have survived. Their agenda was nothing less than the study of all moral and natural philosophy. Polly asked questions, Franklin answered in careful detail, she in turn discussed his answers. The topics they tackled included barometers, insects, rising tides in rivers, why water becomes warmer after being pumped (if, in fact, it does), waterspouts, bubbles in a teacup, the distillation of seawater, fire, electrical storms, his phonetic spelling system, why rain is not salty, why wet clothes do not provoke a cold, and more.

His tone with Polly was anything but flirtatious; it was affectionate and at times verged on reverential:

> After writing six Folio Pages of Philosophy to a young Girl, is it necessary to finish such a Letter with a Compliment? . . . Does it not say that she has a Mind thirsty after Knowledge, and capable of receiving it; and that the most agreeable Things one can write to her are those that tend to the Improvement of her Understanding? It does indeed say all this, but then it is still no Compliment; it is no more than plain honest Truth which is *not* the Character of a Compliment. So if I would finish my Letter in the Mode, I should yet add something that means nothing, and is *merely* civil and polite. But being naturally awkward at every Circumstance of Ceremony, I shall not attempt it. I had rather conclude abruptly with what pleases me more than any Compliment can please you, that I am allow'd to subscribe myself Your affectionate Friend.

To which she replied, in a style that Jane Austen would not have disavowed: "Such a Letter is indeed the highest Compliment. . . . The warmth of your affection makes you see Merit in me that I do not possess. It would be too great Vanity to think I deserve the Encomiums you give me, and it would be Ingratitude to doubt your Sincerity. Continue, my indulgent Friend, your favourable opinion of me, and I will endeavor to be what you imagine me."[10]

His dream was to see Polly marry his son and "become his own in the tender Relation of a Child," and Polly, it seems, was attracted to William, but William decided to marry Elizabeth Downes, the daughter of a Barbados planter. Franklin's disappointment was so keen that he left England less than one month before the wedding. The date of his departure for Philadelphia is traditionally attributed to the fact that his political mission was over, but considering that he had been away from home for five full years on his first mission, it is surprising, even astonishing, that he did not postpone his return for a few more days.

The farewell message Franklin sent from a "wretched inn" in Portsmouth on 11 August 1762, is the one letter in his life in which he admits to being overwhelmed by sadness. The "bad paper" that he found at the inn was adequate, he felt, to tell his Polly that he was afflicted at the thought of never seeing her again, but would it tell *how* afflicted he was? No, it could not. And he ends, "Adieu, my dearest Child; I will call you so; Why would I not call you so, since I love you with all the Tenderness, all the Fondness of a Father? Adieu. May the God of all Goodness shower down his choicest Blessings upon you, and make you infinitely Happier than that Event could have made you."[11]

Franklin and Polly did meet again, some two years later, when he embarked on his second mission to London, but their relationship, while still very cordial, lost some of its elan. Polly, in her thirties, fell in love with the gifted young Dr. William Hewson, and Franklin gave her away in marriage. No more science was discussed; her letters were all about babies and toddlers. She must have really taken to heart the advice Franklin once gave her: "The Knowledge of Nature may be ornamental, and it may be useful, but if to attain an Eminence in that, we neglect the Knowledge and Practice of essential Duties, we deserve Reprehension. For there is no Rank in Natural Knowledge of equal Dignity and Importance with that of being a good Parent, a good Child, a good Husband, or Wife, a good Neighbour or Friend, a good Subject or Citizen, that is, in short, a good Christian."[12]

Polly's happiness did not last long. Shortly before the birth of their third child, Dr. Hewson died of septicemia contracted while performing an autopsy. Franklin's attitude toward the widow became warmly protective. To comfort her, he daydreamed of marrying his own little grandson Benny—whom he had not yet seen and would not meet for years to come—with her last child, Eliza, and of dancing with Polly at the wedding.

On the twenty-fifth anniversary of their friendship, he celebrated their abiding closeness. "It is to all our Honours," he wrote, "that in all that time we never had among us the smallest Misunderstanding. Our Friendship has been all clear Sunshine without any the least Cloud in its Hemisphere."[13]

Polly joined Franklin in Paris with her three children during the winter of 1784–85. Her visit was immensely pleasurable for him, as the pain of a kidney stone kept him homebound. Polly did not fail to express her British contempt for the dissolute French, among whom she included the beloved grandson Temple, who was well on his way, she felt, to becoming a playboy.

Finally, in 1786, the four Hewsons followed Franklin to Philadelphia—never to go home again. Anxious for his religious orthodoxy, Polly was at her friend's bedside when he died. She survived him by only five years and is buried in Bristol, Pennsylvania.

Catharine Ray was in her early twenties when she met Franklin, and Polly Stevenson was eighteen. Georgiana Shipley, another recipient of intensely personal letters, was at the cusp between child and woman—that brief and fragile moment in a girl's midteens. Named after her cousin the duchess of Devonshire, Georgiana was the fourth of the five daughters of Jonathan Shipley, bishop of Saint Asaph, a man whose views grew more liberal as he grew older and who became, along with his whole family, a close friend of Franklin and a champion of the American cause.[14] It was in 1771 at the Shipley summer house in Twyford, near Winchester, that Franklin wrote the first and sprightliest installment of his *Memoirs*, spurred on by the enthusiastic reception given to nightly readings of his work in progress.

Some months later, Georgiana, in great distress, informed Franklin of the death of Mungo, the pet squirrel he had imported for her from America. His letter of condolence is a model of the way an adult should comfort a child. It is grandfatherly in tone—he was well in his sixties at the time—but without a hint of condescension. First, he joined her in lamenting the unfortunate end of poor Mungo, who had escaped from his cage and been killed by a dog. A little praise for the deceased: "He had had a good Education, had travell'd far, and seen much of the World."

Whereupon he introduced her to the healing power of words and the magic of converting sorrow into art: "Let us give him an Elegy in the monumental Stile and Measure, which being neither Prose nor Verse, is perhaps the properest for Grief; since to use the common Language would look as if we were not affected, and to make Rhymes would seem Trifling in Sorrow." [15]

The twenty-two-line epitaph or elegy opens on a somber note:

> *Alas! Poor* Mungo!
> *Happy were thou, hadst thou known*
>   *Thy own Felicity!*
> *Remote from the fierce Bald-Eagle,*
>   *Tyrant of thy native Woods,*
> *Thou hadst nought to fear from his piercing Talons;*
>   *Nor from the murdering Gun*
>   *Of the thoughtless Sportsman*

And it ends on a cautionary note:

> *Learn hence, ye who blindly wish more Liberty,*
> *Whether Subjects, Sons, Squirrels or Daughters,*
> *That apparent* Restraint *may be real*
>   *Protection,*
> *Yielding Peace, Plenty, and Security.* [16]

Only four years after penning this prudent advice, Franklin cast off the "Restraint" that yielded "Peace, Plenty, and Security," in order to sign the Declaration of Independence.

Wife Deborah was soon asked to find a new American squirrel for Georgiana and was given a chance to read the literary output pertaining to the episode. As usual, she promptly set to work and shipped "a verey fine one" after having had mishaps with two other

4. ⌣

Georgiana Shipley Hare-Naylor, one of Franklin's
most devoted adopted daughters. (Engraving by
Samuel Davis in *Century Magazine* [1899], p. 420)

squirrels who ran away even though they had been "bred up tame."
Georgiana, who had a distinct preference for the American variety
of squirrel, which she deemed more gentle and good-humored than
the European, was delighted. She reported that "Beebee" was growing fat and enjoyed "as much liberty as even a North American can
desire." Five years later she told Franklin, then in Paris, that Beebee
was still alive and much caressed; even while old and blind, "he pre-
serves his spirits and wonted activity." [17]

Georgiana herself grew into a beauty. Well versed in modern lan-
guages and the classics, she studied painting under Sir Joshua
Reynolds and was in all respects an accomplished young woman.
She certainly knew how to flirt in writing. Admitting a touch of van-

ity, she wrote Franklin about her sisters and herself, saying that "we have grown excessively conceited of having acquired your good opinion, for we prefer Dr. Franklin's commendation far before the finest things the smartest Macaroni [meaning dandy] could say of us."

Two years of silence ensued as Franklin, back in Philadelphia, assumed a leading role in the Revolution. Almost as soon as he reached Paris, he renewed contact with the Shipley family, and Georgiana's answer—written in secret because her father thought that corresponding in wartime was a dangerous thing—is an explosion of joy. She wondered whether her friend had read Edward Gibbon and Adam Smith, both of recently published renown. She herself was studying Socrates because he reminded her so much of Dr. Franklin. She envied William Temple Franklin for being so close to his grandfather. And she described an electrical machine. One could hardly be more effusive than Georgiana on that 11 February 1777.[18]

She requested a better picture of Franklin than those in the many prints and medals she had seen so far. In case a good painting of him had been made in Paris, she asked for a miniature copy of it. That would make her "the happiest of beings, and next to that, a lock of your own dear grey hair," she continued.[19] In exchange she offered to send him a silhouette of her father and some of her more recent drawings. Franklin obliged, of course, first by sending her one of the small medallions that he distributed among friends as souvenirs and, in early 1780, the hair lock, followed by a snuff box adorned with an exquisite miniature portrait of him on its lid.[20]

She kissed both the hair and the picture a thousand times, she exclaimed. Yes, she could imagine Franklin smiling at her excessive happiness. Still, she had to tell him, the gift would not only make her happier, but also a better person because—she concluded in Latin— her character would be shaped by reflecting on his.

Three young women, three styles, three destinies. Catharine, the warmhearted girl from Block Island, turned out to be the happiest of the three. She kept her exuberance through the hard days of the Revolution and took Franklin's sister Jane Mecom into her house when Jane had to flee from the British occupation of Boston. Even though Jane, quite old by then, did not have an easy temper and was quick to take offense (she was "miffy," said her brother), the two women became and remained close friends.

Polly turned despondent during the five years that separated Franklin's death from her own. She did not get along with the Baches, which is hardly surprising—considering the resentment Sally Franklin must have felt toward this London "rival" who occupied such a prominent place in her father's affection. Polly's son Thomas went to study medicine in Edinburgh, and their correspondence, preserved on microfilm at the American Philosophical Society, resonates with the clash between the homesick mother, longing for England, and the youth who was enamored of America and pined to return there. The Hewsons remained in the New World and produced at least one doctor per generation.

And Georgiana, the star of her lively family? Her life, so full of promise, took an irreversible downward spiral in 1784 when, in defiance of her family, she married the attractive but ineffectual Francis Hare. Scrapped for money, the couple toyed with the idea of settling on a farm in Pennsylvania, and Franklin tried to help them with down-to-earth advice. But work was repugnant to the husband. They spent a vagabond existence in modest European inns on the small pension granted Georgiana by the duchess of Devonshire. Georgiana died in Switzerland in 1810.

They had such different destinies, these three young women who never met one another, and yet they had one thing in common: their memories. Nobody put it better than Mme Brillon, Franklin's Parisian friend, long after his return to Philadelphia: "To have been, to still be, forever, the friend of this amiable sage who knew how to be a great man without pomp, a learned man without ostentation, a philosopher without austerity, a sensitive human being without weakness, yes, my good papa, your name will be engraved in the temple of memory[;] but each of hearts is, for you, a temple of love." [21]

This chapter appears, in a slightly modified form, in the author's recently published *My Life with Benjamin Franklin* (New Haven: Yale University Press, 2000).

PART TWO

Franklin and the Transforming
World for Women

4

SEX AND THE MARRIED MAN:
Benjamin Franklin's Families
Jan Lewis

*For ne'er heard of woman, good or ill
But always loved best her own sweet will.*
—*Poor Richard, 1733*

Is there anything more that can be said about Benjamin Franklin and sex? Claude-Anne Lopez, whose shrewd psychological insights set a standard by which other biographers may be judged, may well have exhausted the subject. Lopez has suggested that Franklin's closest attachments to women outside of his family—Catharine Ray, Margaret Stevenson, Polly Stevenson, Anne-Louise Brillon—were not what we would call "affairs," but instead were intimate, nonsexual attachments of the sort the French called *amitié amoreuse*. Franklin, argued Lopez and Eugenia Herbert in *The Private Franklin* (1975), was most comfortable in relationships that were "platonic but short of the grand passion." They suggested that it was Franklin himself who held back, preferring romance that was "somewhat risqué, somewhat avuncular, taking a bold step forward and ironic step backward, implying that he is tempted as a man but respectful as a friend."[1] This observation is quite astute. It also makes Franklin rather appealing to us today, for ours is an age that prizes irony and suspects that grand passions are at best a sham. Like the women to whom Franklin turned his attention, we are charmed by Franklin's gallantry and, quite frankly, relieved to learn that it was only an elaborate show.

But is this Franklin too modern? Have we read into him too much of our own age, and too little of his? And have we focused too much upon Franklin himself and too little upon the women he wooed? In order to achieve an understanding of Franklin in the context of his own time, we need to shift the grounds of the discussion from his psychology to the situation of women in the eighteenth century. For in the context of prevailing attitudes about masculinity and femininity, as well as the options available to both men and women, it may well have been Franklin's female friends, at least as much if not more than Franklin himself, who set the terms of their relationships.

It was, in fact, Franklin's close friend Mme Brillon who hoped to settle their relationship on platonic terms. As Claude-Anne Lopez described the trajectory of their romance in *Mon Cher Papa*, it seems rather evident that Franklin hoped and indeed pressed for a full-fledged, sexual affair. Franklin, of course, could be quite playful in his addresses to women, and he enjoyed being slightly risqué, but I think that his meaning in his letters to Mme Brillon was clear: As she deflected the elderly widower's advances, he protested, "you renounce and totally exclude all that might be of the flesh in our affection, allowing me only some kisses, civil and honest, such as you might grant your little cousins." He had already told her that every time he saw or thought of her he broke the commandment that enjoined coveting thy neighbor's wife, and, far from feeling guilty, he still hoped to "obtain full possession" of her "person." Moreover, the best way to "get rid of a certain temptation is, as often as it returns, to comply with and satisfy it." And when Mme Brillon attempted to preserve a relationship that was intimate but chaste, Franklin threatened to seek sexual favors elsewhere, faulting her for a "kind of avarice which leads you to seek a monopoly on all my affections, and not to allow me any for the agreeable ladies of your country. . . . What am I receiving that is so special as to prevent me from giving the same to others, without taking from what belongs to you?" [2]

It would appear that Mme Brillon prevailed, and that the relationship continued on the terms that she proposed—intense, deeply intimate, but chaste. And while it may not have offered all of the intimacies and forms of human connection that adult love can provide, it was as far as Mme Brillon, if not her suitor, was prepared to go.

Her reasons, even when expressed in a manner that is sometimes mannered and coy, are impeccable. "You are a man," she wrote, "I am a woman, and while we might think along the same lines, we must speak and act differently. Perhaps there is no great harm in a man having desires and yielding to them; a woman may have desires, but she must not yield." [3] In those brief lines we get a glimpse both of Franklin's attraction for this extremely talented young matron and the danger he presented. They "think along the same lines."

If Mme Brillon had come to believe that she and her American admirer could think, could reason in similar ways, then Franklin had evidently confounded the gender expectations of his era—ones that he himself had helped establish. Several decades earlier Franklin had suggested that woman and man were fundamentally different in their natures: "she wants his Force of Body and Strength of Reason; he, her Softness, Sensibility and acute Discernment." [4] Franklin was hardly original in positing a fundamental difference between male and female nature. In fact, such characterizations were common currency in the eighteenth century. [5] In repeating them, Franklin, like others who wrote about masculinity and femininity, simultaneously held out sexual difference as a fundamental part of nature and as a set of goals toward which men and women should strive.

At the same time, in a series of intimate relationships with women outside his own family, Franklin was able to transcend the very differences between men and women that he himself inscribed. In fact, erasing just such sexual differences seems to have been one of Franklin's goals. "For sixty years, now," he explained, "masculine and feminine things—and I am not talking about modes and tenses—have been giving me a lot of trouble. It will make me all the happier to go to paradise where, they say, all such distinctions will be abolished." [6] And earlier still he noted that the "Rules for Matrimonial Happiness" that he addressed to women were, "with very little Alteration . . . as proper for Husbands as for Wives to practice." Even more than Thomas Jefferson, whose ability to converse easily with women about topics of mutual interest has been noted by Frank Shuffelton, [7] Franklin could make women believe that he and they thought—and felt—the same.

Michael Zuckerman has recently admired this wonderful talent of Franklin's to "get outside himself." "Always," Zuckerman writes, Franklin "could imagine the other." Quoting John Updike, Zuckerman noted the "androgyny" of Franklin's "imagination, from the speech of Polly Baker to his literary gallantries among the ladies of Paris."[8] By assuming the feminine persona, as Silence Dogood or Polly Baker, and by corresponding with a series of educated and intelligent women, Franklin was incorporating women more generally into the "republic of letters" that the Enlightenment created. The republic of letters assumed and asserted a universal human nature; it spoke to human similarities, rather than differences—such as sex. When Franklin pretended to be a woman, Silence Dogood, in order to write about such quintessentially republican topics as freedom of the press; the value of education, particularly for women; and religious hypocrites, he established these principles as universal, transcending gender.

In fact, as Michael Warner has noted, by choosing to write as a woman, Franklin was able to "negate even the particularity of gender." The republic of letters asserted the primacy of the general over the particular, the social over the individual, and an ungendered and anonymous citizenry over the particularities of gender and individuality.[9] Although this assertion of the primacy of society may seem to suggest and even prefigure Rousseau's notion of the "General Will," there is at least one significant difference: if Franklin's idea of the republic rests upon the negation or transcendence of gender, Rousseau's, as a number of feminist scholars have pointed out, absolutely required the subordination of women and their exclusion from the republic.[10]

The body politic, as Franklin conceived it, was ungendered; it was, like his writing, "freed from the localization of the personal, the bodily, the corruptible."[11] Like Franklin, Rousseau attempted to imagine and create a political society that transcended the personal; he could do it, however, only by embodying corruption, by associating it with women's bodies in particular, and arguing that the preservation of male virtue required the control of women and their exclusion from the political sphere.

Franklin, we know, was familiar with at least some of Rousseau's ideas. He condemned the popular French practice of sending babies out to wetnurses, citing Rousseau's "Rights of Children to their Mother's Milk." Rousseau's *Émile* was available in Philadelphia as early as 1763, and it was considerably more popular in America than was his *Social Contract.*[12] Rousseau's misogynistic political theory, presumably, would have been available to Franklin—as well as to other male Revolutionaries—and it is significant that neither he nor they would banish women from the republic that they were creating, at least in such explicit and misogynistic terms.

Franklin, then, was caught between the imperatives of his republicanism, which negated the distinctions of gender, and his own evident appreciation of human sexuality, which, of course, delighted in those very distinctions. Mme Brillon herself may have been caught in her own set of contradictions. An accomplished musician and composer, she was a young matron of some note. She had married a wealthy man twenty-four years her senior in order to satisfy her parents, not herself; he would prove unfaithful. Under the mores that prevailed among the French aristocracy, Mme Brillon might herself have taken a lover—if not Franklin, then someone else. Yet although rumors circulated about her, Mme Brillon's sad assertion that "a woman may have desires, but she must not yield," has the ring of authenticity. The role that she chose for herself—loyal wife and dedicated mother, chaste confidante of great men—might well have suited Rousseau. Caught between the more relaxed sexual mores of the ancien régime and the domesticity that would follow the Revolution, Mme Brillon acknowledged her desire and renounced it.[13]

It is little wonder, then, that Mme Brillon was attracted to Franklin. No doubt it was this capacity of his to draw women into a discourse that negated their gender, and hence the basis for their inferiority in eighteenth-century society, that was part of his appeal to the other accomplished women such as Catharine Ray and Polly Stevenson to whom he formed intimate attachments. Catharine Ray was a vivacious young woman in her twenties when she met Franklin in 1754, when he was visiting his brother in Boston. She would later marry a future governor of Rhode Island, but at this stage in her life, Catharine Greene was evidently flattered by the attention of the celebrated man of science. Franklin acted as her escort on a journey from Boston back to Newport. Franklin would remember the "hours and miles" that he and his female companion, caught in bad weather with improperly shod horses, "talked away so agreeably, even in a winter journey, a wrong road, and a soaking shower." He would also later say that her "Virgin Innocence," like her "lovely Bosom," was as white and cold as snow.[14] Franklin, evidently, had to settle for conversation.

Only three years later Franklin would establish a similar relationship with another intelligent and appealing young woman. In 1758, he went to London, where he lodged with a widow, Margaret Stevenson, and struck up close friendships with both her and her eighteen-year-old daughter, Polly. Franklin quickly transformed the Stevenson house into his home away from home, and the attachments to both women were so great—so entirely comfortable, in fact—that a sexual relationship with neither woman can be ruled out. On the other hand, it seems quite impossible that Franklin would have courted both mother and daughter while maintaining his warm friendship with both. Whatever precise form the relationships took, this much is known for certain, they were close and enduring. Many years later, after she herself had married and been widowed, and after Franklin's wife also had died, Polly Stevenson—then Hewson—moved her family to Philadelphia and was with Franklin when he died.[15]

If we have difficulty in determining the precise nature and extent of Franklin's attachments to women outside his family, perhaps it is because Franklin, too, was confused. He eventually decided that the ideal arrangement would be for Polly to marry his son, William, although William had already fathered a child out of wedlock and was about to marry a woman of his own choosing. Franklin's disappointment is evident in a letter he wrote to Polly. He had hoped that she "might become his own, in the tender relation of a child." Nonetheless, he would still call her his "dearest child. . . . Why should I not call you so, since I love you with all the tenderness, all the fondness of a father?"[16] Somehow, Franklin had to make her his "own," and all that he could think of was to marry her to his son.

It is almost as if Franklin had no word in his vocabulary for a female friend, no way to imagine preserving such a friendship other than by drawing his friend into a formal familial relationship. In 1781, almost two decades after Franklin sought to marry Polly

5. 〰️

Mary (Polly) Stevenson Hewson—Franklin's symboli-
cally adopted daughter, who remained also devoted to
him for more than thirty years and was by his bedside
when he died. (Engraving by Peter Aitken as published in Paul Leicester Ford, "Franklin's Relations
with the Fair Sex," *Century Magazine* [1899], p. 421)

Stevenson to his son William, Franklin would attempt to arrange a
marriage between William's son William Temple, and Mme Brillon's
daughter Cunégonde. "Having almost lost my own daughter because of the wide distance between us [while he was in Europe and
Sally remained in Philadelphia], I hoped to find another one in you,
and still another in your daughter, to take care of my old age."
Franklin would also fantasize about a match between his grandson Benjamin Franklin Bache (Sally's son), and Polly Stevenson
Hewson's daughter Eliza, when the girl was still a toddler.[17]

However we might label Franklin's overtures—whether ardent or ironic, slightly risqué or downright bold—he knew precisely the terms he wanted to use: a young woman "my dear child" or "my very dear daughter," and an older woman, a wife. "Sinners like me I might have said US," Franklin wrote his landlady Margaret Stevenson when she was away visiting, "are condemn'd to live together and tease one another . . . so come home tomorrow."[18] In London and Paris, indeed wherever he went, Franklin would always meet women and easily make new homes.

Yet these women were not Franklin's daughters, nor were they his wives. When he died, Franklin left almost everything he owned to his blood relatives; Polly Stevenson Hewson received only a silver tankard.[19] When all was said and done, Franklin knew the difference between real and fictive kin. But he gave his female friends something he could never provide for his wife or daughter: respect and affection for their minds, and it was this, more than the pose of lover, spouse, or "cher papa," that they seemed to value most of all.

Franklin's letters to Polly Stevenson explained barometers, colors and heat, and rivers and tides—complete with a diagram. He said that hers was "a Mind thirsty after Knowledge and capable of receiving it."[20] Not only must such discussion with so esteemed a scientist and public figure have been deeply flattering to intellectually ambitious young women, it also constituted a form of higher education. On the eve of Franklin's return to the United States, Mme Brillon consoled herself, "Every day of my life I shall remember that a great man, a sage has wanted to be my friend. . . . I shall forever repeat that I spent eight years with Doctor Franklin!"[21]

None of these women denied their femininity. As Lopez and Herbert have pointed out, Catharine Ray was coquettish with the older Franklin, and Mme Brillon could be coy.[22] At the same time, they seemed to want to transcend their femininity, or more precisely, their sexuality. "In paradise," Mme. Brillon fantasized, "we shall be reunited, never to leave each other again! . . . women will not be coquettish, men will be neither jealous nor too enterprising. . . . ambition, envy, conceit, jealousy, prejudices, all will vanish at the sound of the trumpet; a lasting, sweet and peaceful friendship will animate every society." She craved not sexual intimacy, but a pure friendship. "Only friendship, sweet friendship endears my life to me. . . .

There are so many sorrows and so few pleasures for a sensitive being, so many privations for our sex, that without friendship—." [23]

Franklin offered a sort of friendship that contained a recognition of the differences between men and women that the eighteenth century perceived, and transcended them. But such a friendship, between men and women who "think along the same lines," would have perished, Mme Brillon recognized, had it become physically intimate, that is, had it become embodied.

"Let us start from where we are," Mme Brillon had told Franklin. "You are a man, I am a woman, and while we might think along the same lines, we must speak and act differently. Perhaps there is no great harm in a man having desires and yielding to them; a woman may have desired, but she must not yield." It was not that she did not, like Franklin, feel desires. On the contrary, "in the matter of desire, I am as great a sinner as yourself." [24] Women and men might think the same, and they might feel the same impulses, but they simply could not behave in the same way.

Later she would try to explain her position in philosophical terms: "The gentleman, great philosopher that he is, goes by the doctrines of Anacreon and Epicure, but the lady is a Platonist. He wants a fat, chubby love, a love of flesh and bones, spoiled and pampered. . . . the lady tries to blunt his little arrows, while giving him full freedom to run by hills and dales and attack anyone in sight. . . . Platonism may not be the gayest sect, but it is a convenient defense for the fair sex." [25] The compromise that Mme Brillon suggested was to detach the mind from the body, so that she and Franklin might enjoy a love that was deep and intense, but disembodied—and he might seek the pleasures of the flesh—running around and attacking anyone in sight—elsewhere.

Given Mme Brillon's situation as a respectable married woman, her position was wholly reasonable. Of course, given Franklin's advanced age, we may think that there was no danger to Mme Brillon—or hope for Franklin that their affair would have been consummated. Perhaps his age gave him and his confidante license to talk more openly about matters of sex than they would have, had he been younger. Franklin was well known for his playfulness, and his overtures may have been intended, and taken, as charming jokes. Perhaps his attempts to arrange marriages for his favorite young females were nothing more than that, lighthearted ways of expressing his affection.

Yet, in our post-Freudian age, we know that there are really no jokes, that each joke embodies an element of dead seriousness. So with Franklin: what he chose to joke about and the words he chose to express his playfulness are revealing. And so also when Mme Brillion responded to him. Her correspondence with Franklin gave her the opportunity to explore important subjects with unusual candor. The risks of a fully-fleshed affair, particularly when sexual mores were changing, would have been too great; a scandal—not to mention an unwanted pregnancy, could have jeopardized her marriage and social standing.

To be sure, many women in the eighteenth-century Atlantic world would take those risks—and many of them would pay the price. American historians have discovered that over the course of the eighteenth century, an increasing proportion of women were pregnant on their wedding day—as many as 40 percent in the decades just after the American Revolution.[26] Yet any woman who had sexual relations with a man prior to marriage risked a great deal; there was no assurance that her lover would marry her—and she would then face the choice of bearing an illegitimate child or hazarding her life in an abortion.

As Cornelia Hughes Dayton has shown, the increase in premarital sexual relations in the eighteenth century clearly advantaged men and disadvantaged women.[27] Moreover, childbirth itself was risky—with perhaps one in every thirty births resulting in the mother's death. Given high rates of fertility in the colonial period—in fact, the same high rates that Franklin repeatedly extolled—as many as one in five women may have died from causes associated with childbirth.[28]

No wonder that respectable American women would have been extremely cautious about entering into an intimate relationship with the married Benjamin Franklin. And in France, as the sexual mores of the French aristocracy came under attack, married women there also would have thought twice about entering into a sexual relationship with the elderly widower. On both sides of the Atlantic, respectable women of childbearing age would have had every reason to exercise restraint.

In this light, Franklin's "Speech of Miss Polly Baker," far from

demonstrating his ability to "imagine the other," illustrates his inca-
pacity for thinking about female sexuality in other than self-serving
terms. Polly Baker, as Franklin imagined her, was an unmarried
mother who had just given birth to her fifth child. She protested to
the Connecticut court that was about to fine her for bearing a child
out of wedlock that they were turning "natural and Useful Actions
into Crimes." To engage in sexual relations was natural, and to bear
children useful. Polly had not, in her mind, sinned; she had merely
defied convention. She considered herself fundamentally a moral
person; she had not, so far as she knew, "ever wrong'd Man,
Woman, or Child." She had not even burdened her community, for
she had "maintained" her children by her "own Industry." Having
obeyed the biblical injunction to *"Increase and multiply,"* she deserved a "Statue erected to my Memory" instead of the "public Dis-
grace and Punishment" that had been her lot.[29]

"The Speech of Miss Polly Baker," is, of course, one of Franklin's
comic masterpieces. Perhaps we should not take it more seriously
than Franklin would have intended. Yet Polly gave voice to many of
the elements of the Franklin philosophy—a preference for a "natural" rather than a conventional (and often hypocritical) morality;
pride in America's increasing population [30]—at the same time that
she spoke about female sexuality. There was no shame, she suggested, in sex outside of marriage; indeed, the shame fell primarily
upon those who would scorn her. Written by a father, grandfather,
and great-grandfather of children born out of wedlock, Franklin's
essay, ascribed to a female pen, was more than a little self-serving. It
anchored a freer female sexuality in his utilitarian philosophy, ap-
pearing to make it serve the needs of a prospering and Enlightened
society.

Franklin's Polly Baker supported herself and her children through
her own industry, and she triumphed over convention. Her stirring
words convinced one of the judges who heard her case to marry her.
Surely, however, these words must have rung false to any women
who read them. Few young women would have been able to support
five children by their own industry, and fewer still could have as-
sailed the sexual double standard and won. Women in eighteenth-
century society were vulnerable enough; sex outside of marriage only
made them more so.

That Franklin's addresses to women, including Polly Baker's

speech, were self-serving is underscored by the particulars of his own life. Historians are not certain who the mother of Franklin's son William was. It is possible that she was one of the "low Women that fell in my Way" when he was a single man in Philadelphia, impelled by the "Passion of Youth."[31] She might have been, as Franklin's enemies would later assert, a woman named Barbara, a maidservant who worked in Franklin's household. It is also possible that Franklin's own wife, Deborah Read Rogers, whom he married at about the time of his son William's birth—the precise birth date is unknown—was the mother of the child, and that she and Franklin pretended that William was illegitimate to spare her the shame of a premarital pregnancy, although it is hard to see how taking in her husband's illegitimate infant would have been less shameful than her becoming pregnant before marriage.[32]

Whoever William Franklin's mother might have been, it is clear that Franklin engaged in sexual relations prior to his marriage, that his son William was the product of such a relationship, and that although Franklin would acknowledge him as his son, no woman would ever get to claim that she was his mother.

Franklin knew that the male sexual drive was strong. He would describe it variously as the "Passion of Youth" and "violent natural Inclinations." He thought that marriage was its proper "Remedy," although he was willing to suggest other options for men who were unprepared to take that step.[33] In fact, Franklin's views on marriage seem almost wholly practical, and there is every indication that he married Deborah Read Rogers more out of prudence than passion.

Not only did marriage provide a legitimate outlet for men's "violent natural inclinations," but a good wife helped a man get ahead in the world. In one of his essays in the *Pennsylvania Gazette*, Franklin averred: "A Man does not act contrary to his Interest by Marrying; for I and Thousands more know very well that we could never thrive till we were married; and have done well ever since." As Claude-Anne Lopez and Eugenia Herbert have observed, Franklin could easily have been speaking autobiographically when he extolled the economic advantages of a frugal and industrious wife. Well before he had embarked upon his career of public service, which would take him away from home for years at a time, Franklin noted that a man without a wife to carry on in his absence could not leave home with-

out "Detriment" to his business.[34] With the capable Deborah Franklin looking after his interests in Philadelphia, as Sheila Skemp shows
in Chapter 1 of this volume, Franklin was freed to leave home for
decades at a time.

If Franklin's inclusion of women in a republic of letters was forward looking, his views on marriage were at best traditional. Because
he placed more emphasis on practicality than passion in marriage,
Franklin saw nothing wrong in attempting to arrange marriages for
both his son and his daughter and for one of his grandsons. As we
have seen, he imagined marrying his son William to Polly Stevenson
and his grandson William Temple to Cunégonde Brillon, thereby
bringing women he loved into his family. Franklin chose as his
daughter Sally's prospective husband William Strahan Jr., the son of
a good friend and business associate in London. Franklin had become almost a member of the Strahan family, so much so that one of
the little daughters said she wanted to marry him when she grew up.[35]
Franklin had dreamed of the match for years.

These attempts at matchmaking were curious hybrids, grafting a
more modern notion of the family grounded in affection onto the
sturdy stock of marriages arranged to serve the family's economic
and political interests. In selecting wives for his son and grandson,
Franklin followed his own emotions more than those of the young
people in the family or even the notion of a larger family interest. Indeed, it is hard to discern any notion of a family interest or even of a
consistent social position in Franklin's attempts at matchmaking.
Polly Stevenson and William Strahan Jr., were members of the English middle class, although Strahan, as the son of a leading printer
and prosperous merchant, was several rungs above Stevenson on
the social scale. M. Brillon was a wealthy landowner who had held
a significant government position in the years before the French
Revolution.

All of Franklin's matchmaking schemes failed, no doubt because
they were out of line with prevailing practices. The proposed
matches between the Franklin offspring and their intended English
mates foundered when the young people chose spouses of their own,
following the practice that was becoming prevalent among the middle classes. It was Cunégonde Brillon's father, however, who refused
William Temple Franklin as a son-in-law, for reasons that were quite

traditional. As Mme Brillon explained, "We love your [grand]son and believe he has all it takes to become a distinguished person and make a woman happy, but . . . We . . . need a son-in-law able to take over the position of my husband. . . . This position is the most important of our assets; it calls for a man who knows the laws and customs of our country, a man of our religion." [36] Franklin's domestic schemes, which would have enlarged the circle of his affectionate family, made sense neither to young moderns who expected to choose their own mates nor to older traditionalists who made matches primarily to advance the family interest.

The Franklin who was so acutely aware of his own emotional needs could not acknowledge those of the rest of his family, the women in particular. He was displeased when his daughter Sally married a debt-ridden young merchant with whom she had fallen in love. Sally had violated one of the principles that Franklin held dear, that daughters ought to obey fathers and women defer to men. Franklin consistently advised wives to defer to their husbands and study how to please them, and several times he reminded both husbands and wives that a wife owed her husband obedience. [37] In his own family the republican writer was a patriarch—just the sort of father that republican theorists of the family would rail against. Moreover, it might be said that he compounded his original error by supporting and taking under his wing a grandson, William Temple Franklin, who was widely regarded as a coxcomb and a rake, the antithesis of a man of republican virtue. [38]

It would be easy to condemn Franklin as a hypocrite. As Lopez and Herbert have noted, for example, at the same time that he was insisting that the wife and daughter whom he had left in Philadelphia practice the most rigid economies, he was enjoying the splendors of Europe and even talking about buying diamond earrings for one of his surrogate daughters. [39] In fact, so often did Franklin upbraid one or the other of the women in his family for lack of economy, that one suspects that *this* issue—the connection between women and money—was a particularly sensitive one for him. As Ruth Bloch has noted, Franklin's writings, especially his early ones, are permeated with both praise of female economy and condemnation of female profligacy. [40] To a certain limited extent, Franklin may have felt the sort of "patriarchal rage" that Kenneth A. Lockridge has ascribed to William Byrd II and Thomas Jefferson. Insecure colonials in a metropolitan world, such men made women the focus of their frustrations.[41]

Yet at the same time that Franklin made his wife and then his daughter the focus of his conflicted feelings about economy and luxury—one of the key concerns of republicanism—he also created a succession of substitute families in which he could drink tea out of a silver service and fantasize about buying diamond earrings for a surrogate daughter. In a very real sense the first family had made possible the superior surrogates—with wives and daughters more intelligent and captivating than his own. A man does not lose his liberty when he marries, Franklin had written, but increases it. "Having a Wife that he can confide in, he may with much more Freedom be abroad, and for a longer Time."[42]

But Franklin did not run away from family per se, seeking a freedom beyond the family. Everywhere he went, he seemed to re-create new families, with new and more perfect wives and daughters. How many women over the course of his lifetime did he address as "wife" or "daughter"? And how many women called him "father," "mon cher papa"? The family that he created in America, and which generally followed the pattern he set out for all of family life, proved somehow unfulfilling. The patriarchal model in some way let him down. What it could not provide was the companionship of equals or the communion of teacher and student, the ideals of the republican family. If Lopez and Herbert and the others who have studied Franklin are right, and in all of his significant extramarital and postmarital romances he preserved his emotional distance, protecting himself with irony, then perhaps the platonism that Mme Brillon called a convenient defense for the fair sex served Franklin's needs as well.

And so Franklin had two families, one patriarchal and one republican, one for sex and one for love. That he could not—apparently—find love and sex in the same family speaks not only to his own personal failure but to the failure of his, and his contemporaries', politics, as well. Republicanism, which spoke to the universal and sought to transcend the particular, always became entangled in its own contradictions. It addressed women as if they were the equals of men, as if everyone thought along the same lines, but it would not alter the circumstances that made for and perpetuated the continuing inequality. Michael Zuckerman has suggested that Franklin's ability to get outside himself and imagine the other "enabled him to connect his convictions about public life with his perspectives on personal relations. It allowed him to integrate his conceptions of political economy with his predilections in private affairs."[43] It seems to me, however, that connection and integration are precisely what are missing, and the flaw is not so much in Franklin himself but in the republican world he helped fashion.

Inconsistency, however, is far from the worst of sins. The slippage between egalitarian political ideals and patriarchal family forms, between masculine ideals of domestic paradise and women's family dreams, and, finally, between sex and love, made room for negotiation.[44] No one of Franklin's families met all of his needs; nor perhaps did all of them together. The same was probably true for each of the women in his life as well. The cauldron of revolution in domestic, as in political, life was stirred by many spoons, and some of them were held by women.

PETITIONING WITH THE LEFT HAND:
Educating Women in Benjamin Franklin's America
Mary Kelley

On education all our lives depend;
And few to that, too few, with care attend.
—*Poor Richard, 1748*

Five years before his death in 1790, Benjamin Franklin addressed all those concerned with schooling in a newly independent America. Submitting his "Petition of the Left Hand" to "those who have the superintendency of education," he adopted the persona of a young woman who had been denied an education. "The Left Hand" had a right to that schooling, he insisted. Equally important, the same Left Hand had a need for that education should she have to support herself in her adulthood. Both the tone and content of Franklin's comments suggest that he considered women's minds equal to men's. Indeed it was that very premise that led to his claims on behalf of the Left Hand. And yet Franklin's practices with his daughter and son suggest otherwise. Franklin did not provide his daughter, Sally, with an education that was in any way comparable to the opportunities he made possible for his son, William, or for Sally's son, Benjamin Franklin Bache. William was schooled in Philadelphia's most prestigious educational institutions. Benjamin, or Benny as he was known, was taken to Europe for an elaborate education at boarding schools in France and Switzerland. Sally got little more than reading, writing, and arithmetic. Of course, she also got training in spinning, knitting, and embroidery, although those were hardly designed to develop her intellectual potential.[1]

The seeming contradiction between Franklin's principles and his practices was typical of his time. The most enlightened of the Revolutionary generation—and Franklin would surely be included among them—seemed to claim women's intellectual equality with men. But like Franklin they inscribed that equality with difference. Dedicating the education of women to preparation for their traditional role within the household, they defended female education in terms of a woman's social role as wife and mother, not in terms of her individual right to develop her mind. Purely intellectual interests, careers beyond the home, and a voice in the affairs of the newly independent nation—all these remained the domain of men alone.

Nonetheless, women along with men benefited from the newly available opportunities for education in the decades after the Revolution and establishment of the Republic. Building upon the rudimentary literacy taught in locally supported public schools, an increasing number of private academies and seminaries offered a more extended and diversified education to both sexes. In establishing a bridge from basic literacy to sophisticated comprehension, these institutions highlighted the value that Franklin and other members of the Revolutionary generation attached to more advanced education in the early republic. Convinced that only an informed citizenry could sustain the recently established republic, they looked upon schooling as the means by which to prepare that citizenry to meet its obligations.

But why the concern about female education? Were women considered citizens? The prevailing system of gender relations did restrict female citizenship. Women were subject to coverture, a legal tradition that submerged a wife's property into her husband's. They were denied participation in the nation's body politic either as voters or as jurors. Simultaneously, however, subtle but discernible changes were becoming evident. Perhaps most important, the ideology of republican motherhood made the education of white women critical to the survival of the republic. Inscribing domestic obligations with political significance, republican motherhood held women responsible for the inculcation of virtue in their children. Defined as the ability to yield private interests before the needs of the newly established nation, virtue was considered the linchpin of the republic. So too was a republican mother, virtue's teacher. Obviously, then, mothers and wives, as much as fathers and sons, had to become informed citizens.[2]

When the essayist Judith Sargent Murray observed that "female academies are every where establishing," she spoke to this important change.[3] Established in the North and the South during the nineteenth century's opening decades, nearly four hundred of these schools were founded exclusively for women between 1790 and 1830.[4] Local newspapers described the character of these institutions and indicated the rapidity with which they were established in the early republic. Readers of Hartford's *Connecticut Courant* had an increasingly large number of choices—thirty-four academies, all of which admitted women, announced that they were opening their doors in the three decades after 1790. In the second decade of the nineteenth century alone, nine academies, six of which were exclusively female, were established in Hartford and surrounding towns.[5]

This was the decade in which a Mrs. Value announced the opening of her "BOARDING SCHOOL for young ladies" and listed "orthography, reading prose and verse, writing, arithmetic, parsing English grammar, the elements of astronomy on the celestial globe, geography on the terrestrial globe with a correct knowledge of the atlas and maps, history, Blair's lectures, [and] composition" among the subjects that she offered. Students, she noted, would have the added value of her husband, who would "give them a lesson every day (Sundays excepted) in polite manners, dancing, the French language, and music."[6] Towns much smaller than Hartford and its environs also had their academies. William Elliott, a resident of early nineteenth-century Beaufort, South Carolina, then a town with fewer than a thousand inhabitants, told Ann Smith, his future wife, that "Miss Thomson, a Lady from New York, is come to establish a female Academy here." "An author and professed bluestocking," Thomson had made "quite a sensation in our little town," Elliott told Smith. That was probably an understatement.[7]

Institutions such as those founded in Hartford, Connecticut, and Beaufort, South Carolina, introduced their students to subjects such as history, geography, mathematics, and the natural sciences. Their impact was profound. With the exception of Oberlin College, the nation's colleges and universities began to admit women only after the middle of the nineteenth century. The earliest women's colleges—Vassar, Smith, and Bryn Mawr—did not open their doors until 1865, 1875, and 1884, respectively. Founded as a seminary in 1837, Mount Holyoke did not become a college until 1888. For more than a half a century, then, the hundreds of female academies and seminaries were the only institutions that provided women with advanced learning. In a letter dated 21 September 1819, Maria Campbell, a resident of a plantation in Virginia, highlighted their significance. Reminding Mary Humes, then a student at the acclaimed Salem Academy in Salem, North Carolina, that hers was a world much different from that of earlier generations, Campbell told her younger cousin that "in the days of our forefathers it was considered only necessary to learn a female to read the Bible." [8] Institutions such as Salem Academy made Mary Humes a reader of many books.

In addition to this formal system of academies and seminaries, women also educated themselves. Constituting the act of reading as informal education, women immersed themselves in the literature published on both sides of the Atlantic in the years after the Revolution. Women read for information. They read for instruction on topics they themselves had chosen. They read for examples that either strengthened particular identities or invited adoption of alternatives. In joining reading and education, Mary Guion, daughter of a farmer in Bedford, New York, was typical. An entry she recorded in her diary in January 1803 made that relationship explicit: "I can be receiving instruction and improving my mind." [9]

During the seventeenth and eighteenth centuries, women's reading had been primarily religious in character. In a diary that spanned the last forty years of the eighteenth century, Hannah Heaton noted that "i [sic] read constantly and find it teaching." She did exactly that in a daily schedule that took this New Englander from the Bible to the meditations of John Bunyan to the treatises of Thomas Shepard, Solomon Stoddard, and Michael Wigglesworth. [10] Some women in the seventeenth and early eighteenth centuries also read secular literature, including Shakespeare, Congreve, Pope, Fielding, and Dryden among their choices. [11] By the final decades of the eighteenth century, Heaton's exclusive focus on Bibles, treatises, and meditations was no longer typical. Indeed, the evidence from the letters, diaries, and journals of late eighteenth-century women suggests that they read widely and deeply in both religious and secular literature.

South Carolinian Sarah Reeve Gibbes was notable in this regard. Her confidence in taking command of a large body of literature and exercising the skills of a critic was perhaps still more notable. Telling her son, a student at Princeton in the 1780s, that she was pleased he had decided "to make a collection of books," she proceeded to select the authors for him—Shakespeare's "force of human genius," Pope's "chastity of thought," and Dryden's stimulation of "imagination" made them required reading. Swift was problematic. "Happy sallies of wit" notwithstanding, Gibbes found him wanting in "refinement, in many parts his inelegant expressions hurt the delicate reader." The antidote was Sterne's Yorick, who would "correct your feelings." History, Gibbes insisted, would "be most substantially useful, the Roman history particularly will furnish you many noble examples that deserve imitation."[12] Hannah Adams's reading reflected equally capacious tastes. Recalling a New England childhood in which she read "with avidity a variety of books," she acknowledged that she was "passionately fond of novels." But she hastened to add that she was "also an enthusiastic admirer of poetry." Most important, she did not "neglect the study of history and biography, in each of which kind of reading I found an inexhaustible fund to feast my mind."[13] South Carolinian Martha Laurens Ramsay read still more widely. Noting that she "was indefatigable in cultivating an acquaintance with books," her husband David Ramsay recalled that she immersed herself in "natural and civil history, biography, astronomy, chronology, philosophy, voyages, travels, and etc." Simultaneously, Martha Ramsay read the same texts that so engaged Gibbes. Indeed, as her husband noted, she took much pleasure in the "modern works of genius, taste, and imagination, written in the English and French languages."[14]

Nowhere is the engagement with both religious and secular literature more apparent than in the diary of Elizabeth Drinker, a prominent resident of Philadelphia. Begun in 1758 when she was twenty-three years old, Drinker's diary is a window through which we can glimpse a woman seated with her books about her, reading sometimes alone, sometimes in the company of her husband or her children. In an entry that described a visit to a friend, Drinker commented that she had "found her alone, if a person with a [book in hand] can be called so."[15] Such a person could not be called so, at least by a woman who made books her steady companion.

During the forty-nine years that Drinker kept her diary, she left a record of strikingly cosmopolitan reading. Thomas Paine's *Age of Reason*, Joseph Priestley's *Appeal to the Serious and Candid Professor of Christianity*, Benjamin Rush's *Medical Inquiries and Observations*, Mary Wollstonecraft's *Vindication of the Rights of Woman*, John Bunyan's *Pilgrim's Progress*, Benjamin Franklin's *Works*, Erasmus Darwin's *Zoonomia*, Rousseau's *Confessions*, and William Cobbett's *Kick For A Bite* were typical choices. With a ready ease and confidence, Drinker praised and condemned—she damned Paine's writings as "vile"; she remarked that each time she read *Pilgrims Progress* "the better I like it;" she labelled Cobbett's denunciation of Susannah Rowson "rather scurrilous"; she pronounced Franklin's writings "entertaining"; and she dismissed Rousseau, saying "I like him not, or his Ideas."[16]

Drinker's response to women's rights advocate Mary Wollstonecraft was telling. After she had completed *Vindication of the Rights of Woman*, Drinker expressed certain hesitations about Wollstonecraft, although she acknowledged "in very many of her sentiments, she, as some our friends say, speaks my mind." She retreated following the publication of William Godwin's *Memoirs of Mary Wollstonecraft Godwin*. No one reading Drinker's diary could mistake the reason—she had read Godwin's description of Wollstonecraft's affair with Gilbert Imlay and the birth of their child Fanny, both of which were used to villify Wollstonecraft. The objective was not so much the destruction of Wollstonecraft's reputation, although that surely gave her opponents pleasure. Primarily, however, they sought to invalidate her claims on behalf of women. In comparison with many of her contemporaries, Drinker's response was actually mild. She continued to read Wollstonecraft. She described her as a "prodigious fine writer." She went so far as to say that she "should be charmed by some of her pieces." And then she added, "if I had never heard of her Character."[17]

Drinker also read widely in the newly available history, biography, and travel literature. She immersed herself in advice literature, a choice that became common in the nineteenth century. Now and

6. ⌣

Two women celebrate the birth of America and the establishment of rights for men—and women. (Engraving by S. Hill, 1790, in *The Massachusetts Magazine* [1790], frontispiece, Library of Congress, LC USZ62-45,522)

again she permitted herself the pleasure of novels, again a common choice in the nineteenth century. Susannah Rowson's *Charlotte Temple* (which she read at least twice), Henry Brooke's *Fool of Quality*, Agnes Bennett's *Beggar Girl and Her Benefactors*, Laurence Sterne's *Tristam Shandy*, and Maria Edgeworth's *Belinda* were duly recorded in her diary. After she had read Cajetan Tschink's *The Victim of Magical Delusion*, she acknowledged that reading fiction was "a practice I by no means highly approve." And yet she trusted she had not "sinned." Why such confidence in this regard? "I read a little of most things." That Elizabeth Drinker surely did.[18]

Reading, then, served as the vehicle for an informal education that functioned in tandem with the learning offered in academies and seminaries. Simultaneously, reading encouraged women to learn together. In this process of mutual education, women relied upon each other, either for information or for texts themselves. Abigail Adams sent Mercy Otis Warren a volume of Molière, telling her friend that she "should be glad of your oppinion [sic]." Not one to hesitate in expressing her opinion, Adams declared that Molière manifested a "general want of spirit." Worse still, he "ridiculed vice without engaging us to virtue."[19] Amelia Pringle asked Sarah Lance

Huger to lend her either David Hume's *History of England* or David Ramsay's *History of the United States*, both of which were widely read in early nineteenth-century America. Pringle hastened to add, "[I] shall take particular care of them knowing the value of such books."[20] Sarah Jane Bradley read *Advice to Young Ladies*, a volume that a friend had "sent me sometimes since." Bradley looked upon *Advice* favorably, "though I doubt if such books do much good."[21] In response to Eleuthera Du Pont's inquiry, Sophia Cheves confirmed that she had read Scott's *Waverly* twice. She recommended Scott's other novels, some of which she had found equally pleasurable.[22] Eliza Mordecai Myers told her sister Rachel that she had completed Germaine De Stael's *Corinne* in the original French. Her sister should do the same: "I know you will be charmed by it." Myers was now contemplating Stael's *Delphine*, presumably in the original French as well.[23]

The increased educational opportunities, the advanced literacy that resulted, and the increasingly expansive reading broadened women's network of communication and exposed them to a wider variety of perspectives. They fostered a denser and more diversified mental life. And they contributed to a sense of independence. Literacy, of course, entailed a variety of competencies. The ability to decode an already familiar passage from the Bible stood in sharp contrast to sustained engagement with Locke's *Essay Concerning Human Understanding.* Yet each of the individuals engaged with these texts would have been considered literate. The education provided by academies and seminaries and the self-education achieved by reading meant that significantly larger numbers of women were able to command a rapidly expanding print culture, be it in the form of books, periodicals, or newspapers. Lockean epistemology, narratives of conversion, novels, intricacies of biblical theology—all were now included in these women's domain. In a letter to one of her classmates at Mount Holyoke Seminary, Julia Hyde spoke to the implications of an advanced literacy that resulted from women's increased educational opportunities. Telling Lucy Goodale that she ought to "cultivate independence of character," Hyde made reading the means to this end: "In our intercourse with books we have a fine opportunity to do this. Take some book, for instance, and read it and form your own opinion as to its character, its influence, its beauties and its faults. Have an opinion about it, and then, if you like, you can find out what others think and compare your decisions with theirs."[24] In a subtle but critical sense, women such as Hyde were experiencing an enhanced sense of themselves as historical actors.

Simultaneously, women were observing and increasingly were participating in a debate about what an educated woman should do, about what her role should be, and about what her service to the republic should encompass. This debate had an equally profound impact upon women's sense of themselves. In the latter part of the eighteenth century, Americans began to consider the subject of female intellect, a topic that had elicited little concern earlier. The resulting discourse addressed fundamental questions. Were women's minds equal to those of men? Did this equality necessarily imply sameness? Or was it possible for women to be simultaneously equal *and* different in their mental capacities? However these issues were addressed, questions about the purpose of female education remained. Were women to be educated simply to enlarge their minds and to encourage them to become enlightened and articulate individuals? Or was it more appropriate to dedicate their education to a larger social purpose? And if the latter was stressed, to what degree should their education be different from that of their male counterparts?[25]

In developing the idea of an educated woman, commentators almost always did exactly what Benjamin Franklin had done. They juxtaposed female equality against female difference. On the one hand, they insisted that women's minds were equal to men's. Writing in the *American Museum* in May 1792, one J. P. Martin emphasized that no one should "limit merit, nor knowledge, to either sex;" instead, both should be considered "the natural growth of the human mind." Alden Bradford clearly agreed. Speaking at the opening of the local academy in Wiscassett, Maine, in 1808, he told the town's residents that women "possess equally with the other sex quickness of apprehension and accuracy of discernment; and that with equal advantages, they make as great proficiency in any branches of literature."[26]

On the other hand, this particular equality did not mean that education should prepare women for equal roles with men. The same J. P. Martin who had rejected intellectual distinctions between the sexes insisted upon very different intellectual objectives for educated women and men. "Our young men," he declared, "will be emulous to excel the geniuses of the east; our daughters will shine as bright constellations, in the sphere where nature has placed them." Alden Bradford pointedly appended to a defense of female equality grounded in sameness the caveat that "women's employments and pursuits are not the same." In contrast to male counterparts who were developing skills to act upon the world, females should dedicate themselves to becoming "more agreeable and judicious companions and more capable of directing the dispositions and manners of children." [27]

In rejecting the idea that women's minds were lesser and their education useless, these commentators reflected a change in perspective that emerged at the end of the eighteenth century. Indeed, female education was now being represented as necessary for the fulfillment of a woman's newly politicized role as wife and mother. In an address that he delivered before the Young Ladies Academy of Philadelphia, Benjamin Rush justified female education on exactly those grounds. Beginning with what he considered the obvious, Rush declared that a woman's "education should be accommodated to the state of society, manners, and government of the country." In a republic, her role was just as evident—"the instruction of children" and particularly the instruction of "sons in the principles of liberty and government." In Rush's statement we can also locate the origins of one of the oldest clichés in American political life. "It has been remarked," he himself stated, "that there have been few great or good men who have not been blessed with wise and prudent mothers." [28]

Nonetheless, Rush's confidence in women's salutary influence was countered by his conviction that they would also be the harbingers of the republic's decline. Aligning himself with the widely accepted cyclical theory of history, Rush predicted that America would "probably too soon follow the footsteps of the nations of Europe in manners and vices." The signs would be apparent everywhere—language would be corrupted, churches neglected, novels read, and Sundays appropriated for amusement. But the signal tendency would already have been displayed in women's "idleness, ignorance and profligacy." Like so many others in early America, Rush's predictions of the nation's degeneration were gender based. [29]

Joseph Pilmore, who followed Rush to the podium at Philadelphia's Young Ladies Academy, was much more optimistic about the republic's possibilities for survival. The students were indeed fortunate "to live in an age of light and refinement," an age that he was confident would continue if they remembered the lessons of "an education properly calculated for opening the understanding, enriching the mind, and the promotion of virtue." Lest they forget the latter, he stressed that their "delight in learning, [their] diligence in acquiring mental improvements" would always be coupled with their "love of virtue." The next year John Sproat made exactly the same point, telling the students that their education had been designed to "mollify the temper, refine the manners, amuse the fancy, improve the understanding, and strengthen virtue."[30]

Not surprisingly, the justification for female education articulated by Rush, Pilmore, Sproat, and other male advocates defined the woman who was expected to emerge from academies and seminaries and simultaneously circumscribed what she was to do with her education. Deeply marked by gender, this particular model of womanhood defined an educated woman as decidedly different from her male counterpart. In contrast to men who increasingly subscribed to the ideology of individualism, a woman was still expected to define herself in relation to others. Serving husband and children, her education was directed to benefit them, not to fulfill whatever individual potential she might have. There are at least two possible reasons why male theorists constructed this model of behavior. Perhaps they simply could not envision women engaged in any role except that of wife and mother. However, the highly charged character of the rhetoric belies this interpretation, suggesting instead a concern that female education might have unanticipated consequences. Inadvertently, the intensity also highlights the concern, indeed the fear, that one of those consequences could be a challenge to the model itself.

Nowhere was the distinction between expectations for women and men more clearly made than in the pages of the *Port Folio,* a prominent journal launched shortly after the Revolution. Praising the more progressive perspective on women's education, James Milnor nonetheless issued a strongly worded admonition: "Let it be forever recollected, that as a polite and well-informed woman is the most welcome companion of the intelligent of our sex, a female pedant is in all respects the reverse." A cherished "modesty and ami-ableness," both of which were marked as feminine, were juxtaposed against "affectation and conceit of scholastic attainments." The achievements and, more important, the "ostentatious display of the decorations of her mind" made a woman decidedly unwomanly.[31]

Just as important, this woman, who indeed was not a woman at all, appeared to threaten the conventional system of gender rela-tions. It was almost as if she symbolized the system gone awry. An artfully constructed piece titled "Dialogue on Female Education," published in Baltimore's *Portico,* described an alternative system marked by stark reversals in gender attributes and the relations they sustained. Throughout the "Dialogue," the author identified with the advocate Theodosius until the skeptic Eugenius posed the last and most telling question. In wondering whether education would erase a woman's "delicacy and modesty," that is, her femininity, Eu-genius asked rhetorically whether "instead of endeavoring to gain the hearts of the men by engaging manners, they would become their rivals, and be more anxious to vanquish them by strong arguments, than by fascinating manners?" Absolutely not, responded Theodo-sius, telling Eugenius that they could "safely trust to the dispositions implanted in the female breast, to prevent this."[32] Theodosius's con-fidence notwithstanding, his response was not entirely reassuring, at least for those wedded to conventional gender relations. What if "dispositions" were part of a gender system that was socially con-structed rather than natural? What if an education led female stu-dents to challenge those "dispositions" labeled feminine and to develop those considered masculine?

By the last decade of the eighteenth century, women were already beginning to participate in the discourse on female intellect. Al-though they were less visible and their contributions fewer in num-ber, their articles, speeches, and pamphlets demonstrated that women had begun to regard themselves as subjects and were no longer simply objects in a male debate on female intellect. These fe-male commentators also help us to determine the degree to which gender itself shaped the perspective of the participants. Novelist, teacher, playwright, and actress Susannah Rowson established one of the nation's earliest academies dedicated to the education of women. In the addresses she prepared for her students, Rowson made already familiar claims on behalf of female intellect. Insisting that "the mind of a female is certainly as capable of acquiring knowledge as that of the other sex," she placed that knowledge at the service of others. The study of history filled "the mind with entertaining topics of conversation and render[ed] us fit companions for persons of sense and knowledge." Command of literature did much the same, enlivening a woman's ideas and preparing her "to interest and charm those with whom we associate." But Rowson also reminded her students that a woman who pursued knowledge for other ends risked the damning judgment of being "conceited." Indeed, such a woman was so vulnerable to opprobrium that Rowson wrote that "it were better to remain in ignorance, since pedantry and presumption in a woman is more disgusting than an entire want of literary information."[33]

The stereotyping to which Rowson referred was deplored in the aptly titled (and anonymous) *Female Advocate*, a pamphlet that consistently defended a woman's pursuit of learning, whatever the objective. Identifying herself only as "an aged matron," the author condemned those who labeled a learned woman "masculine." If they meant the woman "was a person of reading and letters, a person of science and information, one who can properly answer a question, without fear and trembling," then any woman (or man) should try to become as "masculine" as possible. But, of course, what they meant was that she was "bold, assuming, haughty, arrogant." Poking fun at those who would include women in this category of the "masculine," the author declared her willingness "that the other sex should share it altogether themselves." Actually, however, "masculine" became a negative not because a learned woman displayed these conventionally male attributes, but because gender relations had reserved for her male counterparts "all science, all public utility, all superiority, all that is intellectually great."[34] Whether saddened or defiant, both Rowson and the *Female Advocate* distinguished themselves from their male counterparts. Sensitive to the gender markings attached to learning, they nevertheless rejected the idea that female learning was deviant. Simultaneously, their responses registered an understanding that women were extremely vulnerable to precisely that equation.

Writing under the pseudonym "Constantia," Judith Sargent

Murray was not as sharply critical as the *Female Advocate*. But she was also more decisive and confident than Rowson. The suggestion that women might be less capable was "in this *enlightened age*, totally *inadmissible*." Instead, as she insisted, women's minds were "*naturally* as susceptible of every improvement, as those of men." [35] Murray's peremptory dismissal and her unequivocal statement that women and men had the same intellectual potential might have led her readers to wonder whether she would insist that their education be the same. But in this regard at least, she followed the same path as male participants in the debate on female intellect. Having made equality the linchpin for her defense of education, Murray employed difference to inscribe that education with purpose. Mothers, she declared, "imprint on the opening mind, characters, ideas, and conclusions, which time, in all its variety of vicissitudes, will never be able to erase." [36]

But if Murray aligned herself with male commentators in stressing the primacy of motherhood, she distinguished her position with the suggestion that female education had a secondary purpose preparing women for "independence." Boldly declaring that "the Sex [women] should be taught to depend on their own efforts, for the procurement of an establishment in life," she identified an education that would serve different ends. If women were provided the tools for economic and social independence, they could look calmly upon the fact that marriage was "no more than a probable contingency." [37] Murray did not choose to follow her reasoning to equally logical *and* decidedly radical conclusions. Women who were educated for independence had more options than marriage. As the famous author of *Little Women* (and *Little Men*), Louisa May Alcott, aptly phrased it, they might decide that "liberty is a better husband." [38] But Murray did glimpse another purpose for a woman's education and enthusiastically defended a woman's potential independence.

It was left to Priscilla Mason, a student not more than sixteen years old, to suggest all that might be entailed in the decision to educate women. The setting was Philadelphia's Young Ladies Academy, the speaker the class salutatorian, and the date 1793. Mason's remarkable address seemed decidedly unremarkable at the outset. Beginning with the formulaic expression of gratitude to teachers and trustees, Mason proceeded with an equally formulaic declaration of self-effacement, if not self-deprecation. She was "female," she was "young," she was "inexperienced," and more—on that day in May 1793 she was "addressing a promiscuous assembly," listeners who were both female and male. What could she do but commence with an apology, as indeed she did before launching into her radical departure from the typical address on female education for any late eighteenth-century American, much less one who was female, young, and inexperienced.

Claiming for herself and all women the exercise of authority in public as well as private—"our right to instruct and persuade"—she insisted that this most basic of human entitlements had been denied them. "Our high and mighty Lords," as Mason described men, had "early seized the sceptre and the sword; with these they gave laws to society; they denied women the advantage of a liberal education; [and] forb[ade] them to exercise their talents on those great occasions, which might serve to improve them." Denunciations of the past were joined with declarations about a more auspicious present. "Happily," she told her listeners, "a more liberal way of thinking begins to prevail. The sources of knowledge are gradually opening to our sex." These altered circumstances had not yet changed the boundaries separating the private and the public, and as Mason said pointedly, "the Church, the Bar, and the Senate are shut up against us." Men were still the obstacle. It was they who "first made us incapable of the duty, and then forbid us the exercise." But if Mason remained pointed in her criticism of men, she believed that their recalcitrance could be overcome by women. Speaking directly to her classmates, she offered them a challenge enveloped with a promise: "Let us by suitable education, qualify ourselves for those high departments—they will open before us." [39]

Susannah Rowson, the pseudonymous *Female Advocate,* Judith Sargent Murray, and Priscilla Mason were all able participants in their society's discourse on female intellect. The degree to which gender shaped their perspective was evident in the references to the toll taken by intellectual deprivation. No less, gender informed the readiness with which they embraced calls for the development of women's intellectual potential. The same can be said for a parallel discourse that emerged simultaneously in a setting that has received less consideration from historians. Private rather than public and located in letters, diaries, and journals, it illustrated the almost startling rapidity with which ideas regarding female education spread through a newly independent America. There was a signal difference between these public and private discourses, however. The latter was the domain of women. Certainly, educated men acknowledged the issue in their letters, diaries, and journals. But women who themselves were literate made it a key subject for consideration.

The significance that women attached to education is perhaps most graphically illustrated by those who registered the deprivation condemned by the *Female Advocate* and by Mason. In introducing herself to her sister-in-law Elizabeth Wainwright, Hepsy Howard of Dorchester, Massachusetts, reluctantly acknowledged that Wainwright should "not expect to find in me the well-informed companion." The problem was Howard's education, which had "consisted more in the ornamental than the useful." Hers was a too typical circumstance, "a too general fault in regard to females." It was also a circumstance that Howard proposed to remedy with a female education exactly like that offered males. Should Wainwright object on the grounds that "women thus educated would not be attentive to their domestic concerns," Howard said she had only to look to herself. Declaring that "you are the person I am speaking of," Howard insisted that female intellect need not detract from female obligation: "With all the advantages you profess [,] I do not understand that you neglect a duty belonging to domestic life."[40]

Despite the fact that she had been much more fortunate than Howard in her education, Mary Howell also considered herself deprived, albeit relative to men. A telling entry in her journal described a conversation between herself and a male friend who had insisted upon "the superior pleasures and advantages enjoyed by his sex." Initially Howell had denied any such pleasures. Yes, she had responded, males could vote and defend their country in armed conflict, neither of which Howell considered particular pleasures. Supposedly, the same could be said for advantages. But, her male friend pressed still further, "don't you wish you was a man?" Here Howell had faltered before the interrogation. "I was almost tempted to deny it, convinced that if I did *not*, he would give me no credit for anything I had just advanced, but *truth* brought forward my answer. I was unwilling to send her back, and replied, 'yes,' but merely from a wish to enjoy the advantages of education."[41] The disparities that Howell hesitated to concede served as the basis for Eliza Southgate's call for increased educational opportunities. Writing to her cousin Moses Porter, this resident of Scarborough, Maine, declared that the cultivation of intellect was "a privilege (or I may say duty) that belonged to the human species, and not man[']s exclusive prerogative."[42]

In claiming for themselves the advantages enjoyed by Howell's friend and Southgate's cousin, women employed the rhetorical and ideological strategies of republican motherhood. Writing to the man she would soon marry, New Englander Elizabeth Palmer Peabody echoed Rowson and Murray. Although she granted that women's role and place were different from those of men, Palmer insisted that "the duties they have to fulfill are not less important." The most important were those performed by the mother, who "ought to be capable, to teach the lisping infant to speak with propriety, and as the tender mind expands to fill it with virtuous principles." These duties made female education key to the survival of the republic. "In this view," she told Nathaniel Peabody, "the fate of our Country, is in some degree dependent, on the education of its females."[43] Eliza Southgate made exactly the same point in her journal. During a visit to Lucy Brown Derby, a mother of several children, the still unmarried Southgate was impressed with the "great necessity that Mothers or all ladies should have cultivated minds, as the first rudiments of education are always received from them, and at that early period of life when the mind is open to every new impression and ready to receive the seeds which must form the future principles of the character."[44]

The tensions and contradictions that had been encoded in the idea of an educated woman persisted well into the nineteenth century. Employing the strategies that had been developed by commentators in the years after the Revolution, later generations continued to situate female equality in the context of female difference. Education continued to be defended in terms of woman's conventional role as wife and mother, not in terms of her right simply as a human being to develop individual potential. But later generations also

7. ⌣

Woman in the form of Liberty gives support to the Bald Eagle,
symbol of the Republic. (Stipple engraving and mezzotint by
Edward Savage, published 11 June 1796, Library of Congress,
LC USZ62-15,369)

went beyond those male commentators who had participated in the earlier debate to insist as Murray had done that women be educated for independence, that they be provided with the means by which to support themselves. It was this demand that highlighted their recognition of what women did hold in common: a shared vulnerability in a structurally inequitable society. Here too certain tensions and contradictions remained, perhaps the most prominent being that education for self-support was defended only for unmarried women.

In juxtaposing equality and difference, these nineteenth-century participants highlighted still another continuity that made all the others possible. They employed these juxtapositions because they were readily available, were just as readily recognizable, and most important, were dominant modes of explanation. Ultimately, however, the framework itself made it difficult if not impossible to reconcile equality with difference. That claims continue to be made on this basis today suggests how deeply these juxtapositions inform our contemporary debates. So long as dualities constitute the basis upon which social and political relations are established, hierarchies based on a presumptive difference between women and men are likely to remain. And a Sally Franklin will have a lesser claim on education than will her male counterparts. But if these juxtapositions can be set aside, perhaps the search for more expansive understandings of equality can be undertaken. And then a Sally Franklin will have the same educational opportunity that Benjamin Franklin provided her brother, William, and her own son, Benjamin Franklin Bache.

6

FRANKLIN, WOMEN, AND
AMERICAN CULTURAL MYTHS
Carla Mulford

Dally not with other folks' women or money.
—Poor Richard, 1757

Perhaps more than any other of the "Founding Fathers," Franklin has been credited quite literally with the "fatherhood" of the nation. Franklin the philanderer—not the scientist, the natural philosopher, the diplomat, but the one whom citizens think they know in his intimate domestic concerns, concerns heterosexual and male dominant—seems to preoccupy the public consciousness and dominate the popular stories of many United States citizens. It is true that some Americans interested in Franklin-related history know that he founded libraries, created various useful scientific devices, and served abroad as a diplomat during the Revolution. But many more people "know" better the man who was fond of women and of whom women were fond. Indeed, there seems to exist in the public consciousness a notion about Franklin that must in some way fulfill Americans' notions of themselves as attractively heterosexual. Stories in circulation are told frequently—by both women and men and with affectionate jocularity and confident pseudoknowledge—that Franklin was a bawdy womanizer. One story, in fact, holds that the one-hundred-dollar bill has Franklin's figure on it because that is the number of illegitimate children he fathered.[1]

These stories about Franklin and women in the public conscious-

ness tell us nothing about Franklin's life, but they suggest some interesting things about American culture. Some of the stories about
Franklin in circulation today have had a remarkable resilience
across time. Franklin's reputation with regard to women has come
down to us late in the twentieth century in somewhat the way it
began, ranging between scandal and sainthood and tending ultimately toward indulgence rather than dismissal of Franklin's heterosexuality. Surely it is worth considering these stories about
Franklin in an effort to get to know ourselves and United States culture a little better.[2]

On 5 June 1776, before Franklin had even arrived in France,
Anne Robert Jacques Turgot, retired finance minister and eminent
economist, had sent to Samuel Pierre du Pont de Nemours the Latin
epigram that is perhaps the most famous line ever written about
Franklin—*Eripuit caelo fulmen, sceptrumque tyrannis*—"He stole lightning from the sky, the scepter from tyrants."[3] This international
praise was given Franklin only twelve years after he had been scur-
rilously attacked during the notorious election of representatives to
the Pennsylvania assembly in 1764. With the Quakers in the assembly, Franklin had been supporting the taxation of proprietary lands.
In the pamphlet war that followed, the beginnings of the public stories about Franklin, stories that in one form or another (as this commentary will show) are still circulating in the general culture,
emerged, took hold of some of the populace, and increased specula-
tion about this already talked-about man.

Franklin was being attacked for political reasons, but aspects of
the onslaught were purely personal. In 1763, the illegitimacy of
William Franklin and wild stories about Franklin's treatment of the
boy's mother must have been circulating in London. On October 9
of that year, George Roberts, son of Franklin's friend Hugh Roberts,
wrote to a London Quaker, Robert Crafton:

> In answer to your hint relative to a Certain Gentleman
> [William Franklin] now acting in a public Station—tis gener-
> ally known here his Birth is illegitimate and his Mother not in
> good Circumstances, but the report of her begging Bread in the
> Streets of this City is without the least Foundation in Truth. I
> understand some small provision is made by him for her, but

her being none of the most agreeable of Women prevents particular Notice being shown, or the Father and Son acknowledging any Connection with her.[4]

It is clear from this letter that even in faraway London, questions about William's legitimacy were tied up in the issue of the governance of the colonies. Closer to home, in Philadelphia, as Philip Gleason has described the situation of 1764, "It was apparently well known before the battles of 1764 that Franklin had an illegitimate son, and after the campaign began no one could have been ignorant of it."[5] The anonymous author of *An Answer to the Plot* (1764)—the plot being to bring the province under the control of the Crown rather than the proprietors—charged that Franklin was a womanizer and troublemaker. Characterized as "a Letcher," "plagu'd with fumbling Age," Franklin was said to be a man who "Needs nothing to excite him, / But is too ready to engage, / When younger Arms envite him."[6]

The accusation of lechery was a rather light one compared with the harsh claims raised against Franklin by Hugh Williamson, a staunch supporter of Presbyterians. Williamson used the vehicle of a mock epitaph of Franklin to explicitly address the fact that Franklin had an illegitimate son. While arguing that Franklin was "aiming to overturn The best of Governments," Williamson described Franklin thus: "studious and artfull, tho' conscious of his Guilt, He struggled hard, but in Vain, To screen his Sins From the Sight of the People." The "Sins" Williamson indicated might have been political ones, but Williamson quickly went on to denounce Franklin for his intrigues with women. Insisting that Franklin had mistreated William's mother, "his Hand Maid Barbara, A most valuable *Slave*, The *Foster-Mother* of his last Offspring, Who did his dirty Work," Williamson said Franklin had allowed her only "The *pitiful* Stipend of *Ten Pounds per Annum*, On which he had cruelly suffered her To Starve." According to Williamson, Franklin buried her in an unmarked grave.[7] The anonymously published broadside *The Counter-Medley*, written by schoolmaster David James Dove quickly picked up and ran a version of Williamson's story about Franklin.[8] Franklin lost the assembly election.

Across the Atlantic and more than a decade later, the story as it

was run in the London *Morning Post, and Daily Advertiser* on 1 June
1779, was more deadly—but then so was Franklin's cause, by then,
against England. In the *Post* it was said that Franklin became father
to William Franklin, his "natural son," "by an oyster wench in
Philadelphia, whom he left to die in the streets of disease and
hunger."[9] Thomas Hutchinson, the appointed royal governor of
Massachusetts, who had gone to London to avoid the wartime conflict and threats to his life, commented in his diary entry for 29 August 1779, that William Temple Franklin was "the natural son of his
[Franklin's] natural son, both by street women."[10] In both of these
instances—the diatribes of the election of 1764 and those that arose
in Revolutionary-era England—there are political reasons for the
circulation of the stories. From the perspective of the proprietors
and then the British Crown and loyalist sympathizers, Franklin was
an obstructionist upstart, a miscreant fully deserving of personal
attacks.

Likewise, political motives probably drove those who wrote diatribes about Franklin shortly after his death. The anonymous writer
of the *Memoirs of the Late Dr. Franklin* (London, 1790) announced,
"In private life this philosopher was not exempted from the little im-
perfections and weaknesses of human nature: irregular in his addresses to the Cyprian goddess, the legal partner of his bed
complained of infidelities. It is well known, he had mistresses plenty;
and there are several living testimonies of his licentious amours." As
proof of this, the purported biographer reported the story related by
"A gentleman of Philadelphia, who was very intimate with him."
According to this story, Franklin was observed overhearing two
working women reported to have been fighting over their places in
Franklin's affections, "one of them . . . the doctor's housekeeper,
and the other a comely washerwoman, who had been also honoured
with his intimate acquaintance. The contest was sharp both in
words and blows; the streets re-echoed with their shrieks, and their
caps flew in pieces; while the Doctor, from a window, beheld the bat-
tle, and laughed most heartily." With a sigh the biographer ironi-
cally apologized that "philosophers have their frailties like other
men."[11] Though it was published in London, this account seems to
have been read in the United States, where growing alarm at the out-
come of the fall of the Bastille began to fuel anti-French sentiment.

Not surprisingly, then, about this time in the United States, sto-ries about Franklin's life came into circulation. The *American Mu-seum* of October 1791 reported a story about the aging Franklin's amiably sly handling of a ticklish situation with a French woman. The writer averred, "Doctor Franklin, being in France previous to the revolution, when the true spirit of gallantry was fashion-able, . . . received frequent attentions from the most celebrated beauties." One such "beauty," "being a favourite, was particularly pleased with the old gentleman's company." When Franklin asked why she never invited him for an overnight stay, she "answered, 'she would be happy to be favoured with his company that very night.'—Fortunately, it was summer time," the article went on, and "the old gentleman, a little embarrassed, not expecting so warm a reply" took out his memoranda book, saying that he would make a note of the invitation and that when the nights were longer he would have the pleasure of waiting upon her.[12]

In this tale, Franklin is sought after but chaste, seeming poten-tially outwitted yet wittily in control all along. This particular story made much of two aspects of Franklin's relations with women—that they were attracted to him and that he, though he found them at-tractive, always behaved courteously and with "virtue." Indeed, in treating Franklin's supposed strategies for avoiding amorous and adulatory women, this story marks the beginning of the repeated and favorable representations of Franklin then entering into circu-lation. The stories that follow this line are less trenchant, more "worldly-wise," and revealing of the culture's penchant to see Franklin as a sought-after, heterosexualized, *manly* gentleman. In fact, this story was widely reprinted, for example, in *Beers' Almanac* (Hartford, Connecticut, 1799), and it was reflected even as late as in the writings of Bernard Faÿ.[13]

Meanwhile, even as stories like this entered public consciousness in the late eighteenth century and the turn into the nineteenth cen-tury, William Cobbett (in an attack on Joseph Priestley) found a way to vent his spleen against Benjamin Franklin Bache, whom he called "the son of one of Dr. Franklin's bastards, . . . an avowed atheist."[14] In Cobbett's *The Life and Adventures of Peter Porcupine* (Philadelphia, 1796), Franklin was derisively figured (in the shadow of Peter Por-cupine's affectionately drawn grandfather) as "an almanack-maker, . . . quack, . . . chimney-doctor, . . . soap-boiler, . . . printer's devil, . . . a deist." Unlike the stories that might be repeated about Franklin's children, Cobbett reported of Porcupine's children, "all his children were born in wedlock," thus insinuating that Franklin's were not. The mockery concluded with the implication that Franklin's children deserved to see him "accused of having been a fornicator, a hypocrite, and an infidel."[15]

Following a line of argument similar to Cobbett's, Joseph Dennie hoped to win a highbrow audience for his new journal, the *Port Folio*, and he likewise fumed that Franklin was immoral.[16] Using the clear slur that a first-name-only reference at that time could create,[17] Dennie pronounced that " 'our Benjamin' was no more distinguished for the *originality* of his conceptions, than for the purity of his life, or the soundness of his religious doctrine." Dennie promised "to devote some future speculations to the subject of Dr. Franklin," but in the succeeding months he published only occasionally on Franklin, some scathing remarks here and a brief letter there. Even among Philadelphia's upper crust, it would seem, attacks against Franklin would not sell newspapers.[18]

Indeed, the most serious and scurrilous calumny was reserved for private audiences, in diaries—such as that, for instance, in the 1801 diary of Sylvester Douglas, Lord Glenbervie. Glenbervie wrote down information reported to him at a dinner, on 17 November 1801, by George Hammond, "who was several years our Minister in America" and who "had been secretary with David Hartley when he went to Paris to settle the Commercial Treaty in 1783." Hammond had "thought to obtain favour on his arrival in America [in 1791]," Glenbervie wrote, "by mentioning that circumstance [that he had formerly known Franklin in 1783]." "But," Glenbervie continued, "he found that it was far from a popular topic. Franklin had died two or three years before, and his memory was universally detested. Adams, Jay, King, etc., hated him." According to Glenbervie, Franklin "died very rich," leaving a large inheritance to daughter Sally Franklin Bache, with whom Franklin "was said to have [had] an incestuous intercourse."[19] We can only now wonder what other scurrilous things this son-in-law of Lord North had to say about Franklin.[20]

Generally speaking, the commentary in the United States was less venomous. The talked-about "facts" of the life were beginning to blur into popular, somewhat embellished memory about it. The Revolutionary generation was passing. Interestingly, clear signs of Franklin's growing, masculinized, and heterosexual folk-hero status emerged at the same time when scholars and others—some of them descendants of the Revolutionary generation—began publishing bits and pieces of the Frankliniana surfacing from private hands. While these somewhat partisan writers were beginning to publish interesting relevant materials, the more general populace was treated to a Franklin who personified the virtues of industry, frugality, and civic responsibility. Especially in the Midwest, where oral history might have traveled faster than printed media, Franklin began to be considered, according to Richard C. Wade, the "perfect civic leader."[21] The cult of Franklin as a national hero was beginning to take hold.

Most curiously, Franklin was made a devout Christian, beginning with Mason Locke Weems's fanciful rendering of Franklin-as-Christian in the 1818 version of Franklin's life, called *Life of Benjamin Franklin. With Many Choice Anecdotes and Admirable Sayings of This Great Man, Never Before Published by Any of His Biographers.*[22] By 1836 these Christianized versions of Franklin had taken such hold that Franklin, for Robert Lincoln, became "in his maturer years a believer in divine revelation."[23] It seems that Franklin's deistic writings were almost entirely forgotten. In 1848, Orville L. Holley attributed Franklin's success to "the direct and visible effect of those causes, chiefly of a moral kind, which, for the encouragement of honest effort and virtuous enterprise, a wise Providence has established as the most worthy and legitimate means of attaining success in this life."[24] The generalized language of morality, including references to honesty, virtue, and "wise Providence," mystified the man Benjamin Franklin and created an imitable ideal man in place of the man who had professed deism and an attraction to women, among other things.

In Holley's account, the situation with Mrs. T., James Ralph's woman friend to whom Franklin made advances in Ralph's absence, is explained away as an *attraction* that a benevolent Franklin felt for her virtue. The way in which Holley manipulated Franklin's own story is well worth noting for the extent to which it suggested, first, that Franklin was virtuous and kindly, while second, the actual practice of virtue was the woman's function, not the man's. Pointing out that Mrs. T. had already "forfeited the favor of her friends and lost her business, by means of her connection with Ralph," Holley, undaunted by what Franklin had himself reported in his memoirs, continued that Mrs. T.

> often, in her distress, sent for Benjamin, who generously supplied what money he could spare, for her relief. This was a dangerous intercourse for the young man. His account of it clearly shows that her applications for assistance, proceeded from actual and extreme penury on her part, and honorably acquits her of any artful design of entrapping him. But this freedom from all craft and subtlety toward him, only increased his danger; and in his sympathy for a person of her attractive qualities and infirm virtue, it was but too natural that he should soon feel other and less pure impulses mingling with his benevolence.[25]

Holley's writing of the story suggests that Mrs. T., already having displayed nonvirtuous conduct, brought Franklin into a "dangerous intercourse." The words encode a rigid double standard with regard to male-female relations even as they slip into praise for the seemingly innocent Franklin's benevolence.

Remarkably, Holley found that Mrs. T. had an "infirm virtue" though he "honorably acquit[ted] her of any artful design." This woman drew out Franklin's "sympathy," and thus she received his unsought addresses, according to Holley. Holley concluded that Franklin in this situation was imitable rather than blameworthy in his behavior: "Though his conduct, in one particular, was culpable, yet his ingenious confession of his fault, his honest self-condemnation, and his just reference to fixed religious principle, as the truest and surest restraint upon the passions, make some amend for his transgression; while his generous readiness to relieve distress, is worthy of imitation, as well as praise."[26] In biographies such as this, written during the middle part of the nineteenth century, Franklin's peccadillos more frequently than not were glossed over as insignificant, or else they were not mentioned at all.

Franklin's sexual attractions became the stuff of an affectionate and masculinized sense of national identity. Thus, for instance, in 1836, the same year during which Robert Lincoln announced that Franklin became a believer in divine revelation before he died, the *Southern Literary Messenger* ran a poem, "From the MSS. of Franklin," that made an emblem of a virtuous Franklin. Somewhat like Holley's later Franklin, this one became virtuous *because* he admired women; this one was not a sober pontificator of Poor Richard-like moral maxims. The brief poem did indeed appear in Franklin's Commonplace Book of the early 1730s.[27] As it was printed in the *Southern Literary Messenger* in 1836, the poem read:

> *In vain are musty morals taught in schools,*
> *By rigid teachers and as rigid rules,*
> *Where virtue with a frowning aspect stands,*
> *And frights the pupil with her rough commands.*
> *—But Woman—*
> *Charming Woman, can true converts make—*
> *We love the precepts for the teacher's sake:*
> *Virtue in them appears so bright and gay,*
> *We hear with transport, and with pride obey.*[28]

Here Franklin's little wisdoms from the *Autobiography*, which were then being converted by moralizing teachers and parents to authoritarian and paternalistic lessons, were transformed into the more affectionate and popularized image of a Franklin who was no longer a womanizer but a devotee of those women who are paragons of virtue. The onus for "virtuousness" of course resided in women according to this system, thus suggesting that if men erred, the fault would lie in women's inexact virtue. That such little writings by Franklin were reaching the popular press suggests both the popularity of stories about Franklin for a growing reading audience and the ideological uses to which images of Franklin as ideal man were being put. To the popular imagination, Franklin, male-dominant heterosexuality, and virtue would be registered and linked in a way that has come down to us even in today's culture.

By the middle of the nineteenth century, Franklin's excruciating diplomatic years in France were largely ignored in favor of charming

8. ⌒

Sketch of Franklin and a female friend as observed by Charles Willson Peale at 36 Craven Street in 1767. (Pencil sketch by Charles Willson Peale, 1767, American Philosophical Society)

stories (along the lines of the *American Museum* story of 1791) of chaste love relationships or playfully snatched kisses. An example of this sort of fare appeared in a broadside poem written and circulated by Benjamin Penhallow Shillaber, a very popular journalist, humorist, lecturer, and editor. Shillaber's broadside poem, *A Very Brief and Very Comprehensive Life of Benjamin Franklin, Printer, Done into Quaint Verse, by One of the Types—September 17, 1856*, told of Franklin's supposed reception by the French court. As Shillaber described it, Louis XVI stepped off the throne to meet Franklin,

And the queen frowned not in check,
When this plain republican Mister
Threw his arms about her neck
And very gallantly kissed her![29]

In other words, according to Shillaber's story line, as soon as Franklin appeared on the scene, the typical courtly gestures were overlooked. Here, it is Franklin kissing rather than being kissed, to be sure, but he acted "gallantly," and the queen was not in the least likely to have frowned. Ten years later, reports such as one in the *Once-a-Week* for 16 June 1866 took a more personal tack by treating Franklin's known relations with the Passy circle.[30] The *Once-a-Week* fictionalized Franklin's relations with Mme Helvetius, providing ideal and sentimentalized reasons for their necessary separation and Franklin's return to the United States.

This is not to suggest that during the nineteenth century there remained no curiosity about Franklin's progeny. A little note by one E.L.S. in a December 1869 issue of *Notes and Queries* confused William Temple Franklin and William Franklin, calling Temple "a (natural, as I understood) son of the renowned philosopher, and governor of some place."[31] This note produced a wonderful flurry of activity, with articles in response commenting on the status of the legitimacy or illegitimacy of the Franklin progeny. Five little notes appeared in *Notes and Queries* by way of response. In January 1870, Jno. Kaye Barnes clarified the difference between William the father and William Temple the son.[32] In the same issue, P.A.L. insisted, "There is no question as to the legitimacy of both son and grandson," quoting letters between Franklin and William Franklin.[33] In May, one L.T.A. pronounced William to have been illegitimate, calling him "natural," but William Temple legitimate, calling him "lawful."[34] In October, H.P.B. supported the legitimacy of both offspring and deflected attention instead to William Franklin's disloyalty to his father and country. Referring to the Jared Sparks 1836–42 edition of Franklin's *Works*, H.P.B. asserted that "Dr. Franklin was not the father of any illegitimate son (if by *natural* illegitimate is meant), nor was William Temple Franklin the illegitimate son of any father. But the doctor always felt that William was an *unnatural* son for opposing his father, and espousing the cause of the king during the American revolution."[35] The issue of American patriotism was here clearly tied to the legitimacy of William Franklin in interesting ways, displacing any potential slur upon Franklin by disposing of the son as unpatriotic. The linking of national virtue with Franklin's name was occurring in the late nineteenth century with ever greater frequency.

Then, too, perhaps the efforts of those who insisted upon the legitimacy of both William and William Temple Franklin were fueled by the seeming ill will of Peter Hutchinson, who wrote for the January 1870 issue of *Notes and Queries.* Hutchinson argued that both William and William Temple were illegitimate offspring. Remarking that "Some great men, by the way, are better not looked at too close," Hutchinson recounted a tale told in "the diary in MS. of my great-grandfather T[homas] H[utchinson], governor of the then province of Massachusetts Bay." Reporting a Thomas Hutchinson diary entry for the date 29 August 1779, Peter Hutchinson retold the story, frequently mentioned in nineteenth-century writings, of Franklin's having taken William Temple Franklin to meet the dying Voltaire. Thomas Hutchinson had called the young man Franklin's "grandson (which, by the way, is the natural son of his natural son, both by street women)."[36] This slur would have surprised no one at the time, for Peter Orlando Hutchinson was a direct descendant of Thomas Hutchinson, the last royal governor of Massachusetts. More interesting is that Hutchinson omitted this detail, which he was quick to offer in 1870, from his 1883 and 1886 editions of *The Diary and Letters of Thomas Hutchinson.* In the later publication, editor Peter Hutchinson removed the parenthetical insertion and supplied a footnote that read, simply, "The Editor has here omitted a few words in a parenthesis. They concern genealogy rather than history."[37] Perhaps like Dennie before him, Hutchinson had been chided for emphasizing the negative details of so great a man as Franklin was in the process of becoming in the cultural imagination of the United States.

The specifics of the case aside, it is worth noting that intense interest in Franklin's progeny—whether that interest confirmed the illegitimate picture or the legitimate one—suggests a cultural preoccupation with Franklin's sexuality. That is, even negative stories deriding children out of wedlock indicate that the culture was concerned with (male) virility and with women's virtuousness, if virtuousness is considered a function of female chastity and domesticity. Many social historians have characterized the nineteenth century as ridden with anxieties about femininity, masculinity, and gender roles generally. These commentaries about Franklin's progeny and his reputed promiscuousness provide yet another index to the troubled relations between the sexes. If Franklin's name was being tied up with national identity and national virtue, those qualities were equally a part of the male-female debates centrally at issue during the middle of the century.

Even as they shed additional light on the gendered double standard, some of the specifics of the stories about Franklin's progeny are interesting, too. Franklin, like Thomas Hutchinson, had relations who defended him. William Duane[38] vociferously attacked Elizabeth Cady Stanton for having inaccurately besmirched Franklin's name in a speech she was giving on her lecture tours from 1869 through the 1870s. The virulence of Cady Stanton's attack on Franklin deserves notice here: her comments illustrate *in the very harshness of their negativity* the extent to which Franklin had, by 1870, entered the popular imagination as a national hero—and to Cady Stanton's chagrin, at the expense of women's marital freedoms. The following is from a section of her speech called "Home Life," as that speech is available in Cady Stanton's papers:

> What a record of heartlessness and indifference some of our greatest men have left of their domestic life. Dr. Franklin, that old utilitarian kite-flyer, went to Europe leaving his wife behind him and never saw her face for eleven years. She had shared his poverty, practiced his poor Richard maxims. . . , bred children and nursed them . . . while Benjamin enjoyed the splendors of a court, velvet coaches, good dinners and choice society. Of course, when he came back the poor drudge was no match for the philosopher. . . . That her heart rebelled in her solitude and neglect is manifest in the headstrong acts of her children. He quarreled with his sons and disinherited one of them: thus were the mother's wrongs revenged. . . . The less said of Franklin's private character the better. William Franklin, Governor of New Jersey, was his natural son and how many more of the same sort he had probably Franklin himself never knew. . . . Undazzled by the glories of Franklin stoves and lightning rods, one sees much to disapprove in the life of the great philosopher!![39]

Cady Stanton negatively imaged several of the achievements for which Franklin was then being praised: the kite-flying experiment to identify the nature of lightning; the "rise" from rags to riches (Deborah Franklin was with him when he was poor but not when Franklin "enjoyed the splendors of the court"); his life among the virtuosi of Europe; and the utilitarian inventions such as the development of Franklin stoves and lightning rods. The focus upon Franklin's scientific discoveries, his benevolent utilitarianism, and the wealth and splendor in which he was, late in life, surrounded all provide an index to the ways in which his life was being represented to the general audience. Franklin's scientific contributions, which were assisting domestic comforts and safety, were in effect counterbalancing any negatively moralistic codes that would call into question his relations with women.

Yet Cady Stanton's scathing commentary featured what she configured as a broken family and Franklin's sexual promiscuity. If hers had then been the standard Franklin tale, Cady Stanton's strong tocsin would not have been necessary. That she did center her particular comments on Franklin's sexual proclivities and his progeny suggests the extent to which the illegitimacy of William Franklin and the reports of Franklin's philandering were being overlooked, for the most part, by many of Cady Stanton's contemporaries. It suggests, too, the extent to which the ideology of a national fabric, the popular conception of a national destiny, might have depended upon such neglect of personal circumstances.

But time had changed Franklin's image, as revealed in the vociferous reaction of William Duane, a great-grandson to Franklin. Duane was furious with Cady Stanton for such comments about Franklin, and his ire showed in his anonymously published pamphlet *Remarks upon a Speech Delivered by Mrs. E. Cady Stanton! During the Summer of 1870* (1870).[40] Duane wrote that Franklin did not anticipate being absent so long when he first left for England, that his children were adults when he left, and that Franklin was a good father. Duane vituperated: "Where can we find so great an amount of ignorance crowded into the same space as is exhibited in this portion of Mrs. Stanton's harangue? The display of such ignorance may confirm some persons in their opposition to female politicians. If Mrs. Stanton, who is a bright and shining light (not to say a torch) among these female agitators, knows so little, what must be expected from the rank and file of her followers?" And he rebuked what he called "mannish women [who] mistake a strong will for a strong under-standing." Mocking Cady Stanton and her followers, he said that they were relinquishing their "proper duties" because they wanted to see their names in newspapers. He followed this article with a briefer one, also anonymously published, in 1871. In this brief arti-cle, Duane argued that when Franklin left for England the second time, William Franklin had been married for two years, Francis Franklin had been dead for two years, and Sally Franklin was seven-teen years old. He concluded, "If some women would devote some of the time which they waste upon politics and other subjects outside of their 'sphere,' to the study of history and biography, they would not make so ridiculous a figure when they mount the platform."[41]

Cady Stanton's attack *against* Franklin had revealed the extent to which the ideology of the nuclear family had become crucial to the identity and development of the middle class. Likewise, the viru-lence of Duane's attack signaled middle-class notions of gendered identity. The male-dominant assumptions underlying Duane's de-fenses of Franklin illustrate the pervasiveness of Victorian attitudes about gendered social roles. They imply, as well, that among hetero-sexual men there was a strong cult of masculinity associated with Franklin and those who supported him. Women might have been in-scribed by a cult of domesticity to which Duane evidently adhered, but men were inscribed by the representative opposite of such a cult, one that found the locus for men's actions in politics and public is-sues, in affairs of state that, once enacted, created and enforced a cult of masculinity and its association with nationhood. In a world in which masculine identity was destabilized by men's isolation and alienation and was enforced along ethnic and class and race lines, stories such as those of Franklin's life were needed by white (espe-cially Anglo-American) men—just as stories such as those about Ho-ratio Alger were needed—to identify avenues of possibility for a stable approach both to manhood and nationhood.[42]

At the turn of the twentieth century, Franklin's genius, his print-ing trade, his scientific experiments and their outcomes in practical uses, and his philanthropy were widely celebrated. The unveiling of Franklin statues became common in the nation's cities. Franklin was used as an icon of American achievement. J. J. Flynn's ode, spoken as part of a celebration of an unveiling of a Franklin statue in Lincoln Park, Chicago, 6 June 1896, is fairly representative of the kinds of generalized praise Franklin received:

Wherever truth prevails, throughout the earth,
Wherever reason reigns and minds are free,
Wherever toil commands a cheerful hearth,
Wherever plenty smiles on industry,
Wherever honor's paid to honest worth,
And manhood's robed in manhood's dignity,
Wherever Franklin's words and deeds are known,
The millions claim and love him as their own.[43]

In the generalized praise, the lofty language, the facts of the life are apotheosized into an American nationalist fantasy, one that links "truth," "reason," "toil," and "honor," with "manhood robed in manhood's dignity." The terms are noteworthy not only for the work ethic they both employ and promote but for the higher ideals, such as "truth" and "reason," representatively engaged and valued as transcendently available for enlightened Americans. For the general populace, in the public sphere, Franklin's peccadillos were transformed into favorable signs of his manhood or else happily ignored entirely, largely for the good of the state, it seems, at least at the unveiling of statues.

To be sure, criticisms of Franklin survived, as one speaker noted at a similar unveiling in Philadelphia in 1899. The Honorable James M. Beck, then U.S. Attorney for the Eastern District of Pennsylvania, remarked upon "certain hereditary prejudices, which should have died more than a century ago" but which "continue, by a mysterious kind of atavism to affect our [Philadelphia] people."[44] Such commentary was particularly suitable to the Philadelphia area, where descendants of Franklin's old enemies still remained. Beck pointed out that in Franklin's own day,

there were Philadelphians . . . who disliked him, partly because he was a *novus homo*, or self-made man, partly because of his religious convictions which were heterodox, partly because of the envy which success always inspires, but chiefly because in his long assault on the selfish privileges of the Penns and his constant assertion of democratic principles, he had incurred the dislike and opposition of the select few, who formed what was then called society. Time was when in Philadelphia it was not "fashionable" to visit Franklin. Time *is* when in a small and ever decreasing circle it *is* not fashionable to praise him.[45]

Beck thus retraced the issues that had made Franklin unpopular even as he incited those who might have remained dubious about honoring Franklin to honor him nonetheless because it was the "right" thing to do. What audience member listening to this address would want to be linked with those of the "small and ever decreasing circle" who were not "fashionable"?

At the turn of the twentieth century and during its first few decades, Franklin was praised for his scientific genius, his philosophy, and his rags-to-riches industry. This is not to say that Franklin's relations with women went unnoticed. Indeed, these remained topics of conversation among those who, knowing a few details of the life, praised him—and those who blamed him, too. Among those who held Franklin culpable were Charles W. Eliot and Ellis P. Oberholtzer, who condemned Franklin in a dignified manner but never forgot his tradesman beginnings. At the two-hundredth-anniversary celebration of Franklin's birth, Eliot praised Franklin's trade work as "author, editor, and publisher," but he found fault with Franklin for his treatment of women. To Eliot, Franklin "never seems to have perceived that the supreme tests of civilization are the tender and honorable treatment of women as equals, and the sanctity of home life. There was one primary virtue on his list which he did not always practice. His failure in this respect diminished his influence for good among his contemporaries, and must always qualify the admiration with which mankind will regard him as a moral philosopher and an exhorter to a good life."[46] This critique of Franklin's moral attitudes toward women shows the extent to which Franklin was already apotheosized into an American "Great Man," despite his own admitted "errata." It also reflects the social disdain felt by those who considered themselves Franklin's betters, simply by virtue of their birth into well-known families (this one New England), despite Franklin's international reputation. Indeed, Eliot's haughty critique reveals his own inherited but inflated sense of self-worth.

Ellis Paxson Oberholtzer's comments about Franklin in *The Literary History of Philadelphia* (1906), published in the same year as Eliot's, revealed similar attitudes. Oberholtzer deprecated Franklin, as if wondering aloud how Franklin could have been considered an important writer in his own day. "If we are asked exactly to state what Franklin did to lead David Hume to declare him the first writer in America to gain an international reputation and to be honored in France beyond Voltaire, Rousseau, and Turgot," Oberholtzer wrote, "the task is not an easy one. We are referred to the incomplete autobiography which has been printed in so many languages. . . . We are also urged to consider the wise saws of Poor Richard."[47] Such pretense to puzzlement about Franklin's high reputation as a writer proved to be mere window dressing to a further negative comment about Franklin, this time about his morality:

> We read his bland account of the "errata" of his life in his "Autobiography," his half-proud allusions to his love intrigues that attest to the immorality of his youth, and his foolish fondness for adulation in his old age, not without blushes for the honor of our eighteenth century civilization, if he be set up as the highest type. We know of his duplicity in his business and political relations and couple his name with that of some of the vulgar masters of party management in modern America. To this day there are probably Philadelphians who would disown Franklin and let him revert to the New England from which he came.[48]

Whereas James Beck had wondered about "hereditary prejudices" that caused dislike for Franklin to survive by a "mysterious kind of atavism," Ellis Oberholtzer fanned the flames of moral opprobrium by highlighting Franklin's supposed sexual transgressions. Eliot's and Oberholtzer's deprecations gave witness to a highbrow culture that also, from Franklin's day to their own, enabled the disparagement of trade labor and writing for working people. For both of these men, Franklin's failings might have had less to do with his sexual proclivity than with his pedigree. And like the speech of Cady Stanton, these negative representations of Franklin contrast with the popular positive image of Franklin's rise-to-riches fame, a rise that most United States citizens imaginatively (if not actually) realized for themselves when they retold stories about Franklin's rise from obscurity to fame by virtue of his own industry and frugality.

Class-driven attitudes and concerns about Franklin's intimate domestic relations were explicitly linked in Sidney George Fisher's account of Franklin's illegitimate and legitimate children.[49] Like a few biographers of his generation, Fisher read quite literally the familiar addresses by Franklin—as when he affectionately called younger women "my daughter" in correspondence and in company—as indicative of his paternity. Thus Fisher promulgated the notion that Judith Osgood Foxcroft was actually Franklin's daughter. He also repeated some of the gossip about William's mother, evidently still current during his day, including the Hugh Williamson attack, the one by Reverend Bennett Allen in the London *Morning-Post*, and the defense by Paul Leicester Ford of Deborah Franklin as William's true mother.[50]

Fisher's comments on the relations between the legitimate and illegitimate children placed a special emphasis on class matters. Fisher strongly promoted his belief that Franklin fathered Judith Osgood Foxcroft, then talked of Franklin's daughter Sally's good relations with the illegitimate William Franklin, and then came up with a most surprising conclusion: "This extraordinarily mixed family of legitimates and illegitimates seems to have maintained a certain kind of harmony. The son William, the governor, continued the line through an illegitimate son, William Temple Franklin, usually known as Temple Franklin. This condition of affairs enables us to understand the odium in which Franklin was held by many of the upper classes of Philadelphia, even when he was well received by the best people in England and France."[51] Fisher's comments elucidate turn-of-the-century assumptions fostered by elite groups about class and sexual activity: members of the upper classes (so they said) would not participate in sexual relations outside marriage, and they would not happily receive in their homes men whose "virtues" in this regard were questionable. The clear demarcations about class and nation—that upper-class people in the United States were in some mystical way more "proper" than their European counterparts—did not seem ultimately to have been shared by a majority of Fisher's generation. Indeed, most seem to have found Franklin admirable, despite—and some might even suggest because of—his interpersonal relations with women.

Articles on Franklin's supposed progeny continued, but less steadily, in the twentieth century. Other writers speculated about Franklin's children. Among those considered to be Franklin's illegitimate daughters, in addition to Judith Osgood Foxcroft, were Marianne and Cecilia Davies. Albert Henry Smyth remarked upon the attribution to Franklin of Judith Osgood Foxcroft in the 1906 edition of *The Writings of Benjamin Franklin* by saying: "If all the young women whom Franklin called 'daughter' and who called him 'father' were actually of his flesh and blood, he would have been attended by the largest family that ever dwelt under one roof-tree."[52] Attributions supporting various Franklin fatherings continued, however, and in 1928 Albert Matthews found himself quoting Smyth's humorous 1906 assertion, while refuting Franklin's paternity of the Davies sisters.[53]

More often than not, especially for general audiences of the twentieth century, Franklin's sexual activity has been favorably explained or else denied altogether. In a little pamphlet purchased by the Lawrence Savings and Trust Company of Newcastle, Pennsylvania, as a gift book for distribution in 1910, Wayne Whipple wrote that Franklin's kite experiment might have used a key but that "Franklin's true key was a common-sense view of practical, everyday life." Whipple avoided the detail of Franklin's own *Autobiography*, where Franklin admitted having attempted to take advantage of James Ralph's friend Mrs. T., and says instead that "Ralph took offense at some fancied injury" he supposed Franklin had done him.[54] This shifting of the ground, the substitution of one "truth" for another, signaled common public attitudes about Franklin as they were emerging during the twentieth century. Whipple sought to emphasize how Franklin took every opportunity to find useful employ in the world and to show how thrift toward dollars would make them accumulate. Yet Whipple elided the situation in which Franklin clearly admitted having been an opportunist with his friend and with Mrs. T. Other biographers offered other sorts of "facts" in an effort to clear Franklin's name of supposed moral wrongdoing associated with sexual promiscuity. Thus, for instance, Charles Henry Hart argued in an article in the *Pennsylvania Magazine of History and Biography* that Deborah Franklin was William Franklin's mother.[55]

Still other biographers took different approaches altogether. Paul Leicester Ford, for instance, promoted the notion that mores in the eighteenth century were different from those in this century. The essays that form Ford's *Many-Sided Franklin* were first serialized in the *Century Magazine* in 1898–99,[56] and they first appeared in book form in 1899. The book was reprinted many times during the initial three decades of the twentieth century. The phrasing Ford used is valuable in light of our consideration of the popularization of Franklin as the masculine man: "As he grew in years and wisdom," Ford wrote, "Franklin set himself to conquer his own nature in this failing" (i.e., his passion), "but struggle as he would, his physique was stronger than his will: through all his life he never succeeded in bringing himself to his own standard. . . . Yet, though this incontinence was a matter of common knowledge, and was recurrently used as a subject of attack in political campaigns, his own generation, both men and women, deemed him a moral man."[57] For Ford, the facts surrounding Franklin's supposed promiscuity were not important. What mattered was a recognition, nostalgic in orientation, that times had changed and that what might have been considered immoral behavior at the turn of the twentieth century was not immoral when Franklin lived. In Ford's view, it would seem, Franklin's ungovernable desire was excuse enough for Franklin's promiscuity: Americans could excuse a man who was acting so as to fulfill his "masculine" tendencies.

The ways in which Ford's comments were phrased (and the tremendous popularity of the biography) provide a useful index to turn-of-the-century (white) Americans' cultural attitudes about "virtue," national identity, and masculinity. Ford had said of Franklin that "the career of Franklin teaches very strongly that general ability, rather than special aptitude, is the quality most potent in winning success";[58] that "Franklin was too inherently the statesman not to look further than the mere union of the American colonies";[59] and that "it has been said of Franklin . . . that he must be considered the one true diplomat America has ever produced; and when his services, and the circumstances under which they were rendered, are weighed, the statement seems justifiable."[60] Ford's praise of Franklin bespoke a nationalist impulse of the era. In the configuration Ford upheld, nationalism and Franklin's ungovernable male sexual appetite were inevitably linked in an uncritical way. Such a linking of nationalism with masculinity has survived into the late twentieth century.

The view of Franklin as a masculine man who was as attracted to women as they were to him was promoted also by Franklin's foremost biographer of this century, Carl Van Doren. Van Doren's biography, first published in 1938, has undoubtedly influenced academic opinions about Franklin and women.[61] Its continued use reveals much about the continuing masculinist tendencies of the twentieth century. Speaking of Franklin's later years at Passy, Van Doren commented, "If in France there were new women whom Franklin loved and who loved him, he lost none of his old [women] friends," pointing out that Franklin "kept up an intermittent correspondence with Catherine Greene" and wrote as well to Georgiana Shipley and Polly Hewson. Van Doren expounded upon Franklin and women in terms marked with a masculinist tendencies: "The long life of all of his affectionate friendships helps to define them. Without the brevity of ordinary lust, or the perseverance of obsession, they had a general warmth which, while no doubt sexual in origin, made them strong, tender, imaginative, and humorous beyond the reach of mere desire, with its hard, impersonal appetite. . . . Statesman and scientist, profoundly masculine, he took women into account as well as any other force of nature."[62] Van Doren here made an interesting distinction between affection, imagination, tenderness, and humor, on the one side, and what he called "ordinary lust," obsession, hardness, and "impersonal appetite," on the other. The differentiation distinguished his biographic attitude from that of Franklin's other editors and biographers, especially those such as Jared Sparks, Albert Henry Smyth, and Sidney George Fisher, who sought to clear up the mysteries of Franklin's paternities. It also differed with the biographical essays of Ford, which tended to speak in masculinist terms while placing Franklin in a distinct historical moment when sexual mores differed. Van Doren's Franklin was a Franklin presumably for all time, not a womanizer but one who treated women under the Newtonian assumption that equal opposites attract.

Less serious biographies of the twentieth century have perpetuated the popular notions of Franklin's masculinity that still survive. Take, for instance, the poem on Franklin in *A Book of Americans* (1933) by Rosemary and Stephen Vincent Benét. The Benéts playfully discussed Franklin's attraction to women and his attractiveness to them:

Ben Franklin was the sort of man that people like to see,
For he was very clever but as human as could be.
He had an eye for pretty girls, a palate for good wine,
And all the court of France were glad to ask him in to dine.[63]

The nostalgically affectionate terms rendering Franklin "clever" but "human" reflected a social attitude of forgiveness—indeed, encouragement—of men who find women attractive. A man's having "an eye for pretty girls," in the popular imagination, was not to be disdained (as it had been by the likes of Charles Eliot and Ellis Oberholtzer). Rather it was to be celebrated almost as a mark of American distinction. After all, "all the court of France were glad" to show Franklin their hospitality.

In a more pronounced way, the wonderfully slangy *Odeography of Benjamin Franklin*, written and printed by Earl Emmons in 1929, constructed a Franklin whose lineaments were similar to those described by the Benéts. Beginning with the attestation that "Ben was quite a lusty lad,"[64] Emmons told the story of the *Autobiography* and some aspects of the later years in jaunty verse that celebrated Franklin for all of his endeavors, not the least of which was his way with women. For instance, in treating the problems Franklin faced in London when he found out that Governor Keith had been insincere in his promise of assistance, Emmons wrote:

"Ah well, the plans of mice and men
Gang aft kerflop," reflected Ben,
"This Keith palooka seems to be a kidder,"
And, musing thus, he went and got
Himself a job with Printer Watt,
And likewise got in trouble with a widder.

In fact, most everywhere he went
He showed the same prolific bent
For crashing into amatory muddles,
And though distressed at doing wrong,
His sorrow never lasted long,
And then he'd pull some more erotic huddles.[65]

Some lines late in the poem illustrate quite clearly what Americans have been doing all along with Franklin's reputation for relations with women. Like many other writers who praised Franklin, Emmons worked with a comparison between Franklin and Washington. But Emmons gave the comparison a twist:

> He toured the land and sailed the seas
> And won collegiate degrees
> In numbers that are staggering to reckon;
> He travelled Holland, Belgium, France,
> In all of which he found romance
> And never passed a chance to do some neckin'.

> And on his travels here and there
> He left an incidental heir,
> Or such has always been his reputation;
> Yet History, capricious dame,
> Has given Washington the name
> Of Father of this great and virile nation.[66]

In the eyes of writers such as Emmons who found in Franklin's life and actions admirable qualities worth emulating,[67] the situation of Franklin's intrigues with women was something *also* to be celebrated, not denigrated.[68] Interestingly, those who have accepted without question Franklin's diplomatic skills, his scientific findings, and his nationalist prejudices also seem to have been those who have excused—and often celebrated—Franklin's attractions to women.

In the decades after World War II, as the monumental project of the publication of *The Papers of Benjamin Franklin* was being conceived and then got under way, serious study of Franklin became more specialized, more academic, and less directly accessible to the general reader. Franklin in all of his complexities becomes more and more available to general readers and to scholars with the publication of each new volume of the eminent *Papers* project. Yet the actual details of his life seem to disappear further and further from public consciousness. In the context of popular culture, if we remember that Franklin used bifocals, it might be because, as the *Saturday*

Evening Post reported in 1975, Franklin made bifocals so he could better examine the women seated beside him while still watching those across the room.[69] Academic historians and serious history buffs well know that 1975 also marked the year that Claude-Anne Lopez and Eugenia W. Herbert published their searching biography of Franklin, *The Private Franklin: The Man and His Family*.[70] But the readers of the *Saturday Evening Post* article were a different audience from the one Lopez and Herbert received for their unusual and penetrating investigation into Franklin's domestic circumstances.

Despite the accessibility of an immense amount of detail about Franklin's life and personal relations, general readers today are more likely to know the usual portrait limned about Franklin and women—that he was attracted to them and had many extramarital relations—rather than the one that scholars have come to know of a Franklin well liked by women but probably fairly loyal to his wife, Deborah Franklin. This might have as much to do with a nationalist tendency to equate masculine heterosexualized activity with admirable virility and state power as it is with an interest in knowing the "facts" about Benjamin Franklin. Mystery readers might also these days take delight in Franklin stories that reproduce the notion that Franklin had many illegitimate children, only some of whom are known.

This was the line taken, for instance, in Robert Lee Hall's *Benjamin Franklin and a Case of Christmas Murder* (1990),[71] where, in addition to being given the role of detective, Franklin was given one Nicholas Handy as an illegitimate son. As told in Handy's words, "This fact [Franklin's paternity of Handy] remained a secret between us (he wishing not to discomfit his faithful wife, Deborah, who remained patiently with their daughter in Philadelphia, nor William, who studied at the Inner Temple), I felt no shame in my lineage. T'was a warm coal in my breast, making me proud: Benjamin Franklin, whom the King of France had thanked for his electrical discoveries, was my father!"[72] Handy asserted, as well, that Franklin was well liked by the ladies around him, especially those in the Stevenson household. Indeed, according to Handy, it is not clear whether Mrs. Stevenson or her daughter, Polly, blushed more from Franklin's kisses.[73]

Reporting on Franklin's benevolent and ruminative sadness

about his mother's death, Handy accepted his place in the Stevenson household as a servant to Franklin who was sometimes jealously watched by elder son William Franklin. The Franklin evoked in this narrative proved himself to be benevolent, curious, and kind, one who looked after his offspring even when he did not acknowledge their mothers. For the general reader, tales such as Handy's will always seem more accessible[74] than the more complicated ones available in multivolumed and exhaustive detail in academic libraries across the United States. Franklin has entered the popular imagination in a way that will not easily be modified by academic opinion.

It is likely that general readers will continue to read biographies of Franklin, each with its own perspective on Franklin's complicated relations with women. With the *Papers of Benjamin Franklin* culminating in the final fascinating years of Franklin's life and with the publication of J. A. Leo Lemay's multivolume biography of Franklin, the future of Franklin study looks bright. But one must wonder whether Franklin has become so familiar, so domesticated, that the stories about his heterosexuality and his masculinity function to index citizens' attitudes about his life and accomplishments. Even though we will soon be able to see Franklin in all of his complexities, the public consciousness might prefer to have stories about his sexual capers rather than clarifications about specific rumors. A virile Franklin, at once "masculine," humane and forgivable, resides with us, it seems. *This* Franklin is a familiar memory for us from childhood schoolbooks on. We assume we already know Franklin: Isn't his face, after all, on our one-hundred-dollar bill? And doesn't this represent the fact that he had one hundred illegitimate children? What more do we need to know?

SALONS AND POWER IN THE ERA OF REVOLUTION:
From Literary Coteries to Epistolary Enlightenment
Susan Stabile

> *Women and wine*
> *Game and deceit*
> *Make the wealth small*
> *And the wants great.*
> —*Poor Richard*, 1758

In an undated letter to the celebrated French *salonnière* Madame Helvétius, Benjamin Franklin complimented her highly cultivated art of pleasing as she directed the enlightened conversation of her salon at Auteuil:

> I see that statesmen, philosophers, historians, poets, and men of learning of all sorts, are drawn around you, and seem as willing to attach themselves to you as straws about a fine piece of amber. . . . we find in your sweet society, that charming benevolence, that amiable attention to oblige, that disposition to please and be pleased, which we do not always find in the society of one another. It springs from you; it has its influence on us all; and in your company we are not only pleased with you, but better pleased with one another and with ourselves.[1]

His flattering description of Madame Helvétius's service to male *philosophes* anachronistically befits what has been called the Old Republic of Letters, when salonnières were called *précieuse*, when membership was guaranteed by aristocratic privilege, and when salons were considered schools of *civilité* rather than institutions of enlightenment.[2]

It describes, additionally, the Continental precedent to British-American institutions of conversation that provided a setting for heterosocial interaction and pleasure. This *beau monde*, or "world," it has been argued, was formed in part by the oral culture of salons, which legitimized heterosocial (negatively called "promiscuous") conversation by sublimating desire into the symbols and language of Platonism. According to literary historian David Shields, "It elevated the patroness on a divine pedestal and expunged the body by a rhetoric of spiritual rapport, thereby giving sufficient distance between women and men to permit conversation."[3] The ethic of heterosexual friendship, along with mutual interest and shared taste, thus cemented what Anthony Ashley Cooper, the third earl of Shaftesbury, called the *sensus communis* between *habitués*. But with the emergence of print, Shields suggests, came the pleasures of the written text and the subsequent transformation of the beau monde into the "public sphere."

As it happens, Benjamin Franklin in his extensive social connections and literary exchanges had a considerable transatlantic influence on the contributions of women to these heterosocial institutions of enlightenment—specifically the intermediate stage between "the world" and the "republic of letters" in the technology of handwritten manuscripts. An examination of his role in elevating and expanding the involvement of women in these exchanges of knowledge and power will be the focus of the following pages.

Since Franklin was abroad during the 1760s and until 1785—the dawning years of American salons—his direct influence upon women's intellectual development in the colonies was limited. But he extended his methods of female education from salon conversation in France to familiar letters in America, writing to Lord Kames in 1760 that "Conversation warms the Mind, enlivens the Imagination, and is continually starting fresh Game that is immediately pursu'd and taken."[4] A handwritten analogue to salon discourse, the familiar letter was thus a necessary progression from enlightened conversation for both Benjamin Franklin and his female peers.

9. ⌐

Franklin's neighbor at Passy, Madame Helvétius,
to whom he proposed marriage in 1779, only to be
politely rejected. (Wood engraving for *Century
Magazine* [1899], p. 419)

Serving as an American diplomat in London almost continuously
from 1757 until 1775 and in France from 1776 until 1785—returning
then to Philadelphia to complete his *Autobiography,*[5]—Benjamin
Franklin witnessed a transformation from the aristocratic patronage
of Continental salons to a new republic of letters in the nation's new
capital. A member of such prestigious intellectual societies as the
French Royal Academy of Sciences, the Lodge of the Nine Sisters,
the Royal Society of Edinburgh, the British Royal Society, the Club
of Honest Whigs, and the American Philosophical Society, Franklin
shared his scientific, philosophical, and political expertise with his
intellectual equals.

In England, he frequented coffeehouses and taverns, including

the Dog Tavern and the George and Vulture—the homosocial institutions for political and philosophical discussions.[6] In France, he
participated in heterosocial societies, becoming what Claude-Anne
Lopez has elsewhere called a sociable "pupil" at Madame Helvétius's
"Auteuil Academy" and other French salons.[7] And in Philadelphia,
he influenced an array of members of intersecting female literary coteries—including Elizabeth Fergusson, Annis Stockton, and Anna
Young Smith at Graeme Park and Morven; Deborah Logan, Hannah Griffitts, and Sally Norris Dickinson at Stenton and Fairhill;
and Susanna Wright at Wright's Ferry.[8]

Though Franklin was in London at a time when literary salons
flourished in the company of Alexander Pope, Lady Mary Wortley
Montagu, and Anna Seward (to name but a few of the habitués),
there is no evidence to date of his participation in the London or
Litchfield salons. Even Josiah Quincy's journal, the single most complete account of Franklin's London social calendar, makes no mention of salon visits.[9] He corresponded with editor William Strahan
and his literary circle, including James Boswell, Samuel Johnson, and
David Hume.[10] And he dined with actor David Garrick and visited
litterateur John Hawkesworth on occasion. But the closest he came
to becoming an habitué of a London salon was through the circle of
women connected with the inhabitants of his residence on Craven
Street, who included Margaret and Mary (Polly) Stevenson, Geor-
gianna Shipley, Dorothea Blount, and Mary Barwell.

In September 1770, Franklin wrote *The Craven Street Gazette*, a
parody of newspaper gossip about the court. Caricaturing the aristocratic conventions of the Old Republic of Letters, Franklin turned
domestic mishaps into courtly scandals. He represented his friends
as regal characters (Queen Margaret, Lady Hewson, and Lady Barwell) and himself as the illustrious Dr. Fatsides. At one point, he
even satirized the salon—or at least the British tea table: "We have
good Authority to assure our Readers that a Cabinet Council was
held this Afternoon at Tea; the Subject of which was a Proposal for
the Reformation of Manners."[11] While Franklin ostensibly mocked
the old court paradigm, known for its luxury, gossip, and corruption, he actually described the gynecocracy of the tea table, which
authorized female conversation. Though criticized by its male critics
for its gossip (an alternative history that broke the masculine mo-

nopoly on cultural representation) and fashion (a symbolic form of emasculation),[12] the tea table—in the company of Dr. Fatsides— would perform the same social function as the salon. As members of a "Cabinet Council," the women of the Craven Street circle would make feminine sensibility a political principle that would not only guide their conversations with one another, but also refine and polish the manners of the male habitués.

In addition to the Craven Street circle, Benjamin Franklin visited with American Elizabeth Graeme (later Fergusson) during her London sojourn of 1764–65. Graeme is well known among historians as the prospective daughter-in-law and ardent political critic of Benjamin Franklin. When Franklin was colonial agent to England during the conflict between the proprietors and the Pennsylvania assembly in 1757, he brought his son William, Elizabeth's fiancée, with him for schooling and as a special assistant. Although Graeme's "Dear John" letter to William no longer exists, William's reply as described in a letter of 24 October 1758 to Mrs. Ambercrombie insinuates that her reasons for ending their engagement were arguably political: "The whole Tenor of that Letter, that my Affection was in no wise Abated, she makes it, or would seem to make it, a sufficient Foundation for concluding my Love for her was changed; and for accusing me of 'want of Generosity' in not having frankly told her that my own Levity of Temper, or my Father's Schemes, or my Attachment to a Party, prevented my preserving in the tender Passion that I had professed."[13] Calling Benjamin Franklin and Joseph Galloway a "collection of Party malice," Elizabeth Graeme changed the focus from William Franklin's questionable fidelity to Benjamin Franklin's suspect politics. Thus, she ardently supported the Proprietary party to which her father belonged and steadfastly rejected both the colonial assembly and William Franklin.

But Elizabeth Graeme is better remembered among early American literary scholars as one of America's first salonnières.[14] Although she and her habitués would not have used the term "salon" to describe their intellectual gatherings, her "attic evenings" (as they were called) clearly were modeled after the French and English salons. According to Benjamin Rush, when she was in London, Elizabeth Graeme "sought and was sought by the most celebrated literary gentlemen who flourished in England at the time of the accession of George III to the throne." [15] From Drs. Fothergill and Hawkesworth to Samuel Johnson and Lawrence Sterne, Elizabeth Graeme and Benjamin Franklin would have kept some of the same company.

By that time she apparently had forgotten the political differences she had once had with Franklin. In fact, several of his letters attest to their sociable visits in London and to their mutual friends. In a letter to Deborah Franklin from London, dated 14 February, Franklin wrote: "Miss Betsy Graeme lodges not far from me, and is pretty well." Deborah replied in a letter of 7 April: "and Miss Graeme has wrote all so that she had the pleshur of a visit from you." [16] While no references to their visits are found in the recently published extract from her epistolary London travel journal, Elizabeth Graeme undoubtedly came under Franklin's influence while abroad. [17]

Their reminiscences of London, in fact, are almost identical. When Benjamin Franklin returned to Philadelphia from London in 1763, he wrote to Polly Stevenson about the westward travel of arts and culture, describing England with a metaphor that Elizabeth Graeme would echo two years later: "Of all the enviable Things England has, I envy it most its People . . . more sensible, virtuous and elegant Minds. . . . But, 'tis said, the Arts delight to travel Westward. . . . Already some of our young Geniuses begin to lisp Attempts at Painting, Poetry, and Musick." [18] Franklin probably was alluding to such painters as Benjamin West and such poets as the Schuykill Swains, Jacob Duche, Francis Hopkinson, Thomas Coombe, and Nathaniel Evans—the litterateurs who soon were to become habitués in Elizabeth Graeme's salon. [19]

Similarly, Fergusson set sail for Philadelphia on 3 July 1765 with the ambition to create an American salon based on the heterosocial British model, writing in her travel journal to Betsy Stedman that "upon the whole, I like Engl[an]d much ev'ry Art & Science, every particular Mode of Life, People may indulge the Hobby Horse to the utmost e[x]tent in, . . . Lond[o]n is the Mart for Knowledge & Pleasure, & Goodness & Virtue are by Individuals, as much practised there as anywhere." [20]

Upon her return to what she would call the "Athens of North America," Graeme wrote a retrospective epic poem, "Ode to the Lichfield Willow," celebrating the famous Litchfield group and constructing a literary history of these British salonnières. She described

10. ⌒

Elizabeth Graeme Fergusson, spurned lover of
William Franklin, American poet and salonnière,
inspired by Franklin's epistles. (Stipple engraving,
artist and date unknown, Free Library of Philadelphia, Lewis Collection)

them each in turn: literary critic Dr. Samuel Johnson "with Cynic
Pen Severe / Yet tender as a Child"; essayist Joseph Addison's abil-
ity to temper wit "with Truths Sublime"; actor David Garrick, "who
wou'd e'en *Shakespeares* Muse adorn / And Raise it near Divine";
painter and caricaturist William Hogarth, "who paints the Passions
on the Countenance and makes visible the Human Mind"; epistoler
Hester Thrale (Piozo), whose "Intimacy with Dr. Johnson and her
Pretensions to Partial Fame are well known"; and the young poet
Anna Seward, whom she calls "the *Sappho* of *Britannia's Plain*."[21]
Whether she met any of the members of the Litchfield group is still a
historiographical mystery. But their influence on her poetry is indis-
putable.[22]

She did, however, meet novelist Laurence Sterne during a visit to York, which she recounted in her travel journal:

> We presently fell into a very free Conversation, on his Part a very sensible one, & told me he wished to lengthen the Time, but was under an Engagement to return to his Hermitage the nesct Morning, but desired I would meet him, at the Assembly room in the Ev'ning, I told him I would be there, but questioned in such a Groupe whether I s[h]ould be found—He said he had some interest in Apollo, who would lend him his Torch on such an Occasion. This was no other than Yorick, the celebrated Lawrence Sterne. Author of Tristram Shandy.[23]

Renowned for his participation in French and English salons, Sterne introduced Elizabeth Graeme into a literary salon (or "Assembly of Apollo"), where she would have experienced all the wit and wisdom that Benjamin Rush would later describe.[24]

Though she repeatedly acknowledged the merits of the Litchfield group, and though she was thrilled to attend Sterne's assembly, Graeme saw Benjamin Franklin as particularly instrumental in fulfilling George Berkeley's prophecy of transplanting arts and learning from England to America. In a companion piece to the "Willow" ode titled "Ode to American Genius," Graeme literalized in the willow tree Berkeley's popular heliotropic metaphor, predicting that American literary culture would "to perfection rise / If we the Metaphor pursue / Symbolic of the Wise."[25]

Recalling an anecdote about Franklin bringing a basket made of willow back from Litchfield, she wrote:

> *Through* Franklin's *Hands the Basket past*
> *And flourishd fair to view*
> Franklin *who dons the Lightning's Blast*
> *As [Phoebus's] Laurels do.*

In a detailed footnote about the basket, Graeme not only traced its migration from England to America, but also its cultural value as gift given by Benjamin Franklin to another young woman—Deborah Norris (Logan).

Norris, thus inspired, would eventually create her own salon at Stenton, become the first female member of the Historical Society of Pennsylvania, transcribe and edit the now famous correspondence of William Penn and James Logan, and earn notoriety as a gifted historian and biographer:

> About thirty years past a Basket made of Willow . . . came from England and lay a Winter in a damp Cellar belonging to Dr. Franklin; And in the spring swelld and Budded Showing strong Marks of Vegetation. Dr. Franklin gave it to Miss Deborah Norris, a lady who had a particular taste for Gardening. She had it planted in her Garden near the State House in Philadelphia. It was by her Cherishd and with what Success all in that City know But perhaps they dont know that by much the great part of the Willows which now are so plentifully planted over the State of Pennsylvania took Rise from this Emigration. The Garden which contained the American Parent Stock is now in the Possession of the Widow Norris wife to Charles Norris Esquire.

Giving the willow basket to Norris, Franklin enacted the translatio metaphor (*metaphor* from the Greek meaning to "transfer" or "carry across") that he had mentioned to Polly Stevenson. "Symbolic of the Wise," the willow served as an image for the burgeoning female literary culture that would flourish in Philadelphia by the second half of the eighteenth century.[26]

In addition to introducing British influences into American literary circles, Benjamin Franklin would also share his numerous experiences in the French salons, where he was entertained by Madame Helvétius, Madame Geoffrin, Mademoiselle Lespinasse, and Madame Necker.[27] Through the aesthetics of wit and ease, these women refashioned what was once a noble, leisure institution into one of the Enlightenment. "No longer an extension of seventeenth-century court culture or royal academies," argues historian Dena Goodman, the eighteenth-century salon became a public space where male and female philosophes could freely discuss social, political, and literary issues without the constraints of patronage.[28]

Abbe Morellet, another habitué of the Helvétius salon, acknowledged women's preeminence in intellectual conversation: "The free commerce of the two sexes [is] one of the most powerful principles of civilisation and of the improvement of sociability. This effect occurs by means of conversation." He continued: "To be frank, I have never seen consistently good conversation except where a *salonnière* [*maîtresse de maison*] was, if not the only woman, at least a sort of center of the society." [29] Although women were relegated to domesticity, they could influence and improve men's manners, thereby securing their own place in sociable institutions of polite society in their parlors.

Like Morellet, Benjamin Franklin believed that women had "a certain feel, which is more reliable than [men's] reasonings" that helped to draw sound conclusions from difficult premises. [30] With his simple manner (the wigless Franklin too often was mistaken for a Quaker by fashionable society) and his imperfect French, Franklin looked to the salonnières to "improve both his soul and his French. [31]

Madame Brillon consistently corrected his poor grammar and flawed epistolary style, punctuating his errors with editorial marginalia. But rather than focusing on Franklin as a student, Brillon compared her own pedagogy to that of the formal academy: "I am a female guided by *instinct*, and since you seem to express yourself more forcefully than a grammarian, my *judgment* goes in your favor. . . . yet my *reasonings* might not be more unreasonable than those of your admirable, illustrious Encyclopedists — economists — moralists — journalists—theologians—atheists—materialists—and all imaginable sorts of —ists!" [32] Brillon justified her unorthodox opinion about Franklin's innovative French by indirectly placing the feminized salon among the educational institutions that otherwise precluded women.

In rehearsing the popular definition of "sense" as an instinctual faculty of perception, on the one hand, and as a moral and aesthetic judgment, on the other, she gently satirized Denis Diderot and Jean Le Rond d'Alembert's *Encyclopédie* entry for "wit" (or *espirit*), which "one could define it, ingenious reason." [33] Wit, she well knew, was not a product of academic reason, but rather the hallmark of novelty and variety in salon conversation. Thus, she put herself (and her female instinct) in the "reasonable" company of the famous Encyclopedists.

In addition to learning the refined conversation of the French and improving his poor grammar, Franklin exchanged reading materials and performed his bagatelles (including "The Ephemera," "The Elysian Fields," and "The Whistle") for Madame Brillon, Madame Helvétius, and Madame la Frete. He shared with them his unparalleled knowledge in natural philosophy, science, music, and belles lettres. Since the paradigm for the salon was one of exclusivity and reciprocity, and since Franklin and the salonnières provided mutual instruction, their pleasure and enlightenment were likewise shared.[34]

As Franklin confessed to Madame Helvétius in the guise of a mathematician: "Here is a problem a mathematician would be hard put to solve. Usually, when we share things, each person gets only one part; but when I share my *pleasure* with you, my part is doubled. The *part* is more than the *whole*."[35] Franklin, therefore, was both pupil of and teacher to the French salonnieres.[36]

But as Benjamin Franklin noticed, there was considerable cultural anxiety over the growing female influence in the republic of letters on both sides of the Atlantic. Montesquieu regarded salons as "a kind of republic whose members always actively aid one another. It is a new state within a state." Rousseau, however, argued that "a witty woman is a scourge to her husband, to her children, to her friends, her servants, to all the world." Montesquieu thought that "whosoever observes the action of those in power, if he does not know the women who govern them, is like a man who sees the action of a machine but does not know its secret springs." Conversely, Rousseau thought such female governance and genius would result in a woman "scorn[ing] to stoop to the duties of a woman, and [being] sure to commence a man."[37]

Similarly, in America, ideologues replicated the double talk, demanding the widespread diffusion of knowledge to ensure a literate republic, while discouraging republican women from equal participation in the *res publica*. "Nothing can so well promote the equality of rank, so much talked of and applauded yet so little known in republics as the universality and the estimation of literature," argued one contemporary man of letters. But " 'those masculine women'

who wished to participate in politics, commerce, [or] abstract intellectual pursuits," argued another philosophe, must "learn that the
women's true empire had the heart for its object."[38]

Benjamin Franklin, in truth, also embodied these ideological contradictions, promoting female education while condescending to
call the educated women in his circle by such paternalistic epithets as
"my dear daughter" and "my little pocket wife." Pushing republicanism to its most democratic (and domestic) conclusion, Benjamin
Rush wrote: "Let the ladies of a country be educated properly, and
they will not only make and administer its laws, but form its manners and character" as dutiful Republican mothers.[39] Through "sensible" conversation, then, American women refined men's passions
to develop the moral sense essential to good citizenship.

Responding to these conflicting opinions, the American salonnières, like their French counterparts, created salons of enlightenment rather than of leisure. They complemented performances of
belles lettres with discussions of politics, philosophy, and science.
And they tempered this new intellectual power with displays of sensibility, seasoning dull erudition with ameliorative touches of sociability.[40] Like the French salonnières, they also extended their
heterosocial system to an exclusively female mentoring program:
women would serve an informal apprenticeship to gain the skills
necessary to formalize their own salons.

"Rather than social climbers," Dena Goodman argues, "the salonnières of the Enlightenment must be viewed as intelligent, self-
educated, and educating women who reshaped the social forms of
their day to their own social, intellectual, and educational needs."
And like the French women, who considered the salon a social system that was an egalitarian model for the emerging republic, American salonnieres added republicanism to their aesthetic and political
repertoire.[41]

Unlike the London and Parisian salons, which were often criticized as hotbeds of luxury, fashion, idleness, and gossip, the American salons replicated the classical republican virtues of agrarian
simplicity and egalitarianism. Their pastoralized salons at country
seats such as Graeme Park, Stenton, and Morven were governed by
the democratic principles of reciprocity, equality, debate, and exchange.[42]

While habitué Anna Young Smith recast these civic qualities as

"Duty, Friendship, Liberty, and [platonic] Love," Nathaniel Evans pastoralized them in his poem, "An Ode Written at Graeme Park, 1766":

> *Then shall th' immortal Nine unfold*
> *What sweets the sylvan scenes can give;*
> *In heav'n thy name shall be enroll'd,*
> *And others learn like thee to live.*[43]

Evans commended Elizabeth Graeme for her graceful poetic strains and for the sociability she fostered in her salon. The salonnière, therefore, became an exemplar of republican refinement.

Supplanting personal desires with civic disinterestedness, moreover, heterosocial salons promoted a shared sense of benevolence and politeness among men and women alike. Sociability demanded "a distancing from everyday life and preoccupation with self,"[44] where sociable persons played a role that was distinguished from their private personae. Such distancing from individual desires likewise blurred the boundaries of sexual difference. Annis Stockton described it this way in 1769: "How often when I am reading Mr. Pope's Letters, do I envy that day the knot of friends that seem'd to have but one heart by which they were united and their greatest pleasure was giving each other pleasure."[45] With "but one heart," male and female habitués shared a communal identity.

Like Stockton, Benjamin Rush erased the particularities of sexual categories in his description of Elizabeth Graeme: "The genius of Miss Graeme," he wrote in the *Port Folio* of 1809, was "instructed by the stores of knowledge contained in the historians, philosophers, and poets of ancient and modern nations." "Upon these occasions," he continued, "her body seemed to vanish, she appeared to be all mind." Removing her body from his memory, Rush recovered and inverted the convenient Cartesian theory of the sexless mind. Such a theory not only severed the mind from the body, but also gave gender distinction to the division by associating masculinity with intellect and femininity with gross corporeality. Graeme accordingly shared both sentiments (of "one heart") and ideas (being "all mind") with her male habitués.

The corporeal absence of the salonnière's body underscored the ideological uncertainties about women's concurrent place in the home and the public sphere. Because domestic duties often prevailed, women could not always attend the salons, but relied instead upon written correspondence. "Like the art of pleasing in company," according to eighteenth-century rhetorician Hugh Blair, "letters are conversation carried upon paper, between two friends at a distance, [which provided the] ever agreeable and innocent pleasures that flow from social love, from hearts united by the same laudable ties."[46]

With the same aesthetic of reciprocity, letters continued the ethos of the salon, trading the aural delights of conversation for the tactile pleasures of writing and receiving letters. Simple, easy, and pleasing, letters followed the same rules as speaking in company. As Blair insisted: "The first requisite, both in conversation and correspondence is to attend to all the proper decorums which our own character, and that of others, demand."[47]

While letters served as an appropriate rhetorical proxy for the absent salonnière, they also provided the expected moral examples. As moralist John Bennett suggested: "It is an office particularly suited to the liveliness of your fancy, and the sensibility of your heart; and your Sex, in general, much excels our own, in the *ease* and graces of epistolary correspondence."[48] Since letters were seen as spontaneous and natural effusions of the heart in a plain style; since the sentimental and moral philosophers agreed that women were naturally more effusive and spontaneous than men; and since there were popular strictures against female pedantry, the familiar epistle was an excellent medium for women's educational advancement and moral progress in heterosocial society.

Benjamin Franklin is well known for his instructive epistles to Polly Stevenson (Hewson). Through letters, he taught her about such scientific and philosophical subjects as the absorption of heat by color, the movement of the tide in rivers, the effect of air on barometric pressure, and the possibilities of a phonetic alphabet. In a letter of 1 May 1760 Franklin explicitly described himself as the tutor and Stevenson as the student of both moral and natural philosophy: "If we enter, as you propose, into moral as well, as natural Philosophy, I fancy, when I have fully establish'd my Authority as a Tutor, I shall take upon me to lecture you a little on that Chapter of Duty."[49] While this passage is a testimony to Franklin's commitment to her education, its preceding query is more like a utilitarian endorsement of the improving educational ideology of the eighteenth century: educate women just enough to become better social and moral companions to men (the same justification for their discursive participation in salons). Though letters were aestheticized as a feminine genre that established an epistemology of the human heart, Franklin asserted his "Authority" as tutor by "lecturing" Hewson on her duties as moral arbiter rather than following the epistolary rules of reciprocity.

Franklin asked: "But why will you, by the Cultivation of your Mind, make yourself still more amiable, and a more desirable, Companion for a Man of Understanding when you are determin'd, as I hear, to live Single?"[50] His version of reciprocity, therefore, was marriage. Here Franklin joined the ongoing transatlantic conversation on female education, following Mary Astell and Madame Maintenon and anticipating Benjamin Rush and Judith Sargeant Murray. According to these critics, a woman's cultivated intellect appreciated in value on the marriage market since it increased the heterosociability of the otherwise separated spheres. But, more important, this conservative ideology permitted women's entrance into public discussions of philosophy, science, politics, and belles lettres, while it safeguarded them from being unfairly labeled as masculinized pedants.

Polly Stevenson Hewson upheld her role as a student of moral philosophy in a 1770 poetic epistle to Franklin, crediting her brilliant tutor both with her knowledge of philosophy and her acquisition of virtue: "From whom Philosophy and Virtue too, / I've gain'd—If either can be counted mine: / In you they with the Dearest lustre shine."[51] Similarly, in another short poem, "Dr. Franklin," Hewson followed Franklin's lead in merging the domestic and public, the female and male, domains. The poem was not only a token of appreciation to her mentor, but also evidence of the reciprocity of their epistolary exchange:

Behold the Man in whose Capacious Mind
The Sciences and Virtues are conjoin'd;
Whose Lib'ral Hand is ready to bestow,
While his Heart melts in sympathetic Woe.
Alike in Private Life and Publick Trust
Active, engaging, sensible and just.[52]

As tutor, friend, and correspondent, Benjamin Franklin created for Polly Hewson a private educational system that far exceeded the possibilities of salon conversation. And she fulfilled her meliorative duty of refining men's manners. She softened Franklin's earlier assertion of "authority" by balancing the academic style of his "Capacious Mind" with the sympathy of his melting Heart.

While Franklin conversed with Elizabeth Graeme both in Philadelphia and in London as well as with Deborah Logan at her Stenton salon, most of his influence on these women of letters was through instructive epistles. From personal correspondence to published periodical and newspaper missives, Franklin's epistolary techniques were models of polite intercourse for the Philadelphian salonnieres.[53] Elizabeth Graeme Fergusson fondly alluded to Franklin's early letters to her (which are no longer extant) in a 23 December 1797 epistle to Benjamin Rush: "I have some of the kindest and fondest letters from Dr. Franklin wrote to me when he wished me to have been a member of his family, which had had [sic] vanity taken place, and I had had a mind to have shewn them, would have been circulated thro all the anecdote writers in Europe and America under the article traits of Dr. Franklin's Domestic Character."[54] Fergusson made no mention of his politics (as she had in her earlier letter to William Franklin), but like Polly Hewson, praised the virtue of his domestic character, which served as a model to her and her literary circle.

In her *Memoir of Dr. George Logan,* Deborah Logan also remembered Franklin's domestic character, his epistolary expertise, and his public virtue:

I have myself had the pleasure of being a few times in Dr. Franklin's society. His conversation was easy, and appeared to grow entirely out of the circumstances that presented themselves to the company, yet I observed that if you did not find you had acquired something by being with him[,] it must be placed to the account of your own want of attention. His familiar letters give you a good idea of his conversation,—a natural and goodhumoured (not sarcastic) wit played cheerfully along and beguiled you into maxims of prudence and wisdom. The man who could make the sayings of "Poor Richard" fash-

ionable in France must have had no ordinary powers of conversation. What a pity there should have been any "errata" in
his moral conduct![55]

Logan acknowledged the educative value of conversation with
Franklin, as well the instructive maxims gleaned from his fictional
persona Richard Saunder's annual letters to his "courteous reader."
Although she celebrated Franklin as a literary exemplar for female
letter writers, unlike Hewson and Fergusson, she editorialized on his
moral "errata," which made him an unsuitable model for female
virtue.

Franklin also contributed to the education of the Philadelphia salonnières by suggesting readings and sending books to them along
with his letters. He was a correspondent of several women in their
various networks, including Susanna Wright, Deborah Logan, and
Elizabeth Fergusson. Franklin agreed with Benjamin Rush, who
thought that women should attain a "general intercourse with the
world" through reading. From Philadelphia, he sent to Susanna
Wright John Douglas's *Milton Vindicated from the Charge of Plagiarism
Brought Against Him by Mr. Laude* (1751), William Lauder's *A Letter to
the Reverend Mr. Douglas, occasioned by his Vindication of Milton* (1751),
and Henry Dodwell's *Christianity not Founded on Argument* (1741);
from London, he forwarded to her political pamphlets (1758), *The
Gentleman's Magazine* (November 1751), and an almanac (possibly
Poor Richard's for 1762).[56]

Franklin also highly recommended Milcah Martha Moore's *Miscellanies, Moral and Instructive* (1787) as both a moral and literary
guide for his other female correspondents. In her preface, Moore de-
ferred to the aged and wise Franklin as "one of the most approved
judges of books amongst us" and included a recommendation by
him: "A book containing so many well chosen sentiments, and excellent instructions, put into the hand of our children, cannot but be
highly useful to their rising generation."[57] Benjamin Franklin en-
dorsed her book, which promoted both useful knowledge and virtue
for young republicans.[58]

Taking Franklin's advice, Elizabeth (Graeme) Fergusson read
Moore's collection (possibly even contributed to it) and reciprocated
with a poem, "Lines by a Friend, on reading Mrs. M. Moore's

printed and unprinted extracts for the use of schools, suggested by Dr. Franklin."[59] Like Franklin, Fergusson proposed religious virtue and self-education to the rising women of Philadelphia:

> *Then hear, ye modest fair,*
> *Let not her aims be lost;*
> *Aims, generous, kind, polite, sincere,*
> *Which time and labour cost.*
> *But grateful read the nice mark'd lines,*
> *Where taste and judgment's shewn;*
> *Where virtue all harmonious shines:*
> *And make her choice your own.*

She hoped to instill into the younger female generation all the taste, judgment, and virtue of her female companions. Early American women's intellectual circles thus established through the feminized epistle a sororal mentor system analogous to the one institutionalized by the French salonnières. Letters were associated with the elite reading public of women; literacy with their cultivated virtue.

Franklin's female correspondents in Philadelphia thus developed an epistolary mentoring system that continued the educational goals of the salon. The salonnières would hold one another accountable for preserving the aesthetics and virtues of salon conversation. Younger women, in turn, would model their elders. Hannah Griffitts, for example, saw Susanna Wright as her mentor: "[I] have ventur'd some of my rough Scribles to her hand, whose Judgment equals the nicest Critic, but her Benevolent heart glows with the Generous Candor of friendship, on which I rely." Extending the friendship she once shared with Griffitts's mother, Mary Norris Griffitts, Susanna Wright responded: "Your Mothers social Hour was mine / As kindred minds allied . . . Such wou'd thou be, cou'd Youth to Age / The engaging Hand extend; / Such wou'd I prove the tender Tye, / And fondly call thee Friend."

Having found her own mentor, Griffitts accordingly acted as guide for her younger cousin, Deborah Norris Logan. When Deborah was only three years old, her cousin predicted that "Tho' she can Scarcely Speak a word, she Can well express her own meaning, & let us know, she understands ours, like the rest of her Sex, she is kept under. . . . I think if she lives," Griffitts concluded, "she will make her way Thro' life with a figure." Logan indeed became an important figure and acted as a mentor to several young women, including her cousin Sally Norris Dickinson.

As Dickinson wrote to Logan: "but now, my dear, Cousin has settled her [Character] and has left me to tread in her footsteps: This is now more gratified to admire, and improve me than one of my own years." Logan responded modestly, confessing to Dickinson in a letter of 18 September 1799: "And now, I wave apologies which I ought to make for this letter, so very insignificant that not a line of it interests, without Susan Emlen's Sentiment and Style, or Cousin Rhoad's narration. . . . [This is] a vehicle of my Sentiments of affection which are tender, and unabated, and I feel will continue thro' life."[60]

Through his correspondence with the American salonnières, then, Franklin witnessed the transformation of a heterosocial paradigm into a series of interconnected sororal networks, whose privately circulating manuscript letters had well established a feminized *sensus communis* and ensured the moral conduct of their coterie. Just as they conceptually transformed the domestic parlor into the public salon, so they recast familiar letters—as sociable missive, letter-journal, commonplace book, and poetic epistle—into a social institution of conversation. Like the salon's method of performance and criticism, whereby participants were judged for the pleasure and instruction they reciprocally afforded, letters provided the vehicle for literary exchange and critique, as well as for intellectual argumentation, mutual edification, and the advancement of female virtue.

From pre-Revolutionary France to Revolutionary America, Benjamin Franklin participated in a transatlantic ideological revolution in women's education through both salon conversation and written letters—the sociable institutions where Enlightenment rhetoric on women and enlightened discourse by women succinctly converged. And "if salons were the heart of the Enlightenment," as Dena Goodman has suggested, "letters circulated through them [were] like its life blood.[61]

Through his letters to Continental and republican salonnières, Franklin deftly negotiated the boundaries between the homosocial and sororal republic of letters, and created a curriculum for women's intellectual progress that necessarily ensured their moral development. Perhaps this was his most challenging diplomatic feat, as he once conceded to Madame Brillon: "For sixty years, now, masculine and feminine things—and I am not talking about modes and tenses—have been giving me a lot of trouble. I used to hope that at the age of 80 I would be free of all that. But here I am, four times 19, which is mighty close to 80, and those French ferninines are still bothering me. It will make me all the happier to go to Paradise where, they say, all such distinctions will be abolished."[62]

NOTES

Preface

1. Another valuable participant in the symposium was Elaine Crane, historian at Fordham University, who shared her knowledge of Franklin's world through the special lens of eighteenth-century diarist Elizabeth Drinker. Crane chose not to submit an essay for inclusion in this volume.

Introduction

1. The most accessible source of Franklin's most important writings is the marvelous one-volume compilation by the Library of America titled *Benjamin Franklin Writings*, edited by J. A. Leo Lemay (New York: Library of America, 1987), 5–42, 1115–16 (hereafter *BF Writings*). The Silence Dogood articles appeared in fourteen chatty essays between 2 April and 8 October 1722. But also to get the fullest background on any of Franklin's writings, one should always consult the authoritative *Papers of Benjamin Franklin*, edited by Leonard W. Labaree et al., 40 vols. projected (New Haven: Yale University Press, 1959–), 1:8–45 (hereafter *PBF*). On Polly Baker, see Max Hall's exhaustive *Benjamin Franklin and Polly Baker: The History of a Literary Deception* (Chapel Hill: University of North Carolina Press, 1960).

2. The best compilation of these sayings is Frances M. Barbour, *A Concordance to the Sayings in Franklin's POOR RICHARD* (Detroit: Gale Research, 1974), 41, 127–28, 142, 234–35, 239–40.

3. See the biographical glossary included in this book for information on each of these young women.

4. *BF Writings*, 302–3, 964–66, 1329.

5. See Carla Mulford's chapter below.

6. Bache was scorned as having all of his grandfather's shortcomings and has in recent years enjoyed a new spate of scholarly attention: Jeffrey A. Smith, *Franklin and Bache: Envisioning the Enlightened Republic* (New York: Oxford University Press, 1990), 158–66. James Tagg, *Benjamin Franklin Bache and the Philadelphia AURORA* (Philadelphia: University of Pennsylvania Press, 1991), 378–81. See also the extraordinary work on Bache by Richard N. Rosenfeld, *American Aurora: A Democratic-Republican Returns* (New York: St. Martin's Press, 1997), 208, 364, 843.

7. *Dr. Benj. Franklin and the Ladies: Being Various Letters, Essays, Bagatelles, & Satires to & About the Fair Sex* (Mount Vernon, N.Y.: Peter Pauper Press, 1939).

8. Ibid., 67–69, containing the text of the Rosenbach version described below.

9. Ibid., 67–78.

10. Ibid., 68–69.

11. In his autobiography Franklin acknowledged seven different "errata"—sexual and otherwise—during his early years. See J. A. Leo Lemay and P. M. Zall, eds., *Benjamin Franklin's Autobiography* (New York: W. W. Norton, 1986), 16, 27, 34 (2 cases), 36, 51, 56.

12. The story of "Old Mistresses Apologue" is well-related in *PBF*, 3:27–31, and in

Nian-Sheng Huang, *Benjamin Franklin in American Thought and Culture, 1790–1990* (Philadelphia: American Philosophical Society, 1994), 145–48.

13. *PBF,* 3:27.

14. Ibid., 3:28.

15. Ibid., 3:28–29.

16. Huang, *BF in American Thought,* 145–47; *PBF,* 3:29.

17. *American National Biography,* 24 vols.; (New York: Oxford University Press, 1999), 8:247–48. Ford was murdered by his disaffected brother, Malcolm, in 1902. But by that time he had produced fifty-four articles, forty-nine books and pamphlets, and fourteen works of fiction.

18. *PBF,* 3:29; *American National Biography,* 3:367–69, s.v. "Thomas Francis Bayard." Part of Bayard's concern was that Grover Cleveland was entering into a very-shaky looking nominating and reelection season, losing, of course, both contests.

19. All of the quotations here appear either in Huang, *BF in American Thought,* 146–47, or *PBF,* 3:29. On McMaster's career and tendency to moral judgments, see Harvey Wish, ed., *American Historians: A Selection* (New York: Oxford University Press, 1962), 215–53. On Fisher, see *American National Biography,* 8:19–20, s.v. "Sydney George Fisher."

20. On Neill, see *Dictionary of American Biography* (22 vols.; New York: Charles Scribner's Sons, 1934), 13:408–9, "Edward Duffield Neill."

21. Hoar is quoted in Huang, *BF in American Thought,* 147. On Hoar and his character, see *American National Biography,* 10:888–89, s.v. "George Frisbie Hoar."

22. Phillips Russell, *Benjamin Franklin: The First Civilized American* (New York: Bretano's, 1926), 1.

23. Ibid., 170–74.

24. On Ford, see Huang, *BF in American Thought,* 159–60. Bernard Faÿ, *The Revolutionary Spirit in France and America* (New York: Harcourt, Brace & World, 1927), 95, 96, 101; *The Two Franklins: Fathers of American Democracy* (Boston: Little, Brown, 1933), 49–52; *Revolution and Freemasonry, 1680–1800* (Boston: Little, Brown, 1935), 252–60.

25. Carl Van Doren, *Benjamin Franklin* (New York: Viking Press, 1938), 150–52.

26. Claude-Anne Lopez and Eugenia W. Herbert, *The Private Franklin: The Man and His Family* (New York: W. W. Norton, 1975), esp. 16–29.

27. Esmond Wright, *Franklin of Philadelphia* (Cambridge: Harvard University Press, 1986), see, for example, his description of Franklin's relations with Margaret and Mary Stevenson, 110–12. J. A. Leo Lemay, ed., *Reappraising Benjamin Franklin: A Bicentennial Perspective* (Newark: University of Delaware Press, 1993), wherein the only reference to Franklin and women is that made by Claude-Anne Lopez as she described Franklin's activities while in France, asking the question, "Was Franklin Too French?" 143–53

28. Morton L. Ross, "Poor Richard and 'Playboy': Brothers Under the Flesh," *Colorado Quarterly* 15 (Spring 1967): 355–60, as cited in Huang, *BF in American Thought,* 214.

29. Huang, *BF in American Thought,* 214–15.

30. Both of these articles are cited in Huang, *BF in American Thought,* 227–29. The smut piece was David A. Kaplan, "A Quick Look at the History of Smut," *Newsweek,* 2 July 1990, 48.

Chapter 1

1. Benjamin Franklin, *The Autobiography of Benjamin Franklin,* ed. Leonard W. Labaree et al. (New Haven: Yale University Press, 1964), 129. (Hereafter, *Autobiography.)*

2. See especially Lisa Waciega, " 'A Man of Business': The Widow of Means in Southeastern Pennsylvania, 1750–1850," *WMQ,* 3d ser. 44 (1987): 40–64; Susan Branson, "Women and the Family Economy in the Early Republic: The Case of Elizabeth Meredith," *Journal of the Early Republic* 16 (1996): 47–71.

3. *Autobiography,* 76.

4. See Paul M. Zall, "A Portrait of the Autobiographer as an Old Artificer," in J. A. Leo Lemay, ed., *The Oldest Revolutionary: Essays on Benjamin Franklin* (Philadelphia: University of Pennsylvania Press, 1976), 53–66.

5. Ibid., 89.

6. Admittedly, Read had recently fallen on hard times. He had just remortgaged his Market Street lots (he would die in 1723 before he could regain possession of them). Nevertheless, he had once prospered in Philadelphia, and BF could easily have assumed that his financial reverses were temporary. At any rate, Read was surely in a better financial position than BF himself could hope to be for some time.

7. *Autobiography,* 92.

8. Ibid., 107.

9. Ibid., 129.

10. Ibid., 128.

11. Ibid., 129.

12. See Leonard W. Labaree et al., eds. *The Papers of Benjamin Franklin,* 40 vols. (New Haven: Yale University Press, 1959–), 1:362–70 for details of the transaction. (Hereafter, *PBF.)*

13. DF to BF, [24 May 1767], *PBF,* 14:158.

14. *PBF,* 1:219.

15. I am indebted to Professor Joan Gunderson, of the History Department at California State University, San Marcos, for this line of thought.

16. Franklin, "Song," [c. 1742], *PBF,* 2:353, 354.

17. See especially BF to Catherine Greene, 23 January 1763, *PBF,* 10:191; BF to [Elizabeth Hubbart?], [16 October? 1755], *PBF,* 6:222.

18. Carl Van Doren, *Benjamin Franklin* (New York: Viking Press, 1938), 125; BF to Abiah Franklin, 16 October 1747, [7] September 1749, *PBF,* 3:179, 388.

19. For an excellent discussion of the "intermeshing of male and female concerns" and duties in seventeenth—and eighteenth-century America, see Laurel Thatcher Ulrich, *Good Wives: Image and Reality in the Lives of Women in Northern New England, 1650–1750* (New York: Alfred A. Knopf, 1982).

20. *PBF,* 1:172, 331–32; 2:127.

21. DF to Margaret Strahan, 24 December 1751, *PBF,* 4:225.

22. DF to BF, 8 January 1765, *PBF,* 12:15.

23. *PBF,* 7:162n; BF to William Dunlap, 4 April 1757, *PBF,* 169.

24. *Autobiography,* 129, 144, 145. See also BF to Miss Alexander, 24 June 1782, in Albert Henry Smyth, ed. *The Writings of Benjamin Franklin* (New York: Macmillan, 1906), 8:459.

25. *Autobiography,* 196.

26. See especially Claude-Anne Lopez and Eugenia W. Herbert, *The Private Franklin: The Man and His Family* (New York: W.W. Norton, 1975), 42, 66.

27. BF to DF, 6 April 1766, *PBF,* 13:233; Peter Collinson to BF, 26 January 1754, *PBF,* 5:191; BF to Peter Collinson, 26 June 1755, *PBF,* 6:90; BF Account Books, *PBF,* 10:259, 357.

28. *Autobiography,* 145.

29. DF's Account Book, *PBF,* 12:193, 4.

30. BF to DF, 27 December [1755], 25 January, 30 January 1756, *PBF,* 6:313, 365, 379.

31. Mary Beth Norton, *Liberty's Daughters* (Boston: Little Brown, 1980), chaps. 6–8.

32. Edith B. Gelles, *Portia: The World of Abigail Adams* (Bloomington: Indiana University Press, 1992), 37–56; Ulrich, *Good Wives,* 35–50. See also Joan Gunderson, "Independence, Citizenship and the American Revolution," *Signs* 13 (1987): 59–77.

33. DF to BF, [14 July–15 August? 1766], *PBF,* 13:336.

34. DF to BF, 3 November 1765, *PBF,* 12:351.

35. DF to Peter Collinson, 30 April 1755, *PBF,* 6:24; William Daniel to BF, 21 [?] July 1755, *PBF,* 111; BF to DF, 21 March 1756, *PBF,* 426; BF to DF, 13 December 1766, *PBF,* 13:519, 520.

36. Josiah Franklin Davenport to DF, 22 March 1759, *PBF,* 8:301.

37. BF to DF, 11 May 1765, *PBF,* 12:128. She did, however, consult BF's friends before making the purchase. James Parker to BF, 4 January 1766, *PBF,* 13:13.

38. DF to BF, 12 June [1766], *PBF,* 13:31, 32.

39. DF to BF, 21 February [1765], *PBF,* 12:46; DF to BF, [14 July–15 August? 1766] *PBF,* 13:337; DF to BF, 3 July, [13–18 October? 1767], *PBF,* 14:207, 208, 280–82.

40. BF to DF, 9 December 1764, *PBF,* 11:517.

41. DF to BF, 17 February, [1–8] August 1765, *PBF,* 12:46, 224; DF to BF, [14 July–15 August? 1766], *PBF,* 13:337; DF to BF, [20–25 April 1767], *PBF,* 14:139.

42. WF to BF, [2 January 1769], *PBF,* 16:5, 6.

43. DF to BF, [21–22 January 1768], *PBF,* 15:24.

44. BF to DF 5 April 1757, 21 January 1758, *PBF,* 7:175, 365. It was a task, moreover, that he intended to resume as soon as he returned home.

45. WF to BF, [May? 1767], *PBF,* 14:174, 5.

46. DF to BF, 2 [–25 April 1767], *PBF,* 137.

47. BF to JM, 23 February 1769, *PBF,* 16:50.

48. DF to BF, 13 [–15] June 1770, *PBF,* 17:175, 207; Richard Bache to DF, 3 December 1771, *PBF,* 18:258.

49. Richard Bache to DF, 3 December 1771, *PBF,* 18:258.

50. BF to DF, 22 November 1757, *PBF,* 7:275.

51. BF to DF, 10 June 1758, *PBF,* 8:92.

52. DF to BF, 22 September 1765, *PBF,* 12:271.

53. Ibid.

54. DF to BF, [8–13 October 1765], *PBF,* 12:300.

55. BF to DF, 10 June 1758, *PBF,* 8:93.

56. DF to BF [6–13? October 1765], [8–13 October 1765], 3 November 1765, *PBF,* 12:299, 303, 353.

57. DF to BF, 12 June [1766], *PBF,* 13:32.

58. DF to BF, 4 October 1769, *PBF,* 16:214.

59. BF to DF, 14 February, 4 June, [August] 1765, *PBF,* 12:62, 167, 251; BF to DF, 22 June 1767, *PBF,* 14:195; BF to DF, 19 March 1772, *PBF,* 19:90.

60. DF to BF, [6–13? October 1765], *PBF,* 12:296, 298.

61. DF to BF, 12 January [1766], *PBF,* 13:30.

62. DF to BF, 16 August 1770, *PBF,* 17:208.

63. DF to BF, [24 May 1767], *PBF,* 14:158.
64. DF to BF, 3 July 1767, *PBF,* 207.
65. DF to BF, 20[–27] November 1769, *PBF,* 16:231. See also Thomas Bond to BF, 7 June 1769, *PBF,* 153; DF to BF, 31 August 1769, *PBF,* 188. One thing is sure. If BF read his wife's letters throughout this period and did not realize that she was desperately ill, then he was much less perceptive than historians have led us to believe. They are painful to read, and were no doubt more painful for her to write.
66. DF to BF, 16 August 1770, *PBF,* 17:205.
67. Richard Bache to BF, 16 May 1772, 4 January 1773, *PBF,* 19:144, 20:4, 5.
68. Sarah Franklin Bache to BF, 30 October 1773, *PBF,* 453.
69. DF to BF, 30 June [1772], *PBF,* 19:192.
70. DF to BF, [2 August 1772], *PBF,* 230.
71. *PBF,* 231.
72. BF to DF, 21 January 1758, *PBF,* 7:364, 365.
73. BF to DF, 12 January 1758, *PBF,* 7:359, 360; BF to DF, 10 June 1758, *PBF,* 8:92; BF to DF, 5 March 1760, *PBF,* 9:33.
74. BF to DF, 19 February 1758, *PBF,* 383.
75. DF to BF, [8–13 October 1765], *PBF,* 12:300.
76. DF to BF, [5–8? February 1766], *PBF,* 13:115.
77. BF to DF, 18 April 1765, *PBF,* 12:107. This kind of letter, really nothing but a paragraph acknowledging his existence and hers, increasingly characterized BF's missives to DF throughout the late 1760s and early 1770s.
78. BF to DF, 22 June 1767, *PBF,* 14:193.
79. BF to DF, 1 May 1771, *PBF,* 18:91.
80. DF's letter is, unfortunately, missing. Its contents can only be guessed at based on BF's letter to her of 17 August 1771, *PBF,* 207.
81. DF to BF, 6 April, 29 October 1773, *PBF,* 20:152, 449, 450.
82. BF to DF, 14 August 1771, *PBF,* 18:204, 205; 14 February, 15 July 1773, *PBF,* 20:58, 59, 317–19.
83. DF to BF, [14?]–16 May 1772, *PBF,* 19:141; BF to DF, 1 December 1772, *PBF,* 395.
84. BF to DF, 6 October 1773, *PBF,* 20:436.
85. BF to DF, 7 May, 22 July, 10 September 1774, *PBF,* 21:210, 246, 303.
86. WF to BF, 3 May 1774, *PBF,* 206.
87. Richard Bache to BF, 24 December 1774, *PBF,* 401.
88. BF to WF, 22 March 1775, *PBF,* 593.

Chapter 2

I am grateful to my colleague and editor Claude-Anne Lopez for both published and unpublished data essential in documenting this chapter, to Mary Kelley of Dartmouth College for perspectives on the subject and a good reading of the piece, and to Marian Godfrey of the Pew Charitable Trusts of Philadelphia for some important insights and a careful reading as well.

1. Franklin's will as it appears in Jared Sparks, ed., *The Works of Benjamin Franklin,* 10 vols. (Boston: Tappan Whittemore, and Mason), 9:599–610. There are also substantial files on the history of the will at the Benjamin Franklin National Memorial of the Franklin Institute in Philadelphia and at the American Philosophical Society. It was one of my distinct pleasures shortly after I arrived at the Franklin Institute to assist Mayor Wilson Goode of Philadelphia in appointing a select committee of historians and citizens to determine what should be done with Philadel-

phia's portion of Franklin's trust fund on the occasion of the bicentennial of his death, 17 April 1990. Philadelphia was the first of the four entities receiving funds in 1990 to select a disposition for its funds. Our committee recommended that the funds be transferred to the Philadelphia Foundation, a community foundation, to continue the spirit of what Franklin intended, i.e., to make loans and to guarantee credit for individuals in Philadelphia trained in one of the trades (plumbing, electricity, technologies, carpentry, and the like), to make grants to strengthen trades training programs, and to give awards to individuals demonstrating outstanding proficiency in the various trades. The Commonwealth of Philadelphia followed this plan in part by making half of its funds available to community foundations across Pennsylvania for the same purposes as the Philadelphia initiative. The other half was granted to the Franklin Institute of Philadelphia to continue its program of training students and citizens of Philadelphia in science, technology, and the mechanic arts.

2. Franklin's will, in Sparks, *Works of Benjamin Franklin*, 9:601–2.

3. Franklin's will, in Sparks, *Works of Benjamin Franklin*, 9:599–600.

4. Franklin's will, in Sparks, *Works of Benjamin Franklin*, 9:601.

5. Sheila L. Skemp, *William Franklin: Son of a Patriot, Servant of a King* (New York: Oxford University Press, 1990), 273–74.

6. The respective careers of Franklin's heirs are beautifully detailed in Claude-Anne Lopez and Eugenia W. Herbert, *The Private Franklin: The Man and His Family* (New York: W. W. Norton, 1975), 305–9.

7. Lopez and Herbert, *Private Franklin*, 310–11.

8. Lopez and Herbert, *Private Franklin*, 306–7.

9. I am grateful to colleague Claude-Anne Lopez for additional insights and information on the Bache trip to England, per a phone conversation, 3 December 1993. See also Lopez and Herbert, *Private Franklin*, 306–7. According to Sheila Skemp, *William Franklin*, 274–75, William Franklin provided similar services to Sally's second son and his namesake, William Franklin Bache, two years later when he came to London to study medicine.

10. Information on activities of the Baches in England provided by Claude-Anne Lopez, phone conversation, 3 December 1993. Descriptions of the portraits are inspired by descriptions in Lopez and Herbert, *Private Franklin*, 307.

11. Information on Sally's correspondence with Le Veillard from Claude-Anne Lopez, conversation, 3 December 1993. Information on Franklin's friends and their fate from Lopez and Herbert, *Private Franklin*, 277–78.

12. Information provided by Claude-Anne Lopez, conversation, 3 December 1993. For Le Veillard, see J. A. Leo Lemay and Paul M. Zall, eds., *Benjamin Franklin's Autobiography: An Authoritative Text, Backgrounds, Criticism* (New York: W. W. Norton, 1986), 188.

13. Information provided by Claude-Anne Lopez, conversation, 3 December 1993.

14. Skemp, *William Franklin*, 8–21, 28–29.

15. Lopez and Herbert, *Private Franklin*, 70–72. Hereafter, page numbers from this work are cited parenthetically in the text.

Chapter 3

1. Franklin's relationships with French women have been described in Lopez, *Mon Cher Papa: Franklin and the Ladies of Paris* (New Haven: Yale University Press,

1966). Some passages in this chapter have been reproduced from Claude-Anne Lopez and Eugenia W. Herbert, *The Private Franklin: The Man and His Family* (New York: W. W. Norton, 1975).

2. See William G. Roelker, ed., *Benjamin Franklin and Catharine Ray Greene: Their Correspondence, 1755–1790* (Philadelphia: American Philosophical Society, 1949). See also Leonard W. Labaree et al., eds., *The Papers of Benjamin Franklin*, 40 vols. (New Haven, Yale University Press, 1959–), 5:502n. (Hereafter *PBF*).

3. *PBF*, 5:502–4; 535–37.

4. *PBF*, 6:182–86.

5. *PBF*, 6:96–97.

6. *PBF*, 5:537.

7. *PBF*, 6:225.

8. William Franklin, Franklin's only surviving son, was born out of wedlock (c. 1729) to an unknown mother, but was promptly recognized and given the Franklin name. He followed first in his father's footsteps, then took a law degree in London and was appointed royal governor of New Jersey. He sided with the loyalists during the Revolution, went to London in exile in 1781, and died there in 1813.

9. *PBF*, 22:350; 23:292. Emma Thompson is a tantalizing figure. All we know about her comes from the spirited letter she wrote Franklin on 6 February 1777 from Saint Omer in northern France. Her sympathies lay, no doubt, with the Tories. She called Franklin "you arch Rebel," but admitted humorously that her two most welcome visitors were women with whom she played whist, "tho friends to your Cause." After asking Franklin's advice about where she should settle, given her slender means (Brussels? Lille?), she confessed ruefully that she still admired him: "For tho I know you a Rebel and myself a right Loyal, tho you deserve hanging and I deserve pensioning, still I feel you my Superior, feel a return of the great Respect I ever held you in, and feel, alas, unhappy, thinking I have been too bold" (*PBF*, 23:291–92). His answer, two days later, was roguish: "You are too early, Hussy (as well as too saucy) in calling me Rebel; you should wait for the Event which will determine whether it is a Rebellion or only a Revolution. Here the Ladies are more civil; they call us *Les Insurgens*, a Character that usually pleases them. And methinks you, with all other Women who smart or have smarted under the Tyranny of a bad Husband, ought to be fix'd in *Revolution* Principles, and act accordingly" (*PBF*, 23:296–99). Their one exchange of letters implies that they had friends in common and had enjoyed a teasing kind of relationship, but Emma Thompson herself eludes us completely.

10. *PBF*, 9:216–19. Their scientific exchanges appear mostly in this volume of the papers.

11. *PBF*, 10:142–43.

12. *PBF*, 9:121.

13. See Whitfield Bell Jr., " 'All Clear Sunshine': New Letters of Franklin and Mary Stevenson Hewson," *American Philosophical Society Proceedings* 100 (1956): 521–36.

14. *PBF*, 18:136–37.

15. *PBF*, 19:300–302.

16. The "Mungo Elegy" has been put to fittingly noble music by Martin Mangold.

17. *PBF*, 21:396–97; 29:408. Deborah also sent a couple of squirrels to the Shipleys' great friends, the Spencer family, direct ancestors of Diana, Princess of Wales.

18. *PBF*, 23:303–6.

19. *PBF,* 29:407—9.
20. *PBF,* 31:44—45.
21. Lopez, *Mon Cher Papa,* 314.

Chapter 4

1. Claude-Anne Lopez and Eugenia W. Herbert, *The Private Franklin: The Man and His Family* (New York, W. W. Norton, 1975), 56.

2. Quoted in Claude-Anne Lopez, *Mon Cher Papa: Franklin and the Ladies of Paris* (New Haven: Yale University Press, 1966), 44, 40, 44; and Carl Van Doren, ed., *Benjamin Franklin's Autobiographical Writings* (New York: Viking Press, 1945), 437.

3. Quoted in Lopez, *Mon Cher Papa,* 40.

4. "Old Mistresses Apologue," 25 June 1745, in *Benjamin Franklin Writings* (New York: Library of America, 1987), 302. Hereinafter *BFW.*

5. For a summary, see Mary Beth Norton, *Liberty's Daughters: The Revolutionary Experience of American Women, 1750—1800* (Boston: Little, Brown, 1980), 110—14; and E. Anthony Rotundo, *American Manhood: Transformations in Masculinity from the Revolution to the Modern Era* (New York: Basic Books, 1993), 11.

6. "Rules and Maxims for Promoting Matrimonial Happiness," 8 October 1730, in *BFW,* 155; Quoted in Lopez, *Mon Cher Papa,* 25.

7. Frank Shuffelton, "In Different Voices: Gender in the American Republic of Letters," *Early American Literature,* vol. 25 (1990): 289—305.

8. Michael Zuckerman, "The Selling of the Self: From Franklin to Barnum," in Barbara B. Oberg and Harry S. Stout, eds., *Benjamin Franklin, Jonathan Edwards, and the Representation of American Culture* (New York: Oxford University Press, 1993), 164.

9. Michael Warner, *The Letters of the Republic: Publication and the Public Sphere in Eighteenth-Century America* (Cambridge: Harvard University Press, 1990), esp. 82—87; quotation on 87. And see, for example, Franklin's letter published in the *New-England Courant,* 8 July 1723, signed "Abigail Twitterfield," which humorously asserts the republican belief that literature should address human similarities, rather than differences: ministers "ought not to calculate their Discourses to the Circumstances of themselves and Families, when they are *marryed, bereav'd of near Relations,* or have *Children born to them,* &c. but should study *to know the State of their Flocks in general. . . . (BFW,* 56.)

10. See, for example, Joan B. Landes, *Women and the Public Sphere in the Age of the French Revolution* (Ithaca: Cornell University Press, 1988), chap. 3; Carole Pateman, *The Sexual Contract* (Stanford: Stanford University Press, 1988); and Lynn Hunt, *The Family Romance of the French Revolution* (Berkeley and Los Angeles: University of California Press, 1992).

11. Warner, *Letters of the Republic,* 87.

12. Jay Fliegelman, *Prodigals and Pilgrims: The American Revolution Against Patriarchal Authority, 1750—1800* (New York: Cambridge University Press, 1982), 29—35, 275 n. 52.

13. For Mme Brillon, see Lopez, *Mon Cher Papa;* for changing sexual mores, see Sarah Maza, "The Diamond Necklace Affair Revisited (1785—86): The Case of the Missing Queen," in Lynn Hunt, ed., *Eroticism and the Body Politic* (Baltimore: Johns Hopkins University Press, 1991), 63—89.

14. Franklin to Catharine Ray, 11 September 1755, *Autobiographical Writings,* 93; Franklin to Ray, 4 March 1755, *BFW,* 478. See also Lopez and Herbert, *Private Franklin,* 55.

15. Lopez and Herbert, *Private Franklin.*

16. Franklin to Polly Stevenson, 11 August 1762, in *Autobiographical Writings,* 135.

17. Quoted in *Mon Cher Papa,* 92; Franklin to Polly Hewson, 8 July 1775, *Autobiographical Writings,* 410; *Private Franklin,* 201.

18. Franklin to Mme Brillon, [Oct.-Nov. 1782], in *Autobiographical Writings,* 489; Franklin to Margaret Stevenson, *BFW,* 828.

19. Lopez and Herbert, *Private Franklin,* 306, 313.

20. Franklin to Mary Stevenson, 11 June 1760; 13 September 1760; n.d., *BFW,* 768–75, 777–81; quoted in Lopez and Herbert, *Private Franklin,* 83. The exception may have been Margaret Stevenson, who, according to Lopez and Herbert, was most like Deborah Franklin of all Franklin's female friends and who may well have hoped to marry him after Deborah died. Lopez and Herbert, *Private Franklin,* 84, 201.

21. Quoted in Lopez, *Mon Cher Papa,* 120.

22. Lopez and Herbert, *Private Franklin,* 57; Lopez, *Mon Cher Papa,* 34.

23. Quoted in Lopez, *Mon Cher Papa,* 68, 102.

24. Quoted in Lopez, *Mon Cher Papa,* 40–41.

25. Quoted in Lopez, *Mon Cher Papa,* 47.

26. Robert A. Gross, *The Minutemen and Their World* (New York: Hill and Wang, 1977), 217, 235; Daniel Scott Smith and Michael S. Hindus, "Premarital Pregnancy in America, 1640–1971," *Journal of Interdisciplinary History* 5 (1975): 537–70.

27. Cornelia Hughes Dayton, "Taking the Trade," *WMQ,* 3d ser., 48 (1991):19–49. See also Kathleen Brown, *Good Wives, Nasty Wenches, and Anxious Patriarchs: Gender and the Politics of Identity in Colonial Virginia* (Chapel Hill: University of North Carolina Press, forthcoming), chap. 9.

28. John Demos, *A Little Commonwealth: Family Life in Plymouth Colony* (New York: Oxford University Press, 1970), 66, 131; Jan Lewis and Kenneth A. Lockridge, " 'Sally Has Been Sick': Pregnancy and Family Limitation Among Virginia Gentry Women, 1780–1830," *Journal of Social History* 22 (1988): 5–19.

29. "The Speech of Miss Polly Baker," the *Maryland Gazette,* 11 August 1747; first printed 15 April 1747, in *BFW,* 305–8.

30. See *BFW,* 368, 723.

31. *The Autobiography,* in *BFW,* 1371.

32. Lopez and Herbert, *Private Franklin,* 22–23; Esmond Wright, *Franklin of Philadelphia* (Cambridge: Harvard University Press, Belknap Press, 1986), 42–43. Deborah Read Rogers was married to another man, John Rogers, who had deserted her at the time that she entered into her common-law marriage with Franklin. Rogers never reappeared.

33. *The Autobiography,* in *BFW,* 1371; and "Old Mistresses Apologue," in *BFW,* 302.

34. 4 March 1734/5, *BFW,* 250; Lopez and Herbert, *Private Franklin,* 32.

35. Lopez and Herbert, *Private Franklin,* 76–77, 82–83.

36. Quoted in Lopez, *Mon Cher Papa,* 95.

37. "Reply to a Piece of Advice," in *BFW,* 251; "Rules and Maxims for Promoting Marital Happiness," in *BFW,* 152.

38. Fliegelman, *Prodigals and Pilgrims;* Jan Lewis, "The Republican Wife: Virtue and Seduction in the Early Republic, *WMQ,* 3d ser., 44 (1987): 696–721.

39. Lopez and Herbert, *Private Franklin,* 223.

40. Ruth H. Bloch, "Women, Love, and Virtue in the Thought of Edwards and Franklin," in Oberg and Stout, eds., *Franklin, Edwards, and American Culture,* 144–47.

41. Kenneth A. Lockridge, *On the Sources of Patriarchal Rage: The Commonplace*

Books of William Byrd and Thomas Jefferson and the Gendering of Power in the Eighteenth Century (New York: New York University Press, 1992).

42. "Reply to a Piece of Advice," *The Pennsylvania Gazette*, 4 March 1734/5, in *BFW*, 250.

43. "Selling of the Self," in Oberg and Stout, eds., *Franklin, Edwards, and American Culture*, 164–65.

44. Of course, the problem of integrating love and sex is not one that our generation can claim to have solved. For a suggestive discussion of how the post-Revolutionary generation of educated men and women attempted to resolve this issue, see Lucia McMahon, " 'While Our Souls Together Blend': Narrating a Romantic Readership in the Early Republic," in Peter N. Stearns and Jan Lewis, eds., *An Emotional History of the United States* (New York: New York University Press, 1998), 66–90.

Chapter 5

1. Benjamin Franklin, "A Petition of the Left Hand: To Those Who Have the Superintendency of Education," in *Benjamin Franklin: Writings, Library of America* (New York: Literary Classics of the United States, 1987), 1115–16. I am indebted to Larry Tise for sharing this document with me. Earlier versions of portions of this chapter appeared in " 'Vindicating the Equality of Female Intellect': Women and Authority in the Early Republic," *Prospects: An Annual of American Cultural Studies*, 17 (1992): 1–27.

2. Linda Kerber identified republican motherhood in her classic article "The Republican Mother: Women and the Enlightenment—An American Perspective," *American Quarterly* 28 (1976): 187–205. See also Rosemarie Zagarri, "Morals, Manners, and the Republican Mother," *American Quarterly* 44 (1992): 192–215. Jan Lewis demonstrated the equal significance attributed to a wife's influence on her husband in "The Republican Wife: Virtue and Seduction in the Early Republic," *William and Mary Quarterly*, 3d ser., 44 (1987): 696–721. In an analysis of the implications of literacy, Harvey Graff has highlighted the value that Western culture more generally has attached to literacy. See *The Literacy Myth: Literacy and Social Structure in the Nineteenth-Century City* (New York: Academic Press, 1979), esp. 1–48.

3. Judith Sargent Murray, [Constantia], *The Gleaner*, 3 vols. (Boston: I. Thomas and E. T. Andrews, 1798), 3:189.

4. Lynne Templeton Brickley, " 'Female Academies Are Every Where Establishing': The Beginnings of Secondary Education for Women in the United States, 1790–1830" (unpublished qualifying paper, Harvard Graduate School of Education, 1982), 48–49. The schools are listed in appendix C. Brickley notes that this list "is just a beginning and only meant to be suggestive."

5. *The Connecticut Courant*, 18 May 1795; 17 April, 6 November 1797; 5 March, 7 May, 17 December 1798; 20 May, 17 June 1799; 6 January 1800; 26 October 1801; 8 February, 24 May, 21 October 1802; 2 November, 16 November 1803; 10 April, 30 October 1805; 6 April, 9 April, 23 July 1806; 13 July 1808; 19 April, 30 August 1809; 6 June 1810; 21 December 1813; 15 March, 4 May, 13 May 1814; 15 April, 22 April, and 29 April 1817.

6. The advertisement for Mrs. Value's academy appeared in the *Connnecticut Courant* on 21 December 1813.

7. William Elliott to Ann Smith, 6 June 1817, Elliott Papers, Southern Historical Collection, University of North Carolina at Chapel Hill.

8. Maria Campbell to Mary Humes, 21 September 1819, Campbell Papers, Special Collections, Manuscript Department, Duke University.

9. Diary of Mary Guion, January 1803, New-York Historical Society, New York.

10. Hannah Heaton, "Experiences or Spiritual Exercises." A typescript of the diary is deposited at the Connecticut Historical Society, Hartford, CT. Quoted in Barbara E. Lacey, "The World of Hannah Heaton: The Autobiography of an Eighteenth-Century Connecticut Farm Woman," *WMQ*, 3d ser., 45(1988): 288–89.

11. In her research on colonial women's reading, Mary Alice Baldwin found that women also included *The Spectator*, Price, Giovanni Marana's *Turkish Spy*, *The Tatler*, Burton's *Anatomy of Melancholy*, Addison, and Richardson's *Pamela*. Titled "The Reading of Women in the Colonies Before 1750," Baldwin's essay on this subject is deposited with her papers in the Duke University Archives, Duke University.

12. Sarah Reeve Gibbes to John Gibbes, 30 September 1783, Gibbes-Gilchrist Papers, South Carolina Historical Society, Charleston.

13. Hannah Adams, *A Memoir of Miss Hannah Adams, Written by Herself with Additional Notices by a Friend* (Boston: Gray and Bowen, 1832), 4–5.

14. David Ramsay, *Memoirs of the Life of Martha Laurens Ramsay* (Charleston: Samuel Etheridge, 1812), 12, 36. Ramsay's pride in his wife's intellectual achievements may have led to exaggeration in one instance. In describing the relish for learning that Martha Ramsay had displayed from an early age, he claimed that "in the course of her third year she could readily read any book, and, what is extraordinary, in an inverted position." That is, indeed, extraordinary.

15. See entry dated 22 June 1801 in Elizabeth Sandwith Drinker, *The Diary of Elizabeth Sandwith Drinker*, ed. Elaine Forman Crane (Boston: Northeastern University Press, 1991).

16. See 1 September 1796, 4 June 1797, 20 March 1795, 7 March 1800, 13 September 1800, in Drinker, *Diary*.

17. See 22 April 1796; 31 January, 6 March 1799, in Drinker, *Diary*.

18. See 1 January 1796, in Drinker, *Diary*.

19. Abigail Adams to Mercy Otis Warren, 11 December 1773, *Massachusetts Historical Society Collections* 72 (1917), 19.

20. Amelia [Pringle] to Sarah Lance Huger, [c. 1820], Bacot-Huger Papers, South Carolina Historical Society, Charleston.

21. Diary of Sarah Jane Bradley, entry dated 5 November 1848, Special Collections, Dartmouth College, Hanover.

22. Sophia Cheves to Eleuthera Du Pont, 27 November 1822, Cheves Papers, South Carolina Historical Society, Charleston.

23. Eliza Mordecai Myers to Rachel Mordecai Lazarus, 22 May 1831, Myers Family Papers, Virginia Historical Society, Richmond.

24. Julia Hyde to Lucy Goodale, 26 September 1839, Mount Holyoke College/Archives, South Hadley. Linda K. Kerber and Richard D. Brown have also commented on some of these issues. See Kerber, *Women of the Republic: Intellect and Ideology in Revolutionary America* (Chapel Hill: University of North Carolina Press, 1980), 192–93; Brown, *Knowledge Is Power: The Diffusion of Information in Early America, 1700–1865* (New York: Oxford University Press, 1989), 160–96.

25. Some of the analysis that follows appeared in an earlier form in "Vindicating the Equality of Female Intellect: Women and Authority in the Early Republic," *Prospects: An Annual of American Cultural Studies* 17 (1992): 1–27.

26. J. P. Martin, "Extract from an Address on Female Education," *American Museum* 11, no. 5 (6 May 1792): 219–20; and Alden Bradford, *An Address Delivered at the Opening of the Academy, Wiscassett, Maine* (Hallowell, Me.: Cheever, 1808), 13.

27. Martin, "Extract," 220; and Bradford, *Address*, 13.

28. Benjamin Rush, *Thoughts upon Female Education* (Boston: Samuel Hall, 1787), 5–6. Shortly after founding the Young Ladies Academy of Philadelphia early in 1787, John Poor began to invite speakers to address the students at their quarterly examinations. Rush's speech was the first in the series of writings, all of which were published separately but also included as part of a pamphlet describing the academy. An excerpt from Rush's essay was included in *The American Lady's Preceptor*. Published in 1810 and issued in nine subsequent editions, this collection of essays, historical sketches, and poetry was, as the subtitle suggests, "designed to direct the female mind in a course of pleasing and instructive reading." Rush would have been pleased by the appearance of such a volume.

29. Rush, *Thoughts upon Female Education*, 20, 21.

30. *The Rise and Progress of the Young Ladies Academy of Philadelphia* (Philadelphia: Stewart & Cochran, 1794), 6, 11–12, 26. Ann D. Gordon has examined Philadelphia's Young Ladies Academy in "The Ladies Academy of Philadelphia," in Carol Berkin and Mary Beth Norton, eds., *Women of America* (Boston: Houghton Mifflin, 1979), 69–91.

31. James Milnor, "On Female Education," *Port Folio*, 3d ser., 1 (1809): 388.

32. Anonymous, "Dialogue on Female Education," *Portico: A Repository of Science and Literature* 2, no. 3 (September 1816): 215.

33. Susannah Rowson, "Concluding Address for 1810," in *A Present for Young Ladies; Containing Poems, Dialogues, Addresses, As Recited by the Pupils of Mrs. Rowson's Academy* (Boston: John West, 1811), 151–52.

34. Anonymous, *The Female Advocate* (New Haven: Thomas Green and Son, 1801), 3, 21.

35. Murray [Constantia], *The Gleaner*, 3:191, 197.

36. Ibid., 2:6. Lest her readers then wonder what she would consider an adequate education, she immediately told them that mothers would need at least a command of English, French, geography, and astronomy. She added that it should not be considered "*unsexual,* if they were capacitated to render the rudiments of the Latin tongue familiar."

37. Ibid., 3:219.

38. Journal of Louisa May Alcott, 14 February 1868, in Ednah D. Cheney, *Louisa May Alcott, Her Life, Letters, and Journals* (Boston: Roberts Brothers, 1889), 197.

39. Priscilla Mason, "Salutatory Oration" in *The Rise and Progress of the Young Ladies Academy of Philadelphia*, 90, 91, 92, 93. Following this address, Mason disappeared from the historical record.

40. Hepsy Howard to Elizabeth Wainwright, 29 June 1801, Peter Wainwright Papers, Special Collections, Manuscripts Department, Duke University.

41. Journal of Mary Howell, 21 May 1799, Manuscripts, Connecticut Historical Society, Hartford.

42. Eliza Southgate to Moses Porter, 1 June 1801, in Clarence Cook, ed., *A Girl's Life Eighty Years Ago: Selections from the Letters of Eliza Southgate Bowne* (New York: Scribner's, 1903), 60.

43. Elizabeth Palmer to Nathaniel Peabody, 17 February 1800, Peabody Family Papers, Massachusetts Historical Society, Boston. Elizabeth Palmer Peabody was the

mother of Elizabeth Peabody, Mary Peabody Mann, and Sophia Peabody Hawthorne. I am indebted to Megan Marshall for sharing this letter with me.

44. Journal of Eliza Southgate, 6 July 1802, in Cook, *A Girl's Life Eighty Years Ago*, 109—10.

Chapter 6

1. This story has circulated among graduate students in English at Penn State University since 1992, when then M.A. student Chad Hayton mentioned it to other students who were studying for an examination that included questions about Franklin. Hayton's source for the story might have been a former teacher!

2. My goal in this discussion is to provide a summary history of the ways in which Franklin has been "storied" across the centuries, with particular regard to his relations with women. For a discussion of the use of Franklin to create a national (bourgeois) myth, see my essay "Benjamin Franklin and the Myths of Nationhood," in A. Robert Lee and W. M. Verhoeven, eds., *Making America / Making American Literature* (Atlanta, Ga.: Rodopi, 1996), 15—58. For an analysis of the ways in which the figure of Franklin has affected American culture, see my essay on the literary and material cultural renderings of Franklin, "Figuring Benjamin Franklin in American Cultural Memory," *New England Quarterly* 71 (1999): 415—43. A good summary of Franklin in intellectual history appears in Nian-Sheng Huang, *Benjamin Franklin in American Thought and Culture, 1790—1990* (Philadelphia: American Philosophical Society, 1994).

3. This is commented on in Alfred Owen Aldridge, *Benjamin Franklin, Philosopher and Man* (Philadelphia: Lippincott, 1965), 276.

4. ALS in the Charles Morton Smith Papers at the Historical Society of Pennsylvania, as quoted in Leonard W. Labaree et al., eds., *The Papers of Benjamin Franklin*, vol. 11 (New Haven: Yale University Press, 1967), 370—71. Hereafter cited as *PBF*.

5. Philip Gleason, "A Scurrilous Colonial Election and Franklin's Reputation," *WMQ*, 3d ser., 18(1961): 76.

6. Anonymous, *An Answer to the Plot* (Philadelphia: Armbrüster, 1764). This derogatory broadside suggested that the Germans might, as a strategy, offer Franklin a young woman to distract him from his political maneuvers.

7. [Hugh Williamson], *What Is Sauce for a Goose Is also Sauce for a Gander. Being a Small Touch in the Lapidary Way. Or Tit for Tat, in Your Own, Way. An Epitaph on a Certain Great Man* (Philadelphia: [Armbrüster], 1764), 6—7. This mock epitaph spoke slightingly of Franklin's scientific experiments and the honors he received in Europe, and it accused Franklin of political leveling.

8. [David James Dove], *The Counter-Medley* ([Philadelphia]: [Armbrüster?], 1764). This broadside, largely a response to Isaac Hunt's broadside verses aimed at Dove called *The Medley* (1764), attacked Franklin ("the Man, who leads a Patriot's Life") among some others, "being," the subtitle of *The Counter-Medley* attests, "a proper Answer to all the Dunces of the Medly and their Abettors." For background on Dove, see Joseph Jackson, "A Philadelphia Schoolmaster of the Eighteenth Century," *PMHB* 35 (1911): 314—32.

9. "Characters of some of the Leading Men in the present American Rebellion," *The Morning Post, and Daily Advertiser*, 1 June 1779, 4. Washington and Franklin were discussed in this article, which concluded about Franklin thus: "Perhaps antient or modern history scarcely furnishes an example of such consummate hypocrisy, and

hitherto successful duplicity; and if the axe, or the halter, are to be employed on this occasion, it were much to be wished the first example could be made of this hoary traitor." This article was published anonymously, but it was attributed to Reverend Bennett Allen by Sidney George Fisher in *The True Benjamin Franklin* (Philadelphia: J. B. Lippincott, 1899), 107.

10. The diary entry was mentioned by P. Hutchinson, in "Dr. Franklin," *Notes and Queries*, 4th ser., 5 (15 January 1870): 70.

11. [Andrew Allen? and James Jones Wilmer?], *Memoirs of the Late Dr. Benjamin Franklin* (London: A. Grant, for the author, 1790), 90—91. This memoir has typically been attributed to James Jones Wilmer, and it has been reviewed thoroughly by Betty Kushen, "Three Earliest Published Lives of Benjamin Franklin, 1790—03: The *Autobiography* and Its Continuations," *Early American Literature*, 9 (1974): 39—52. But see also a commentary on authorship by Paul M. Zall in "Letter to the Editor," *Early American Literature* 10 (1975): 220—21. Zall questions Wilmer's participation in the preparation of the memoir's most caustic remarks about Franklin.

12. Anonymous, *American Museum* 10 (October 1791): 176.

13. That is, Faÿ, like some other biographers, seems to have enjoyed thinking that Franklin avidly sought the attentions of Madame Brillon and Madame Helvétius and that he proposed to the latter, thus furthering a popular conception of Franklin as having been "a ladies' man" while in France. Dorothy Medlin usefully refutes these stories about Franklin and the view that Franklin was in contest with Turgot for the hand of Madame Helvétius, in "Benjamin Franklin's Bagatelles for Madame Helvétius: Some Biographical and Stylistic Considerations," *Early American Literature*, 15 (1980): 42—58. For Faÿ's interpretation of Franklin as a weakened and feeble old man who sought attentions of attractive women see Faÿ, "His Excellency Mr. Franklin: The Last Loves of the First American," *The Forum* 79 (March 1928): 321—24; and *Franklin, the Apostle of Modern Times* (Boston: Little, Brown, 1929), 453—500.

14. William Cobbett, *Porcupine's Works, Containing Various Writings and Selections, Exhibiting a Faithful Picture of the Unites States of America* . . . , 12 vols. (London: Cobbett and Morgan, 1801), 1:140n.

15. William Cobbett, *The Life and Adventures of Peter Porcupine, with a Full and Fair Account of All His Authoring Transactions . . . by Peter Porcupine Himself* (Philadelphia: William Cobbett, 1796), 11.

16. Joseph Dennie, "Epistolary. For the Port Folio," *Port Folio*, ser. 1, 1, no. 21 (23 May 1801): 165. In an introductory remark to a reprinted letter, Dennie attacked Franklin as immoral. Dennie had earlier promised to attack Franklin in a series of essays, but he somewhere along the way evidently decided that the positive reputation of Franklin was growing rather than dwindling. See Dennie's "An Author's Evenings. From the Shop of Messers. Colon and Spondee," *Port Folio*, ser. 1, 1, no. 7 (14 February 1801): 53—54. See also, Lewis Leary, "Joseph Dennie on Benjamin Franklin: A Note on Early American Literary Criticism," *PMHB* 72 (1948): 240—46.

17. It is true that Franklin was, during the century, more and more frequently called by his first name in publications, especially for children. The first-name reference in a book designed for children would serve to make the figure of the man more affable and familiar, less austere, and more imitable. For a highbrow audience in turn-of-the-century Philadelphia, however, the first-name reference would have served to demean Franklin, casting him in the intended and denigrating subservient light of a mere tradesman.

18. See Dennie, "An Author's Evenings," *Port Folio* 1 (14 February 1801): 53–54; "The Farrago—No. V," *Port Folio* 1 (4 April 1801): 110; and other *Port Folio* issues: 1 (23 May 1801): 165; 1 (10 October 1801): 325; 2 (23 January 1802): 24; 2 (20 March 1802): 87; 3 (12 March 1803): 87; 3 (3 September 1803): 287; and 4 (June 16, 1804): 187.

19. Sylvester Douglas, *The Diaries of Sylvester Douglas (Lord Glenbervie)*, ed. Francis Bickley 2 vols. (London and Boston: Constable and Houghton Mifflin, 1928), 1:285–87.

20. Glenbervie was son-in-law of Frederick North, second Earl of Guilford, better known as the colonies' enemy, Lord North. See *The Diaries of Sylvester Douglas (Lord Glenbervie)*, 1:v.

21. Wade pointed out that cities in the Midwest were frequently modeled on those of the East, particularly on Philadelphia. Commenting that "the Quaker City spirit went beyond streets, buildings, and improvements, reaching into a wide range of human activity," Wade reported that "the highest praise that Western towndwellers could bestow upon a fellow citizen was to refer to him as their own 'Benjamin Franklin.' " See Richard C. Wade, *The Urban Frontier: Pioneer Life in Early Pittsburgh, Cincinnati, Lexington, Louisville, and St. Louis* (Cambridge: Harvard University Press, 1959), 318–19.

22. According to Melvin Buxbaum, in this edition: "Weems did for Franklin what he did for Washington. Franklin is idealized, sanitized, and Christianized, and is the embodiment of all the Poor Richard virtues." Buxbaum differentiated this edition of the life from the two earlier editions: "This edition, though little more than a paraphrase of the *Autobiography*, is Weems' creation. The earlier editions of 1815 and 1817, on the other hand, are almost entirely by Franklin and so he rather than Weems must be considered author of these editions." See Buxbaum, *Benjamin Franklin, 1721–1906: A Reference Guide* (Boston: G. K. Hall, 1983), 65–66. Buxbaum's volumes have been invaluable to me in my search to examine the Franklin's posthumous reputation.

23. Robert A. Lincoln, "Benjamin Franklin," in *Lives of the Presidents of the United States, with Biographical Sketches of the Signers of the Declaration of Independence . . .* (New York: N. Watson, 1836), 348–52.

24. O. L. Holley, *The Life of Benjamin Franklin* ([New York: Cooledge and Bro., 1848]; reprint., Philadelphia: G. G. Evans, 1860), 9–10.

25. Ibid., 87.

26. Ibid., 88.

27. While it is possible that Franklin copied the verse into the Commonplace Book from some other source, it seems likely that the verse is his own. The Commonplace Book, housed in the Ferdinand Dreer Collection at the Historical Society of Pennsylvania, Case 34, is datable to the year 1732. It contains drafts of letters, articles for the *Pennsylvania Gazette*, and notes on the Junto.

Interestingly, the poem appears in the copybook just below a notation about "The great Secret of succeeding in Conversation." Both the "Secret" and these verses are printed in *PBF*, 1:270.

I wish to thank Philadelphia historian George Boudreau for drawing my attention to the original copybook.

28. This verse to some extent poeticizes a Poor Richard maxim: "The proof of gold is fire; the proof of woman, gold; the proof of man, a woman."

29. Shillaber, *A Very Brief and Very Comprehensive Life of Ben: Franklin, Printer, Done into Quaint Verse, by One of the Types—September 17, 1856* ([Boston?]; n.p., n.d.). The standard reference materials for Shillaber do not list this poem as among his oeu-

vre, and they largely treat, instead, his wonderfully funny character, Mrs. Partington. See John Q. Reed, *Benjamin Penhallow Shillaber* (New York: Twayne, 1972) and Clyde G. Wade, "B. P. Shillaber (1814–1890)," in *Dictionary of Literary Biography*, vol. 11: *American Humorists, 1800–1950*, part 2: M—Z (Detroit: Gale Research, 1982), 434–38. Readers might note with a smile that the Wade article on Shillaber begins thus: "B.P. Shillaber made his way into literature over the same indirect route taken by a Bostonian of an earlier day, Benjamin Franklin."

30. R. P., "The Last Love—Episode in the Life of a Philosopher," *Once-a-Week* 14 (16 June 1866): 653–58. This account was plagiarized more than sixty years later in a briefer account in 1934 by M. M. Hughes, "Benjamin Franklin—Lover," *Cornhill Magazine* 149, no. 889 (January 1934): 101–6.

31. E. L. S., "Dr. Franklin," *Notes and Queries*, 4th ser., 4 (25 December 1869): 558.

32. Barnes cited Sparks as his authority. Jno. Kaye Barnes, *Notes and Queries*, 4th ser., 5 (15 January 1870): 70.

33. P. A. L., *Notes and Queries*, 4th ser., 5 (15 January 1870): 70.

34. L. T. A., *Notes and Queries*, 4 ser., 5 (28 May 1870): 518.

35. H. P. B., "William Temple Franklin," *Notes and Queries*, 4th ser., 6 (8 October 1870): 311–12.

36. P[eter Orlando] Hutchinson, "Dr. Franklin," *Notes and Queries*, 4th ser., 5 (15 January 1870): 70.

37. Peter Orlando Hutchinson, ed., *The Diary and Letters of His Excellency Thomas Hutchinson, Esq., . . .Compiled from the Original Documents Still Remaining in the Possession of His Descendants*, 2 vols. (London: Sampson Low, Marston, Searle, and Rivington, 1886), 2:276.

38. This is probably William Duane (1808–82), great-grandson of Franklin. See the Franklin family genealogy in *PBF*, 1:lxiv, lxxvii.

39. Cady Stanton's speech was delivered in various forms from what seems to have been 1870 on. It is a speech on marriage and divorce that examines the connection between indissoluble marriage vows, women's subjugation to men, and the necessity for more reasonable divorce laws so that women had legal recourse for ill treatment. The text of this version of the speech has been taken from the Elizabeth Cady Stanton Papers at the Library of Congress, as printed in Ellen Carol DuBois, ed., *Elizabeth Cady Stanton, Susan B. Anthony: Correspondence, Writings, Speeches* (New York: Schocken Books, 1981), 117. It seems likely that this version of the speech was very similar to the one delivered in Philadelphia in the summer of 1870.

40. [William Duane], *Remarks upon a Speech Delivered by Mrs. E. Cady Stanton! During the Summer of 1870* (Philadelphia: Merrihew and Sons, 1870).

41. [William] D[uane], "Dr. Franklin and Mrs. Stanton," *Historical Magazine*, 2d ser., 9, no. 1 (January 1871): 50. The attribution to William Duane is by Melvin Buxbaum, in *Benjamin Franklin, 1721–1906: A Reference Guide*, 158.

42. Two useful studies of manhood in Victorian America are Mark C. Carnes's *Secret Ritual and Manhood in Victorian America* (New Haven: Yale University Press, 1989) and David Leverenz's *Manhood and the American Renaissance* (Ithaca: Cornell University Press, 1989). For the uses to which fictional heroes could be put, see Carnes, 124–27.

43. J. J. Flynn, "Franklin," as printed in the *Inland Printer* 18, no. 1 (October 1896): 87.

44. James M. Beck, "Address of Hon. James M. Beck," in *Ceremonies Attending the Unveiling of the Statue of Benjamin Franklin, June 14, 1899. Presented to the City of Philadelphia by Mr. Justus C. Strawbridge* (Philadelphia: Allen, Lane, and Scott, 1899), 42–43.

45. Ibid., 43.

46. Charles William Eliot, "Franklin as Printer and Philosopher," in *Record of the Celebration of the Two Hundredth Anniversary of Benjamin Franklin . . .* (Philadelphia: American Philosophical Society, 1906), 1:55–70.

47. Ellis Paxson Oberholtzer, *The Literary History of Philadelphia* (Philadelphia: George Jacobs, 1906), 46–58, at 48.

48. Ibid., 47.

49. Sidney George Fisher, *The True Benjamin Franklin* (Philadelphia: J. B. Lippincott, 1899), esp. 104–31.

50. Ibid., 106–13.

51. Ibid., 105–6.

52. Albert Henry Smyth, *The Writings of Benjamin Franklin,* 10 vols. (New York: Macmillan, 1906), 6:102n.

53. Albert Matthews, "Marianne and Cecilia Davies and Benjamin Franklin," *Notes and Queries* 155, no. 22 (1 December 1928): 390–91. The article Matthews was refuting was Andrew de Ternant's "Marianne and Cecilia Davies and Benjamin Franklin," *Notes and Queries* 155, no. 14 (6 October 1928): 245.

54. [Wayne Whipple], *Franklin's Key. A Brief Biography of the Greatest American* (Philadelphia: Franklin Printing Co., 1910). The attribution is by Melvin Buxbaum, in *Benjamin Franklin: A Reference Guide, 1907–1983* (Boston: G. K. Hall, 1988), 19.

55. See C[harles] H[enry] Hart, "Who Was the Mother of Franklin's Son? An Inquiry Demonstrating that She was Deborah Franklin," *PMHB* 35 (1911): 308–14.

56. Separate essays, which later were combined to form chapters of his book, appear in the *Century Magazine,* vols. 57 and 58, from November 1898 through October 1899. *The Many-Sided Franklin* was first published in book form in 1899, and it went through numerous reprintings in the first three decades of the twentieth century. Indeed, some more recent authors still refer to Franklin as "many-sided."

57. Paul Leicester Ford, *The Many-Sided Franklin* (New York: Century, 1899), 267.

58. Ibid., 308.

59. Ibid., 432.

60. Ibid., 457.

61. Carl Van Doren, *Benjamin Franklin* (New York: Viking, 1938).

62. Ibid., 653–54.

63. Rosemary Benét and Stephen Vincent Benét, "Benjamin Franklin, 1706–1790," *A Book of Americans* (New York: Farrar and Rinehart, 1933), 37.

64. Earl Emmons, *Odeography of Benjamin Franklin* (New York: Ayerdale Press, 1929), 17.

65. Ibid., 24.

66. Ibid., 35.

67. In the foreword to the book, Emmons wrote, "I respect and admire Ben Franklin more than I do any other man I ever have studied, read about or known. I think he is by far the greatest white man this country ever produced and certainly there is no one in world history who contributed more enlightenment, comfort, safety and general good to mankind than he" (Ibid., 11).

68. After cataloging the several areas in which his own life was like Franklin's, Emmons continued that "I have been credited with having a sense of humor as well as a somewhat philosophical turn of mind. I have been suspected of immoralities and have written things which caused censorious persons to break out into goose pimples. I, too, am an old newspaper man myself. So, while not at all comparing myself to the

glorious Franklin, it happens my life has been such that we do have several points of contact; more, I think, than can be claimed by the majority of Franklin biographers" (Ibid., 11–12).

69. Starkey Flythe Jr., "Two Hundred Years of Girl Watching," *Saturday Evening Post* 247, no. 5 (July-August 1975): 50–51, 54.

70. Claude-Anne Lopez and Eugenia W. Herbert, *The Private Franklin: The Man and His Family* (New York: W. W. Norton, 1975).

71. Robert Lee Hall, *Benjamin Franklin and a Case of Christmas Murder* (New York: St. Martin's Press, 1990). See also Hall's earlier *Benjamin Franklin Takes the Case* (New York: St. Martin's Press, 1988). I first learned of these titles from Virginia Ward of the Library Department of the Franklin Institute, when I delivered this essay in its first version, as a talk, on 9 April 1994. I would like to thank Virginia Ward for bringing this lively little mystery to my attention.

72. Hall, *Benjamin Franklin and a Case of Christmas Murder*, 31.

73. See ibid., 4, 26, 33.

74. In a telephone conversation on 18 May 1994, with Nancy Remley, a representative of the mass market publicity department of St. Martin's Press, I learned that the Hall title was being marketed for the general reader and for readers of mysteries. This very accessible book incorporates in surprising ways many of the biographical details about Franklin available to Franklin scholars and history buffs.

Chapter 7

I would like to thank J. A. Leo Lemay for sharing with me his unparalleled expertise on Benjamin Franklin. My thanks also to Martha Slotten, who generously lent me her copy of Elizabeth Graeme Fergusson's 1789 manuscript commonplace book and to David Shields for kindly furnishing me with his copy of Polly Hewson's manuscript poetry from the McCall Family papers.

1. While the letter is undated, the editors of the Franklin *Papers* suggest October 1778 as the appropriate date. Leonard W. Labaree et al., eds., *The Papers of Benjamin Franklin*, 35 vols. (New Haven: Yale University Press, 1959–) 27:670–71. (Hereafter *PBF.*)

2. Dena Goodman, "Enlightenment Salons: The Convergence of Female and Philosophic Ambitions," *Eighteenth-Century Studies* 22 (1989): 330. See also Donna C. Stanton, "The Fiction of *Preciosite* and the Fear of Women," *Yale French Studies* 62 (1981): 107–34. See Londa Schiebinger, *The Mind Has No Sex? Women in the Origins of Modern Science* (Cambridge: Harvard University Press, 1989), 153. For other intelligent discussions of eighteenth-century French salons that challenge the traditional view, see Dena Goodman, *The Republic of Letters: A Cultural History of the French Enlightenment* (Ithaca: Cornell University Press, 1994); "Enlightenment Salons: The Convergence of Female and Philosophic Ambitions," *Eighteenth-Century Studies* 22 (1989): 329–50; "Seriousness of Purpose: Salonnieres, Philosophes, and the Shaping of the Eighteenth-Century Salon," *Proceedings of the Annual Meeting of the Western Society for French History* 15 (1988): 111–18.

3. David Shields, *Civil Tongues and Polite Letters* (Chapel Hill: University of North Carolina Press, 1997), 45.

4. *PBF*, 9:6.

5. Although born in Boston, Franklin considered Philadelphia his home, as he wrote in the opening of part 3 of his *Autobiography*: "I am now about to write at home,

Aug[ust] 1788." in *Benjamin Franklin: Writings*, ed. J. A. Leo Lemay (New York: Library of America, 1987), 1395.

6. See Carl Van Doren, *Benjamin Franklin* (New York: Viking Press, 1938), 420–21.

7. Claude-Ann Lopez, *Mon Cher Papa: Benjamin Franklin and the Ladies of Paris* (1966; reprint, New Haven: Yale University Press, 1990), 3.

8. For a history of these interconnected literary networks, see Karin Wulf and Catherine Blecki's introductions to Wulf and Blecki, eds., *Milcah Martha Moore's Book: A Commonplace Book from Revolutionary America* (University Park: Pennsylvania State University Press, 1998) and my unpublished dissertation, " 'By a Female Hand': Letters, Belles Lettres, and the Philadelphia Culture of Performance, 1760–1820" (University of Delaware, 1996).

9. "Journal of Josiah Quincy, Jun. During his Voyage and Residence in England from September 28, 1774 to March 3rd, 1775," *Massachusetts Historical Society Proceedings* 50 (1917): 433–71.

10. Maurice Quinlan, "Dr. Franklin Meets Dr. Johnson," *PMHB* 73 (1949): 34–44.

11. *PBF*, 17:221.

12. I borrow these cultural definitions of gossip and fashion from David Shields's thorough discussion of tea tables in *Civil Tongues and Polite Letters*, 99–140.

13. Simon Gratz, "Some Materials for the Biography of Elizabeth Fergusson, nee Graeme," *PMHB* 39 (1915): 263–67. See also Sheila L. Skemp's discussion of the Franklin-Graeme affair in *William Franklin: Son of a Patriot, Servant of a King* (New York: Oxford University Press, 1990). While Skemp makes a convincing argument that William Franklin ended their affair, my interpretation of the failed courtship is consonant with David Shield's recent evaluation. See Shields, *Civil Tongues*, 137–38.

14. For representative biographical information on Elizabeth Graeme Fergusson, see Martha Slotten, "Elizabeth Graeme Ferguson: A Poet in the 'Athens of North America,' " *PMHB* 108, no. 3 (1984): 259–85; Pattie Cowell, *Women Poets of Pre-Revolutionary America 1650–1775* (Troy: Whitson, 1981), 101–11; Theodore Bean, *History of Montgomery County* (Philadelphia: Everts & Peck, 1884), 360–65, 880–902; Mary Maples Dunn, "Elizabeth Graeme Ferguson," in Edward T. James et al., eds., *Notable American Women* (Cambridge: Harvard University Press, Belknap Press 1971), 610–11; Elizabeth Ellet, *Women of the American Revolution* (Philadelphia: G. W. Jacobs, 1900), 219–32; Thomas Glenn, *Some Colonial Mansions and Those Who Lived in Them* (Philadelphia: Henry T. Coates, 1897), 367–98; Gratz, "Elizabeth Fergusson" *PMHB* 39 (1915): 257–321, 385–409; 41 (1917): 385–98; [Benjamin Rush], "Account of the Life and Character of Mrs. Elizabeth Ferguson," *Port Folio*, n.s., 1 (June 1809): 520–27; Ellis P. Oberholtzer, *The Literary History of Philadelphia* (Philadelphia: George W. Jacobs, 1906), 76–83; M. Kathrine Jackson, *Outlines of the Literary History of Colonial Pennsylvania* (New York: AMS Press, 1966), 92–101; Anne Hollingsworth Wharton, *Salons Colonial and Republican* (Philadelphia: Lippincott, 1900), 13–24; Chester T. Hallenbeck, "The Life and Collected Poems of Elizabeth Graeme Fergusson," (master's thesis, Columbia University, 1929); and Anne Ousterhout's forthcoming biography, *Elizabeth* (University Park: Pennsylvania State University Press, 2002).

15. Quoted in Glenn, *Some Colonial Mansions*, 389.

16. *PBF*, 12:62, 101.

17. The extract is included in Wulf and Blecki, *Milcah Martha Moore's Book*, 200–17.

18. *PBF,* 10:232–33. The translatio motif was common in Franklin's writing. Both his 1733 plan for the Library Company of Philadelphia and his 1743 prospectus for the American Philosophical Society describe Philadelphia as "the future Athens of America." *PBF,* 1:321.

19. Thomas Coombe was a member of the Craven Street circle during his visit to London and would have seen Franklin there. In addition, Polly Stevenson wrote a poem in his honor, "To the Reverend Mr. Coombe on the day of his taking holy Orders" (1772), which survives in manuscript at the Historical Society of Pennsylvania. Franklin also sent to William Strahan in London poems by Philadelphia litterateurs Thomas Godfrey, Nathaniel Evans, and Francis Hopkinson. *PBF,* 10:167–68n.

20. See Wulf and Blecki, *Milcah Moore's Book,* 216.

21. Both this ode and "The Ode to American Genius" are in Fergusson's commonplace book to the five Willing sisters, formerly in the possession of Lady Strawbridge, but now at Graeme Park Historic Site, Horsham, Pennsylvania.

22. The influence of the Litchfield group as well as the famous Bluestocking poets is evident in many of Fergusson's manuscript poems, including "A Farewell to the Muses written by a Young Woman soon after Marriage," which she transcribes in her 1796 commonplace book, Historical Society of Pennsylvania. In stanza 41, she wrote: "In *Carters, Mores, Sewards,* and *Smiths* we view / In verse mean vice oppose; *Genlis* and *Burney* nobley show / Their talents great in Prose."

By this time, the Bluestockings were well established in print both in England and America. Elizabeth Carter had published *Poems upon Particular Occasions* (1738) and *All the Works of Epictetus* (1758). Hannah More had published *The Search After Happiness: A Pastoral Drama* (1773), *Sir Eldred of the Bower and the Bleeding Rock* (1776), and *Essays on Various Subjects, Principally Designed for Young Ladies* (1777). Anna Seward had published "A Rural Coronation" in F. N. C. Mundy's *Needwood Forest* (1776), *Elegy on Captain Cook* (1780), *Monody on Major Andre* (1781), and *Louisa, A Poetical Novel* (1784). Charlotte Smith had published *Elegiac Sonnets* (1786), *Emmeline: The Orphan of the Castle* (1788 and 1794). Madame de Genlis published *Adelaide and Theodore* (1783), *Alphonso and Dalinda* (1787), and *Age of Chivalry* (1799), while Fanny Burney was known for *Harcourt* (1780), *Cecilia; or Memoirs of an Heiress* (1783), and *Evelina* (1784).

On the connection of Bluestockings to salons, see Evelyn Gordon Bodek, "*Salonnieres* and Bluestockings: Educated Obsolescence and Germinating Feminism," *Feminist Studies* 3 (1976): 185–99; and Sylvia Harcstark Myers, *The Bluestocking Circle: Women, Friendship, and the Life of the Mind in Eighteenth-Century England* (New York: Oxford University Press, 1990).

23. See Wulf and Blecki, *Milcah Moore's Book,* 201.

24. On Sterne and European salons, see Chauncey Brewster Tinker, *The Salon and English Letters: Chapters on the Interrelations of Literature and Society in the Age of Johnson* (New York: Macmillan, 1915). See, too, Benjamin Rush's anonymously published account in the 1809 *Port Folio,* 520–27.

25. The manuscript poem is in Fergusson's 1789 commonplace book written for the five Willing sisters and recently acquired by Graeme Park, 103–5.

26. Graeme spent the rest of the poem cataloguing the habitués of her salon: Thomas Godfry, the "Genius Child . . . whose Verse and Hours beguild"; the "Darling" Nathaniel Evans, who "sweetly breathd, / Melifluous native airs"; Thomas Coombe, who "happier wove this Cypress Wreath. / And there the Garland won"; Jacob Duche, like Homer's Ulysses, was "Slow tho Sure our Hearts Engage / Soft as Descending Snows"; Annis Boudinot Stockton's "plaintive pen complains . . . in ele-

gance of woe" only to switch to odes to Washington "in lofty Period flow." And Anna Young (Smith) was "The Smoothest of Parnassian Maids!" Ibid.

27. Goodman, "Enlightenment Salons," 330–31.

28. For differing approaches to the emergence of the seventeenth-century French salon, see Jürgen Habermas, *The Structural Transformation of the Public Sphere: An Inquiry into a Category of Bourgeois Society*, trans. Thomas Burger (Cambridge: MIT Press, 1992), and Carolyn Lougee, *Les Paradis des Femmes: Women, Salons, and Social Stratification in Seventeenth-Century France* (Princeton: Princeton University Press, 1976).

29. Morellet, "De la Conversation," in *Melanges de litterature et de philosophie du 18e siecle*, 4 vols. (Paris, 1836), 4:77, 129–30.

30. 23 November 1780, quoted in Lopez, *Mon Cher Papa*, 82.

31. Lopez, *Mon Cher Papa*, 39.

32. Quoted in Lopez, *Mon Cher Papa*, 81 (emphasis added).

33. While the lexicon of sensibility (from sense, sentiment, and sensibility) was complex throughout the eighteenth century, G. J. Barker-Benfield offers a sound historiographical interpretation of its etymology in *The Culture of Sensibility: Sex and Society in Eighteenth-Century Britain* (Chicago: University of Chicago, 1992); quoted in Barbara Stafford, *Body Criticism: Imaging the Unseen in Enlightenment Art and Medicine* (Cambridge: MIT Press, 1993), 178.

34. See Elizabeth Goldsmith, *Exclusive Conversations: The Art of Interaction in Seventeenth-Century France* (Philadelphia: University of Pennsylvania Press, 1988).

35. Undated letter from Benjamin Franklin to Madame Helvetius, Bibliothèque Nationale, Paris, and the Library of Congress. Quoted in Lopez, *Mon Cher Papa*, 271.

36. For a discussion of Franklin's reading on education, see Edwin Wolf II, "Franklin's Library," in J. A. Leo Lemay, ed., *Reappraising Benjamin Franklin: A Bicentennial Perspective* (Newark: University of Delaware Press, 1993), 319–31. Besides his own 1745 work, *Thoughts on the Education of Youth*, Franklin owned copies of Obadiah Walker's *Of Education* (London, 1677); Milton's *Paradise Lost*, including "a Tractate on Education" (London, 1730); Locke's *Some Thoughts Concerning Education* (London, 1732); Charles Rollin's *The Method of Teaching and Studying the Belles Lettres* (London, 1737); and David Fordyce's *Dialogues Concerning Education* (London, 1745). See also Claude-Anne Lopez, "Benjamin Franklin and William Dodd: A New Look at an Old Cause Celebre," *Proceedings of the American Philosophical Society* 129, no. 3 (1985): 260–67 for a discussion of Franklin's recommendation for boarding school teacher Mrs. Brodeau.

37. Quoted in Amelia Gere Mason, *Women of the French Salons* (New York: Century, 1891), 127–28; Jean Jacques Rousseau, *Emilius; or a Treatise of Education. Translated from the French*, 3 vols. (Edinburgh: A. Donaldson & J. Reid, 1763), 3:104–5.

38. Richard Beresford, *A Plea for Literature, More Especially the Literature of Free States* (Charleston: Harrison & Bowen, 1793), 20; Dr. John Gregory, *A Father's Legacy to His Daughters* (London: printed for William Strahan, 1774; Philadelphia: Joseph James, 1787), 61.

39. Benjamin Rush, "Some Thoughts upon Female Education," in Michael Meranze, ed., *Essays: Literary, Moral, and Philosophical* (Schenectady: Union College Press, 1988), 51. For further reading on the French critics, see Stanton, "The Fiction of Preciosite," and Katharine A. Jensen, "Male Models of Feminine Epistolarity; or, How to Write Like a Woman in Seventeenth-Century France," in Elizabeth Goldsmith, ed., *Writing the Female Voice: Essays on Epistolary Literature* (Boston: Northeastern University Press, 1989), 25–45.

40. See Lopez, *Mon Cher Papa*; Carolyn Lougee, *Le Paradis des Femmes: Women, Salons, and Social Stratification in Seventeenth-Century France* (Princeton: Princeton University Press, 1976); Joan Landes, *Women and the Public Sphere in the Age of the French Revolution* (Ithaca: Cornell University Press, 1988); and Sara Muleg, "Women and the *Encyclopedie*," in Samia Spencer, ed., *French Women and the Age of Enlightenment* (Bloomington: Indiana University Press, 1984), 259–71.

41. Goodman, "Enlightenment Salons," 332–33; 340.

42. The Americans follow the democratic French salon model discussed in Goodman, "Enlightenment Salons," 350.

43. Evans's poem is printed in Theodore Bean's *History of Montgomery County* (Philadelphia: Everts & Peck, 1884), 362–63.

44. Shields, *Civil Tongues*, 35.

45. Annis Stockton to Elizabeth Fergusson, 1769, quoted in Lyman H. Butterfield, "Morven: a Colonial Outpost of Sensibility," *Princeton University Library Chronicle* 6 (November 1944): 3.

46. Hugh Blair, "On Epistolary Writing," Lecture 38, in *Lectures in Rhetoric and Belles Lettres*, 3 vols., 2d ed. (London: William Strahan & T. Cadell, 1785), 1:67.

47. Ibid.

48. Reverend John Bennett, *Letters to a Young Lady*, Letter XLVI, in *The Lady's Pocket Library*, 3d ed. (Philadelphia: Matthew Carey, 1797), 101.

49. *PBF*, 9:102.

50. Ibid.

51. Manuscript poem is in the McCall Family Commonplace Book, Historical Society of Pennsylvania.

52. Ibid.

53. In addition to Franklin, the Philadelphian belletrists also read female models of exemplary letter writing, including Madame Stephanie de Genlis's *Adelaide and Theodore, or Letters on Education* (London, 1783) and Hester Mulso Chapone's *Letters on the Improvement of the Mind* (London, 1773; Philadelphia, 1785), as well as the published letters of Madame Sevigne, Madame Maintenon, and Anna Seward.

54. *PBF*, 7:177n.

55. Deborah Norris Logan, *Memoir of Dr. George Logan of Stenton*, ed. Frances A. Logan (Philadelphia: Historical Society of Pennsylvania, 1899), 39.

56. Franklin counted Wright among his intellectual equals, sending political pamphlets to both Speaker Isaac Norris and Susanna Wright. See his letter to Deborah Franklin of 19 February 1758, *PBF*, 7:382. On 9 July 1759, Franklin sent Susanna's brother, James Wright, a copy of Madame Maintenon's letters, which she certainly would have read. See *PBF*, 8:411.

57. Milcah Martha Moore, *Miscellanies, Moral and Instructive* (Philadelphia: printed for Joseph Jones, 1787; London: reprinted by J. Philips, 1787), 4.

58. Milcah Moore also includes in her commonplace book a transcribed letter presumably from Benjamin Franklin to an unidentified [T] H., where he explains his theories of Good Works: "The Faith you mention has doubtless its use in the World. I do not desire to see it diminished nor would I lessen it in any man, but I wish it was more productive of Good Works, Works of Kindness, Charity, Mercy & public Spirit, not Holliday keeping, sermon reading, or having performed Church Ceremonies." Further memorializing Franklin as a virtuous model for her sorority, Moore follows the letter with the epitaphs of Benjamin Franklin and of Josiah and Abiah Franklin.

59. The poem is included in Fergusson's 1796 commonplace book presumably written for Elias Boudinot or Benjamin Rush, which is housed at the Historical Soci-

ety of Pennsylvania. A published version appeared in the *Columbian Magazine* 2 (June 1788): 350.

60. Hannah Griffitts to Susanna Wright, November 1762, Norris Family Papers, Historical Society of Pennsylvania; "S. W. to Fidelia in answer to the foregoing" is published in Wulf and Blecki, *Milcah Martha Moore's Book*, 151; Hannah Griffitts to Susanna Wright, 15 April 1763, Norris Family Papers, Historical Society of Pennsylvania; Sally Norris Dickinson to Deborah Logan, undated letter, Logan Papers, Historical Society of Pennsylvania; Deborah Logan to Sally Norris Dickinson, 18 September 1799, Loudon Papers, Historical Society of Pennsylvania.

61. Goodman, "Enlightenment Salons," 340.

62. *PBF*, 25:200n; Lopez quotes this 6 January 1782 letter in *Mon Cher Papa*, 25.

A BIBLIOGRAPHICAL NOTE ON FURTHER READINGS

This Bibliographic Note focuses on the basic and most reliable texts for gaining an access to Benjamin Franklin and his extraordinary career. For finding their way through the considerable literature on Benjamin Franklin and women, readers should refer to the endnotes to the preceding chapters.

One way of getting into Franklin is through his famous *Autobiography*, printed and reprinted in hundreds of editions from his death to the present. The best-documented version is the authoritative Norton edition, *Benjamin Franklin's Autobiography*, edited by J. A. Leo Lemay and P. M. Zall (New York: W. W. Norton & Co., 1986). Another approach, through collected autobiographical extracts, is edited by Esmond Wright and titled *Benjamin Franklin: His Life as He Wrote It* (Cambridge: Harvard University Press, 1989).

One can also approach Franklin through his collected writings. The most accessible collection is the massive volume (1,605 pages) in the Library of America series, *Benjamin Franklin: Writings* (New York: Literary Classics of the United States, 1987). The next level of comprehensiveness is the early-twentieth-century but still reliable edition by Albert Henry Smyth, *The Writings of Benjamin Franklin*, ten vols. (1907), also available in reprint editions.

The Franklin bible, to be completed in forty volumes in connection with the 300th anniversary of his birth in the year 2006, is *The Papers of Benjamin Franklin*, edited by Leonard W. Labaree and colleagues (New Haven: Yale University Press, 1959–). Carefully illustrated and indexed volume by volume, this is a treasure trove of Franklin literature and writings.

Although there are hundreds of books about various facets of Franklin, he has never attracted a biographer capable of creating a literary classic covering all of his storied career. It is unfortunate that he did not get further in telling his own story in the *Autobiography*, which only covers up to July 1757, when Franklin, at age fifty-one, and son William made a tourist pilgrimage from Falmouth via Stonehenge and Salisbury on their way to London. Except for his habit of jumping forward and backward in the *Autobiography*, we miss almost entirely his fifteen years as Pennsylvania Assembly agent in London, his Revolutionary year in Philadelphia during 1775—76, and, totally, his nine years in Paris and his twilight years in Philadelphia from 1785 until his death in 1790.

Readers will note elsewhere in this volume the story of biographers and how they treated Franklin's relations with women. But biographies that can be profitably read today would be Carl Van Doren's *Benjamin Franklin* (New York: Viking Press, 1938), which is thorough but tedious, and Esmond Wright's *Franklin of Philadelphia* (Cambridge: Harvard University Press, 1986). The best biographical treatment of Franklin, however, is still Claude-Anne Lopez and Eugenia W. Herbert's *The Private Franklin: The Man and His Family* (New York: W. W. Norton & Co., 1975), which gets at the heart of Franklin—the very human being, with feet of clay, a mind of genius, and an odd family arrangement.

As for Franklin's relations with women, not much will help add to what one will find in these pages. But let me mention again the superb *Mon Cher Papa: Franklin and the Ladies of Paris*, by Claude-Anne Lopez (New Haven: Yale University Press, 1966), and the little piece that surely no one will be able to find easily, *Dr. Benj. Franklin and the Ladies* (Mount Vernon, N.Y.: Peter Pauper Press, 1939).

One of the most useful tools for keeping track of what Franklin did, and when and where he was during his many peregrinations at home and abroad, is a good chronology of his life, the best of which was issued by the Friends of Franklin Inc. under the title *Benjamin Franklin, 1706—1790: A Chronology of the Eighteenth Century's Most Eminent Citizen* (Dubuque, Iowa: Kendall/Hunt Publishing Co., 1996). Ordering and price information for this handy publication can be found on the Friends of Franklin website: www.benfranklin2006.org or obtained by e-mail at fof@benfranklin2006.org or by mail at P.O. Box 40048, Philadelphia, PA 19106.

NOTES ON THE CONTRIBUTORS

Mary Kelley is currently the Mary Brinsmead Wheelock Professor of History at Dartmouth College, where she teaches in the History Department and the Women's Studies Program. A graduate of Mount Holyoke College, she has also served on the Board of Trustees of her alma mater. She received her M.A. from New York University and her Ph.D. in history from the University of Iowa. She served as President of the American Studies Association during 1999–2000 and has served as trustee of the American Antiquarian Society. She has also served on the editorial boards of the *Journal of American History, American Quarterly, William and Mary Quarterly,* and *New England Quarterly.* In addition to numerous articles, she is the author of *Private Woman, Public Stage* (1984), has edited important writings of Catharine Maria Sedgwick (1993) and Margaret Fuller (1994), and co-authored *The Limits of Sisterhood* (1988). At present, she is completing a book on the transformative role of formal education in the lives of nineteenth-century American women.

Jan Lewis is Professor of History at Rutgers University, Newark, New Jersey. She received her A.B. from Bryn Mawr College and her M.A. and Ph.D. degrees from the University of Michigan. She is the author of *The Pursuit of Happiness: Family and Values in Jefferson's Virginia* (1983). She co-edited (with Peter N. Stearns) *An Emotional History of the United States* (1998) and (with Peter S. Onuf) *Sally Hemings and Thomas Jefferson: History, Memory, and Civic Culture* (1999). She has written many articles on early American and women's history and is currently completing the second volume of the Penguin History of the United States.

Claude-Anne Lopez is Editor Emerita of *The Papers of Benjamin Franklin* (35 vols.; 1957–), on which she worked from 1954 until her semiretirement in 1987. A native of Belgium, she studied classics at the University of Brussels (undergraduate) and at Columbia University (graduate). Among her numerous books and articles are four important works: *Mon Cher Papa: Franklin and the Ladies of Paris* (1966); *The Private Franklin: The Man and His Family* (with Eugenia Herbert,

1975); *Le Sceptre et la Foudre: Franklin en France* (1990); and *My Life with Benjamin Franklin* (2000). She has served as a consultant, on and off screen, for many television documentaries and other public programs.

Carla Mulford teaches early American literature and culture and American studies and Native American studies at Penn State University, University Park. The founding president of the Society of Early Americanists, she has served on numerous journal editorial boards, including *Early American Literature, American Literature, Eighteenth-Century Studies,* and *The Pennsylvania Magazine of History and Biography.* She has published scholarly volumes related to several Franklin associates and contemporaries: John Leacock, Annis Stockton, William Hill Brown, and Hannah Webster Foster. She has also edited two books, *American Women Prose Writers to 1820* (with Amy E. Winans and Angela Vietto) (1999) and *Teaching the Literatures of America* (1999). Among her thirty published articles are several recent essays on Benjamin Franklin. She is completing a book-length study of Franklin titled *Benjamin Franklin and the Ends of the Empire* (forthcoming).

Sheila Skemp is Professor of History and Acting Director of the Gender Studies program at the University of Mississippi. She is the author of *William Franklin: Son of a Patriot, Servant of a King* (1990); *Benjamin and William Franklin: Father and Son, Patriot and Loyalist* (1994); and *Judith Sargent Murray: A Brief History* (1998). She is currently completing a cultural biography of Judith Sargent Murray.

Susan Stabile is Assistant Professor of English at Texas A & M University, College Station, Texas. She received her Ph.D. from the University of Delaware, where she studied with the prolific Franklin scholar J. A. Leo Lemay. She has published several articles on early American women writers, and is currently working on two book projects, *Beyond the Writing Closet: The Material Culture of Women's Manuscripts* and *Commonplace: An Anthology of Early American Women's Poetry.*

Larry E. Tise is a private-practice historian living and working in Philadelphia. Born in Winston-Salem, North Carolina, and with degrees from Duke University (A.B., 1965; M.Div., 1968) and the University of North Carolina at Chapel Hill (Ph.D., 1974), he has spent much of his career as a history executive, serving as Executive Director of the North Carolina Division of Archives and History (1975–81), the Pennsylvania Historical and Museum Commission (1981–87), the American Association for State and Local History (1987–89), and the Benjamin Franklin National Memorial (1989–96). He conducts historical research and provides history services for clients throughout the United States, Europe, and the West Indies. He advises foundations, corporations, and individuals on the establishment of distinguished awards for human achievement. He is author of more than fifty articles and books on many facets of history and historical work, including *Proslavery: A History of the Defense of Slavery, 1700–1840* (1987) and *The American Counterrevolution: A Retreat from Liberty, 1783–1800* (1999). He is currently writing a sequel to *American Counterrevolution* covering the years 1800–1848, a reference book on the world's most distinguished awards, and a source book of documents and photographs on the experiences of the Wright Brothers on the North Carolina Outer Banks between 1900 and 1911.

INDEX